Parents and Teachers

To Ian and to Mum
With love.

Parents and Teachers:
Power and Participation

Carol Vincent

Falmer Press

(A member of the Taylor & Francis Group)

London • Washington, D.C.

UK   The Falmer Press, 4 John Street, London WC1N 2ET
USA The Falmer Press, Taylor & Francis Inc., 1900 Frost Road,
         Suite 101, Bristol, PA 19007

First published in 1996

A catalogue record for this book is available from the British Library

Library of Congress Cataloging-in-Publication Data are available on request

ISBN 0 7507 0517 5 cased
ISBN 0 7507 0518 3 paper

Jacket design by Caroline Archer

Typeset in 10/12pt Garamond by
Graphicraft Typesetters Ltd., Hong Kong.

Printed in Great Britain by Biddles Ltd., Guildford and King's Lynn on paper which has a specified pH value on final paper manufacture of not less than 7.5 and is therefore 'acid free'.

Contents

Acknowledgments

This book is based on research originally conducted for a PhD which I started in 1989. Over the past six years I have accumulated sufficient acknowledgments to outdo even the most verbose of Oscar award winners. Listed here are my most outstanding debts.

Without the many contributions of 'City' workers and residents, this project would have floundered. Particular thanks are due to the parents and teachers at 'Hill St' and 'Low Rd' schools who gave freely of their time, despite the many pressures upon them, and to City's education officers, the coordinators and the Parents' Centre workers for their sustained welcome and interest in the research. I wish them all well in their future work.

I would also like to acknowledge the financial support of the Economic and Social Research Council (ESRC) between 1989 and 1992 which made it possible for me to work full-time on this research.

Acting first as my supervisor, and now as a highly-valued friend and colleague, Barry Troyna's intellectual and personal contribution to this project has been incalculable. He has been and continues to be extremely generous in terms of the enthusiasm, time, patience, effort and gratuitous insults that he has expanded in support of my work! I am greatly indebted to him. Not least among his achievements has been to introduce me to a branch of knowledge I had previously considered arcane, even irrelevant — the study of Tottenham Hotspur, still the only football team whose players I can name.

Grateful thanks also go to several other researchers. They have not all been directly involved with this work, but they have all been instrumental in keeping me going! Chief amongst these is undoubtedly Sarah Neal (life would be much bleaker without the pub and the 'phone), and also David Gillborn, Sue Heath and Gabrielle Rowe. A special vote of thanks must go to Sally Tomlinson for all the encouragement and interest she has shown me. Stephen Ball, Sharon Gewirtz and the other regular participants at the Kings' College 'parental choice' seminars have provided a congenial and intellectually stimulating forum from which I have greatly benefitted. Other people to whom I owe thanks include Michele Harrison and Pam Wilkie (for reminding me there is life beyond the university sector) Wendy Ball, John Wrench (for their supportive periods of supervision), and also Tony Booth, Andrew Brown, Jennifer Evans and Phil Woods.

Finally I would like to thank Ian Loveland, to whom this book is dedicated.

Without his complete and unfailing calm, support, encouragement and belief in me, I would not have embarked upon this research project, and certainly not managed to complete it.

London, summer 1995

I acknowledge the permission of the editors of *British Educational Research Journal* and *British Journal of Educational Studies* for allowing me to include substantially revised versions of material which appeared in earlier editions of the journals.

Preface

Since 1979, successive Conservative governments have sought to define parents as consumers of the education system with considerable influence over the way in which the producers — teachers — operate. As a result, 'parent power' has become an increasingly common phrase, as advocates and detractors of parental choice of school argue for the merits and demerits of recent reforms. But away from such hotly contested and high profile issues, there lies the question, how do parents experience relationships with their children's teachers once their child is at a school?

This book is about that subject; the factors that shape and influence relationships between parents and teachers. At the heart of the book is an analysis of parent–teacher relationships in an inner-city borough, drawn from a two year study which I conducted between 1990 and 1992. These data, gathered primarily through in-depth interviews with parents, teachers and others involved in education locally, are presented within a historical, political and social context. The analysis examines the changing nature of relationships between home and school over the last thirty years, and, in particular, the current emphasis given to parents as consumers of education.

Readers can approach this book in different ways depending on their particular area of interest. The book starts with a sociological and historical analysis of parental roles within education, and then proceeds to consider events and relationships in five primary schools and a local authority parents' centre. Therefore, the book can be read sequentially; alternatively, some readers may prefer to start with the chapters describing events at the schools and the Parents' Centre (chapters 4–8), and then return to the more theoretically-based opening chapters. The following chapter summary provides a guide.

Chapter 1 explores the themes of power and participation in relationships between professionals and non-professionals. The discussion is arranged around a number of key themes: power, empowerment, participation, community and citizenship, and it is illustrated with a brief review of the development of community education. The chapter analyzes the way in which non-professionals are excluded from decision-making processes. In education, this results in individual parental involvement being the primary mechanism through which parents can gain access to the inner workings of a school. *Individual* parental involvement, of course, does not include the possibility of challenging established professional interests in the same way that *collective* parental participation might.

Chapter 2 provides a historical framework, by detailing the changing ways in which the prevailing political discourse defines 'appropriate' parental involvement. The chapter includes a critique of the concept of the parent as a consumer. Chapter 3 contains an appraisal of recent developments and initiatives in home–school relations, and provides a typology of the roles currently on offer to parents: the *supporter/learner*, the *consumer*, the *independent* and the *participant*. Chapter 4 introduces the borough of 'City', the area where the fieldwork took place. Here I describe the locality, City Council and local education authority and introduce the two main case study schools, Hill St and Low Rd. Chapter 5 takes a further critical look at the existing home–school literature, and, in particular, the way in which issues of ethnicity, social class and gender are overlooked. I argue that neglect of these dimensions results in a superficial discussion of ways to enhance home–school relations. I continue by illustrating, with reference to Hill St and Low Rd schools, the centrality of ethnicity, social class and gender in structuring parent–teacher relationships. Chapter 6 focuses on relationships at Hill St and Low Rd, concentrating on two areas, the curriculum and discipline, which are particularly revealing of the nature of parent–teacher relationships in the schools. Chapters 7 and 8 are concerned with the role of mediators in the parent–teacher relationship; chapter 7 analyzes the troubled history of a local authority initiative to place three home–school coordinators in three primary schools in City, whilst chapter 8 concentrates on the establishment of a borough-wide Parents' Centre, independent of any one school, to provide advice and support to parents.

Future developments in home–school relations are the subject of the concluding chapter, chapter 9. Here I return to the themes of the opening chapter, reconsidering them in the light of the material gathered in City. Several commonly cited initiatives to improve home–school relations are considered, including various school-based developments, as well as the broader solutions proffered by writers influenced by communitarian theories and ideas. The book concludes by emphasizing the need for definitions of community and citizenship which centralize heterogeneity and diversity, and therefore can form the basis for a reconsideration and redefinition of home–school relations in the direction of greater parental participation.

Chapter 1

Parents, Power and Participation

Introduction

'No parents beyond this point' — such signs could once be seen in schools around the country, symbolizing the clear division between home and school. These notices reflect attempts by educators to preserve schools as islands of professional expertise, of calm, order and learning, situated apart from their teeming, disorganized, unknowing surroundings.

Such a view of schools requires them to maintain their separateness from the families of those taught. This has been a distinctive theme in teacher ideologies, an attitude especially common towards working class families since the early days of state education. The nineteenth century educator, James Kay-Shuttleworth, saw teachers as missionaries, 'gentilizing' their pupils in preparation for manual employment (Maclure, 1990; Grace, 1978). However, whilst teachers could have an effect on their pupils, their parents were 'beyond the pale', as is evident in the views of this teacher working in a Ragged school in 1850;

> The women swore and shrieked . . . Never before was such a noise heard. I did not believe that human beings resident in this Christian metropolis could so behave. (quoted in Grace, 1978, p.32; see also Ballard, 1937; Gautrey, 1937)

Over a century later, a teacher in 'City' LEA described to me the same need to preserve the school from the influence of those outside its gate.

> It's such a tough, strained area the school is in. So we try and foster a feeling of morality in school, that it's good to be calm, and to do good things, and to work hard to gain an end.

Another interpretation of the school's role centres on its ability to 'convert' or even to 'save' the people living in its locality. This necessitates the school abandoning its isolation and trying to forge links with individuals, families and groups in the surrounding area. However, the nature and purpose of those links are highly specific as the following quotation, referring to a community development project in Birmingham, shows.

> The staff and management committees of St Paul's resource centre and school soon discovered that no matter how much progress they made in the school day all their good work could be swiftly undone overnight, at the weekend, and in the holidays by *unsupportive* aspects of the community . . . The only solution which made sense was for the staff both to teach well and to reach out to the growth and strong points within the community to ensure that they became resilient enough to overcome its negative features *and to support the efforts of the school.* (Atkinson, 1994a, p.33, my emphasis)

Dick Atkinson's analysis assumes that local communities *should* share the school's agenda and priorities, and does not accord any validity to those who do not. It is this disjunction between home and school, and responses to it from both parties, which provide the main theme for this book.

This introductory chapter explores the themes of power and participation in the relationships between professionals and lay people. It analyzes the pressures towards professional dominance which exclude non-professionals from decision-making processes. In education, this results in individual parent–teacher relationships being the primary mechanism through which parents can gain access to the inner workings of a school. *Individual* parental involvement, however, does not offer the same degree of 'threat' to established professional interests as the possibility of *collective* parental participation. This opening chapter develops a theoretical framework in which to locate and explore this assertion.

First, the chapter briefly explores the concept of power, in order to identify the potential for change to current patterns of power and control. The populist and frequently cited solution, 'empowerment', is also examined, and found wanting when measured against the complexities of existing power relationships. Second, the chapter looks at social democratic and New Right approaches to three key concepts central to the debate about parental roles in relation to state education: increasing lay *participation* in state institutions, the discourse of *community* and the discourse of *citizenship*. The New Right/social democratic division is employed because the comparison illuminates both the social democratic consensus of the post-war period and the grounds on which the New Right challenges that agenda. This chapter asks whether either social democratic or New Right approaches help realize alterations in the way in which power is exercised and particular groups are included or excluded. Third, this chapter presents a brief appraisal of community education which provides an illustration of many of the earlier points concerning social democratic definitions of participation, community and citizenship. Community education is an appropriate focus because many of its supporters have argued for a redistribution of power within the education system, away from professionals and towards parents and other local residents. The chapter concludes that, although there are theoretically opportunities for working class parents to participate collectively in the education system, the number of pressures that operate against this is great. This therefore ensures that *individual* parental involvement remains the primary route by which parents can gain access to the state education system.

A Note on Language — The Concept of 'Condensation Symbols'

One of the aims of this book is to deconstruct and examine the usage of certain common terms, such as 'participation', 'partnership', 'community', 'citizenship' and 'empowerment'. All have positive connotations. Like 'participation', 'partnership' is a diffuse concept. It implies a broad spectrum of ideas embracing equality, consensus, harmony and joint endeavour. 'Community' is a term commonly used to give a positive flavour to other concepts with which it is linked, hence 'community care'. 'Citizenship' suggests a secure and positive partnership between the individual and the state. 'Empowerment' implies redistributing control and influence in favour of the disadvantaged and deprived. Edelman (1964) defines such terms as 'condensation symbols'. They 'condense' specific emotions into a particular word or phrase, so that its usage provokes those emotions. However the exact meaning of these condensation symbols is not clearly defined. Indeed they are often kept vague to attract maximum support. Over time, the words gain assumed meanings which are rarely critically scrutinized. Thus their usage may obscure more than it illuminates. This chapter focuses on concepts of 'participation', 'community' and 'citizenship', terms which offer further examples of the phenomenon of 'condensation symbols', but first it considers conceptions of power.

Power, Parents and Professionals

Much of the current home–school literature acknowledges the imbalance in power which structures relationships between parents, especially working class parents, and education professionals (Dehli and Januario, 1994; David, 1993; Merttens and Vass, 1993; Jowett *et al.*, 1991; Tizard *et al.*, 1988; Bastiani, 1987a and 1988a). This inequality is seen as stemming from the discrepancy between the professional knowledge of teachers and local government officers, and anyone who does not work in, and has limited access to those spheres. For specific groups of parents, such as working class and/or ethnic minority parents, that discrepancy is compounded by the dislocation between the cultural framework of their own lives and that of the school. This chapter continues with a few introductory points on the way in which 'power' can be understood.

The work of the Italian neo-Marxist, Antonio Gramsci, is useful here. Gramsci argued that power is exercised, not simply through the coercive apparatus of 'the state',[1] (for example, the army, police, law courts and prisons), but also through the institutions of 'civil society'. Gramsci defined civil society as consisting of a complex network of social relations, embedded in a range of institutions and organisations, such as the churches, schools, political parties, trade unions, the family and voluntary groups. Participation in all these arenas is by consent, rather than coercion (Simon, 1993).

The language of dominant and subordinate groups is totalizing, appearing to suggest an exclusive dichotomy, and therefore has to be treated with care. However, Gramsci did not suggest that subordinate groups were 'powerless', in the face of an all-powerful ruling group. Indeed, Gramsci accepted that individuals of whatever social status have some residual power (he gives as an example, the idea of parents exercising power over their children, (Gramsci, 1971, p.265). However, his emphasis remains on the hierarchical structure of power. Renate Holub (1992) summarizes his position as follows.

> Some social groups possess more economic, social and cultural power than others, and since this imbalance of power is neither easily challenged nor readily changed, there is a directedness to power relations. (p.29)

Gramsci argued that socially dominant groups endeavour to maintain control over other groups by gaining their 'active consent' to the status quo, a process he referred to as *hegemony*. It is through the institutions of civil society, through the assumptions, values and beliefs propagated by the churches, schools, political parties, and so on, that the hegemony of the dominant social group is exercised. However, the ruling class's ideology is not inculcated smoothly. Instead, Gramsci viewed civil society as composed of many sites of struggle at different levels.

He allows, therefore, for the possibility of collective resistance from a subordinate group which might lead to negotiation and concession by the ruling faction (Buci-Glucksmann, 1980). Gramsci argued that the outcome of such struggles is open-ended, which allowed him to foresee the possibility of working class groups developing their own hegemony with which to supplant that of the ruling group. This might occur in a limited fashion, perhaps temporarily in one locality. Thus, Gramscian theory allows for the possibility of 'space' within the education system for working class parents to challenge the hegemony of the existing system.

However, it is not clear from such a large-scale, macro-analysis how such a process takes place, and how the 'active consent' of subordinate groups is won or withdrawn. In posing this question, Henry Giroux (1983) emphasizes the neglected role of agency, or human activity.

> Theories of the state focus primarily on macro and structural issues, resulting in a mode of analysis that points to contradictions and struggle, but says little about how human agency works through such conflicts at the level of everyday life and concrete school

relations . . . The driving force of culture is contained not only in how it functions to dominate subordinate groups, but also in the way in which oppressed groups draw from their own cultural capital and set of experiences to develop an oppositional logic. (1983, pp.281–2; see also Arnowitz and Giroux, 1993, p.90)

Later chapters of the book (chapters 5 and 6) contain examples of particular parents developing 'an oppositional logic' in regard to their children's education, and, more specifically, their role within it. However, this position does not lead them into direct confrontation with, or resistance to, the school. Instead, they maintain a separateness, an *independence* (see chapters 3 and 6) from the school, and its view of 'appropriate' parental behaviour. In this way, their 'oppositional logic' remains implicit. This is unsurprising if we consider the structural constraints which operate upon agency; that is, the way in which the patterns of social relationships, and the workings of institutions create limits and obstacles to change. Giroux (1994) comments,

> As Antonio Gramsci has pointed out, people often find themselves positioned within forms of knowledge, institutional structures and social relationships that have a 'creeping or quiet' kind of hegemony about them. The forms of domination they produce or sustain are not so obvious, not so clear. For instance, dominant groups often invite people to deskill themselves, by promoting what might be called regimes of common sense; in this case people are presented with narratives about their lives, society and the larger world that naturalize events in order to make it appear as if particular forms of inequality and other social injustices are natural, given or endemic to questions of individual character. (p.157)

Again, later chapters contain examples of the process which Giroux describes, particularly in relation to the discourses surrounding 'appropriate' parenting, (see chapters 3, 5 and 6 on the parent as 'supporter/learner', 'sensitive mothering' and the 'good parent' respectively).

On a related point, Iris Marion Young (1990) argues that power in modern societies is widely dispersed through the actions of many agents. She cites Foucault (1977) as suggesting we should look beyond a model of power as,

> ruler and subject . . . and instead analyze the exercise of power as the effect of often liberal and 'humane' practices of education, bureaucratic administration, production and distribution of consumer goods and so on. The conscious actions of many individuals daily contributes to maintaining and reproducing oppression, but those individuals are simply doing their jobs or living their lives, and they do not understand themselves as agents of oppression. (pp.41–2)

Thus, agency is constrained by the hegemony embedded, not just within the practices and understandings of institutions, but also within a whole range of social relationships and regularities. This point is illustrated by chapters 7 and 8.

The success of attempts to alter these social and institutional practices depends, in part, upon the specificities of a particular situation. As noted earlier, Gramscian theory holds that it is possible for socially subordinate groups to develop their own hegemony temporarily, and in a particular locality. Sophie Watson, writing about the incursion of feminists into public sector institutions in Australia comments,

> The ability of feminists to influence the political agenda and to achieve reforms is inevitably a result of specific political and economic relations, of the composition of bureaucratic and political players, of localized powers and resistance, and of the strengths of 'feminisms' within and outside the political structure. (Watson 1990b, p.19)

However, such incursions are played out 'on a terrain already structured by power' (Hatcher and Troyna, 1994, p.167). Thus discourses which advocate fundamental change and which might be harmful to powerful, established interests are vulnerable to reformulation or marginalization (Watson, 1990b); a point which is illustrated by the review of community education later in this chapter.

Empowerment

The frequently cited solution to the problem of unequal power relations between groups is the process of 'empowerment'. The term 'empowerment' became common currency amongst the political left during the 1980s (Troyna, 1994; Gore, 1993). Definitions varied, and were often inexplicit, but tended to centre around the notion of people taking greater control over aspects of their own lives.[2] In education, the social democratic definition of empowerment embodies a simplistic view of social justice, whereby the involvement of parents can be achieved by teachers and other education professionals, 'giving' some of their power to parents, and thereby creating conditions in which an equal partnership between teacher and parent can flourish (Gore, 1993). However, as the preceding paragraphs suggest, 'empowerment' used in this sense, is too simplistic and imprecise a notion to be able to address the complexities of power relations in late twentieth century societies. There are three main points here.

First, the idea that teachers can 'empower' others emphasizes agency, but ignores the considerable limitations imposed on agency by the contexts in which teachers and other education professionals work (Gore, 1990). As chapters

7 and 8 show, even when educational professionals are placed in an apparent position of advocates, speaking on behalf of, and in support of, parents, their actions are constrained by the norms and values of the professional roles and environments within which they work. Second, the concept of empowerment views power as a quantifiable property. It suggests that power 'given' to a subordinate group is consequently lost by the former power-holders. However, as Foucault (1980) argues, power operates at many levels within society. This means it is exercised in a multiplicity of situations by individuals who employ and experience power at different points and in different relationships, with the result that they 'are always in the position of simultaneously undergoing and exercising this power . . . Individuals are the vehicles of power, not its points of application' (p.98). Third, Jennifer Gore (1990 and 1993) argues that understanding power as exercised, rather than possessed requires us to be attentive to the specific context in which 'empowerment' is said to be taking place, rather than advocating generalized initiatives.

On closer examination, strategies which claim they are about *empowering groups* might be more accurately described as *enabling individuals* (see Wolfendale, 1992). That is, they focus on giving individuals skills to create areas of greater freedom and control in their lives. For instance, many adult education classes would fall into this category. However, because these effects are limited to individuals, a process of enabling does nothing to affect the structural constraints which enforce rigid boundaries on many peoples' lives (O'Hagan, 1991b; Troyna, 1994). As Gus John (1990) comments,

> If there is one criticism I have of the concept of adult education it is that . . . it has to do with enabling people to do things on an individual basis, that is creative and productive and minimises stress . . . as distinct from being a project that is about empowering people as groups and collectivities within the communities in the context in which they operate, and by context, I mean as black people, or women or residents in an estate. (p.139)

Thus if empowerment is to retain any validity as a coherent concept, it might be better defined as a precursor of collective citizen participation; a process of setting in motion actions and attitudes that lead to groups of people, generally considered to have little access to state decision-making processes, acting *collectively* to change the conditions shaping their lives, and in addition improving their quality of life within those boundaries. In theory, therefore, parental participation in their children's education could be empowering for parents, allowing them some measure of control over a welfare state institution, which is perceived as crucially important to future life chances, and that has traditionally been largely closed to lay intervention (CCCS, 1981; Ranson, 1990). A policy based on this alternative notion of empowerment would concentrate on developing a participatory ethos within schools so that parents shared decision-making powers with educational professionals.

Participation, Community and Citizenship

This section of the chapter examines several theories concerning relation-ships between government, institutions, professionals and lay constituents. As a complete critical examination of 'participation', 'community' and 'citizen-ship' would each take a book in themselves, this section serves merely to highlight points which are particularly germane to an understanding of the relationships between parents and schools. Social democratic approaches to these concepts are outlined first, as social democracy is seen as the basis on which the post-war consensus was established; namely, 'the idea that social progress could be achieved through gradual state intervention', (David, 1993, p.33). The 1970s and 1980s witnessed the dislocation of social democratic hegemony in the face of a strong challenge from the New Right, and therefore each of the three concepts are re-examined according to New Right values and beliefs.

Participation

Theorizing Participation: Social Democratic Approaches

Philip Woods (1988) argues that 'participation is not necessarily associated with the achievement of any particular social or moral purpose' (see also Richardson, 1983). In contrast, I argue that different conceptions of participa-tion can make particular kinds of outcomes more likely.

The ideology of citizen participation in a social democratic society assumes the desirability of a fully participative democracy. Advocates of citizen par-ticipation argue that the classic vehicle for achieving such a society — the electoral process — is too blunt a tool as it renders citizens passive between elections, concentrating power exclusively within the governing elite (Carr, 1991). Only through the process of participation itself can the 'informed con-sent' of those governed be achieved (Pateman, 1970; Ward, 1976; Miliband, 1984). Such involvement in the management of state institutions would allow citizens to develop a sense of 'ownership' over organisations previously per-ceived as alienating and/or patronizing (Dale, 1989; Seddon *et al.*, 1990).

Some commentators have perceived the situation to be unproblematic. Thus pluralist theories assert that the political system consists of diverse inter-est groupings competing openly for access to power. Robert Dahl (1961), studying American local politics, concluded that,

> The independence, penetrability and heterogeneity of the various seg-ments of the political stratum all but guarantee that any dissatisfied group will find spokesmen in the political stratum. (p.93)

However Bennington (1977), writing about the 1970s Community Develop-ment Projects, described 'flaws in the pluralist heaven' (Schattschneider, 1960), noting that community participation in decision-making was, in effect, restricted by existing decision-makers who allowed it to operate only in directions they deem to be acceptable. Steven Lukes (1974), in a critique of pluralism, comments that,

> the diversity and openness that Dahl sees may be highly misleading
> if power is being exercised within the system to limit decision-making
> to acceptable issues. (pp.36–7)

Bacharach and Baratz develop this point by highlighting the processes by which an agenda is formed. They quote Schattschneider (1960);

> All forms of political organisation have a bias in favour of the exploita-tion of some kinds of conflict and the suppression of others, because
> organisation is a mobilisation of bias. Some issues are organised
> into politics while others are organised out. (Bacharach and Baratz,
> 1970, p.8)

Ken Newton's (1976) study of decision-making in Birmingham provides an example of this point. He identified a 'limited or partial' pluralism; namely, for some pressure groups the system does operate in a broadly pluralist manner. These groups have effective links with decision-makers, their opinions are heard and influence policy. The character of the 'successful' groups varied depending on the issue involved, but they were often professional and busi-ness associations (also Eade, 1989; Cochrane, 1993). Newton comments,

> some interests are difficult to aggregate while others are represented
> by organisations which, because of the social and economic position
> of their membership, have a weaker set of political weapons than
> opposing groups — consumers as against producers, tenants as against
> landlords, pedestrians as against motorists. (1976, p.227)

Lukes, however, believes that the picture is still incomplete. He argues that the most subtle and insidious form of power is non-decision making. This extends beyond the form that Bacharach and Baratz describe, which is the exclusion by power holders of various issues from the agenda against the wishes of others. Lukes argues that issues may be excluded by decision-makers, without provoking dissent from other groups, even though raising those issues on a public agenda might prove to be in the latter's interests. He continues by noting 'the many ways in which potential issues are kept out of politics, whether through the operation of social forces and institutional practices or through individuals' decisions' (Lukes, 1974, p.24).

'Manipulating the Ambiguity of Participation' (Croft and Beresford, 1992, p.38)

Even when initiatives with the aim of increasing citizen participation do develop, the process is far from straightforward. There are two main points here. First, that attempts to increase participation may prove illusory in substance. Second, that participatory initiatives are primarily designed to legitimate the more general action of the institution concerned. Thus they may result in bringing a few, previously excluded, *individuals* into the decision-making process, but do little to affect the position of excluded *groups*. The first assertion is well-supported by empirical research. One well-known example is Arnstein's (1969) ladder of participation. This has eight 'rungs' indicating different amounts of citizen power, although all are subsumed under the label of participation. At the bottom, for instance, are what she terms 'manipulation' and 'therapy'. These masquerade as opportunities for citizen participation but would be more accurately described as opportunities for the decision-makers to inform, 'educate' or even 'cure' those citizens involved. The ladder progresses through stages of involvement which allow participants to voice their opinions but retain executive powers for the decision-makers. Transference of power occurs at the top two rungs only, 'delegated power' and 'citizen control' (Harlow and Rawlings, 1984, p.440).

Similarly, Gibson's study of black community groups and their relationships with local authority officers defines the majority of their interactions as fitting his 'advisory' or even 'illusion' models of participation (Gibson, 1987). Even when exercises in increasing community participation are underway, not all citizens can respond to the initiative (Croft and Beresford, 1993). Newton's (1976) study of voluntary groups in Birmingham showed that groups with the least radical aims were most able to establish fruitful relationships with local authority officers. Class, ethnicity and gender may all be important factors in determining opportunities and willingness to participate. Although data in this area are sketchy there is, unsurprisingly, evidence that white, middle class people remain most likely to take up voluntary positions in local groups (Thomas, 1986). Indeed Croft and Beresford (1992) conclude that, 'typically participatory schemes have mirrored rather than challenged broader oppressions and discriminations' (p.33).

Thus we begin to sense the gap between the reality and the rhetoric of citizen participation. This obfuscation can result in the same language being used for initiatives with widely differing aims. On this second point, Nicholas Beattie quotes Pennock's (1979) four reasons for introducing participatory democracy: it could serve to *legitimize* institutional or governmental activity; to make it more *responsive* to its clients or electorate; to aid the *personal development* of individuals who become more closely involved in matters affecting their lives; or to *overcome the alienation* of groups supposedly served by that institution (Beattie, 1985, p.5). The first two — 'responsiveness' and 'legitimacy' — can be fulfilled without transferring power. They are conservative in character, their main aim being to ensure the smooth running of the institution. Aims three and four — 'personal development' and 'overcoming alienation', differ in that they are both concerned with minimizing the powerlessness felt by those formerly excluded from the system (*ibid.*). Both these aims, but especially the last, require fundamental changes in existing structures and attitudes, which, as the typologies suggest, are attained less frequently.

Theorizing Participation: New Right Approaches

The rise of the New Right[3] during the 1970s and 1980s has severely disrupted social democratic principles. One result of this is the emphasis which has been placed upon a particular version of participation which derives from economic neo-liberalism. This advocates an enterprise culture in which the market operates free from state constrictions, and is reflected in the calculated move away from collective state provision towards an individual client orientation discernible throughout state welfare policy since 1979 (Adler *et al.*, 1989). In this perspective, citizens are assigned the role of individual consumer and exercise power through the operation of consumer choice. The preeminence of the individual affects the possible forms of citizen participation, as it serves to marginalize collective activity, which in turn, deters potential alliances between individuals with similar interests (John, 1990). Additionally, the consumerist approach to user involvement means that the consumer's power comes from her ability to withdraw her 'custom' from an organization, rather than to participate in its running. Any changes in an institution or service resulting from an aggregate of individual choices in a particular direction are viewed as the supposedly neutral effect of market forces (see chapter of this book; Ranson, 1988; Jonathan, 1993). In relation to education, many commentators assert that the apparent increases in power open to individual parents appear tokenistic, or of use only to a minority (Whitty and Menter, 1989; Ball, 1994a). Yet as Harland (1988) notes, the significance of introducing ostensibly participative processes, such as increased parental choice, lies not just in their outcome, but in the very act of introducing them.

> The state has apparently made an honest attempt to accommodate the views of those concerned . . . having done so its policies *and* its right to enforce them are rescued from legitimation deficit. (p.98, original emphasis)

Despite the many flaws in implementation, social democratic forms of collective participation do offer the possibility of enhanced lay influence over state institutions. New Right concepts of participation offer individuals the possibility of 'exiting' from public sector institutions, but not participating in their management (Bash and Coulby, 1989). To use Hirschman's terms, parents-as-consumers are offered 'exit' but not 'voice'; that is the chance to leave a school, but not to participate in its development (Hirschman, 1970; Ball, 1987).

Community and Citizenship

Theorizing 'The Community': Social Democratic Approaches

Used as a condensation symbol, the connotations of 'community' are always positive. Consequently it is often employed to add a 'warm' and humane gloss to other concepts. 'Community care' is a prime example, giving an impression of a level of care unobtainable from impersonal bureaucracies and institutions. 'Community spirit' is another. The term's positive associations derive from Tonnies' influential work. He distingushed two ways of ordering society — *Gemeinschaft* (community) and *Geschellschaft* (association). The former refers to typical (or stereotypical) rural lifestyles, centred around agriculture and the home. Shared beliefs, continuity and collaboration pervade all areas of life. In contrast, association is linked with city life, underpinned by trade and charac-terised by heterogeneity and a corresponding alienation (Tonnies, 1955).

Concepts of urban alienation were to exercise a strong hold on many sociologists, writing in the early and mid-twentieth century, whose work con-centrated on the generation or loss of community. Louis Wirth, for instance, argued that in urban settings, people's primary relationships with their close friends and families were weakened by the demands of city life, and that rational institutions (for example, the police or social services) could not adequately compensate for the resulting fragmentation (Wirth, 1964; Knox, 1982). His conclusions were questioned by Herbert Gans who suggested that many inner city residents were relatively permanent members of 'urban villages', which contained cohesive social networks based on shared ethnicity and social class (Gans, 1977; Young and Wilmott, 1957). This became an increasingly influential view of community, stressing as it does the locality-as-community, and assuming traditional, homogeneous, contained social networks, whose members share values, assumptions and beliefs.

However, urban localities are now increasingly heterogeneous in terms of social class and ethnicity. Residents in one particular area, say a housing estate, may be divided in many ways, not least by differences in class, ethnicity and religion (Thomas, 1986; Harrison, 1983). Yet, this trend, which Gilbert (1992) refers to as 'the "pluralization" of social life' (p.55), also has positive consequences. The recognition of diversity, for example, is important because, as Sallie Westwood notes, the concept of community as homogeneous and cohesive also has the effect of ignoring, or suppressing any differences.

The contradictions and fractures of gender, ethnicity and age divi-sions to name the most important, melted and were not constructed as the central part of 'communities'. Thus community was located within a consensus and constructed around the hegemony of white Englishness and homogenized as 'the community', becoming itself the subject/object of educational interventions. (Westwood, 1992, p.234).

Despite such criticisms, perceptions of area-based communities with spatially defined social networks, affected the development of ideas about community education, and remain highly influential. Thus schools are encouraged to assume that a cohesive community should exist 'out-there'. If it does not appear to do so, then the school may attempt, single-handedly, to resolve the deficiency (Jeffs, 1992).

Theorizing Citizenship: Social Democratic Approaches

One of the most influential commentators on citizenship was TH Marshall (1950) writing in the immediate post-war period. His conception of citizenship had three component parts: *political* (for example, the right to vote), *civil* (for example, individual freedoms — of speech, right to hold property, right of access to courts etc.) and *social*. By 'social', Marshall meant access to welfare rights which would protect citizens from poverty and allow them to participate fully in society. Marshall viewed the welfare state as the guarantor of these social rights, and indeed the period from 1945 until the early 1970s witnessed the establishment and growth of the welfare state. However, as time went on, Marshall's vision was obscured by the growth of other aspects of the expanding and professionally-led social democratic welfare state (Ranson, 1990; Cole and Furbey, 1994). For instance, the state was presented as an agent of reform, and public sector professionals were allocated a key role within that project, on the grounds of their expertise. As Paul Wilding (1982) comments,

> Fundamental to the power of professionals in policy-making and administration is an acceptance of their right to define needs and problems. It underpins their power and provides a necessary legitimation for its exercise. (p.29)

Similarly Patrick McAuslan (1980), writing about land-use planning, refers to this phenomenon amongst bureaucrats as the *ideology of public interest*. This describes the belief that administrators can, and should, define what is in the 'general' interest and then act on those terms. Such a stance encourages a rather passive model of citizenship, and the resulting inequality between professional and lay person has obvious consequences for the way in which a situation or problem is defined and the 'solution' formulated. The inequality becomes more pronounced if imbalances in professional knowledge are compounded by unequal possession of more general social, cultural and financial resources.

Theorizing 'The Community': New Right Approaches

Thus the social democratic approach to community and citizenship centred around the gradual expansion of social rights through the development of the welfare state. The rationale was to secure a reasonable standard of living which was essential if a sense of belonging to, and an ability to participate in, 'the community' were to be fostered. By contrast, the predominant New Right approach emphasizes 'a society in which free individuals pursue their own interests in the marketplace according to agreed rules of conduct' (Upton, 1987, p.21). In New Right rhetoric, 'community' is commonly portrayed as an unproblematic aggregation of individual choices. For example, by responding to the pressures of their local 'market', schools and other public institutions will develop in line with the specific desires of their local community,

> Schools and hospitals are institutions at the heart of a local com-
> munity. They can and should command the loyalties both of staff
> and parents, of pupils and patients. If they are free from elaborate
> bureaucratic control, they can develop their own distinct characters;
> they belong to the neighbourhood, not to Whitehall. (Willetts, cited in
> the Hillcole Group, 1993, p.5)

The American commentators, Chubb and Moe see similar results arising from their proposals to curtail democratic political control of schools, and replace it with a largely unfettered market in education:

> Schools would be legally autonomous, free to govern themselves as
> they want, specify their own goals and programmes and methods . . .
> select their own student bodies . . . Parents and students would be
> legally empowered to choose among alternative schools, aided by
> institutions designed to promote active involvement. (Chubb and Moe,
> 1990, p.226)

Both observations rest on the assumption that the dominance of the market will result in consensus between clients and producers, which will, in turn, lead to a regenerated sense of 'community'. However, Fazal Rizvi (1993) asserts that this is little more than the rhetoric of 'romantic localism', an effort to make more palatable a system that is increasingly controlled by the centre (p.155).

Theorizing Citizenship: New Right Approaches

New Right conceptions of citizenship (in many respects in direct opposition to Marshall's citizenship of entitlement), appear to have gained considerable ground. The success of the New Right in this area can be explained to some extent by the inadequacies and partial realizations of the social democratic definition of citizenship. Dawn Oliver notes that, 'in the last two decades or so, the elements of the citizenship of entitlement as conceived by Marshall have been eroded, and the weakness of the legal and political foundations of that conception has been exposed' (1991b, p.36).

There are two main strands to the New Right version of citizenship: the neo-liberal emphasis on the citizen as consumer, and the neo-conservative concept of the 'active citizen'. One of the most contentious aspects of New Right ideology is its attempt to redefine social democratic notions of citizenship in terms of consumerism. In an article on the Citizen's Charter,[4] Taylor (1992) criticizes the way in which the two concepts are bound together and asks,

> Is citizenship constructed simply through the public world of consumerism or equally through the social relations of reproduction and the family . . . Is the content of citizenship something to be handed down in a charter or something that should be built on the self-advocacy of citizens? (p.93)

Similarly, Ranson (1986) suggests that an awareness of the interaction between individuals is missing from the market model of citizenship. Consumers make individual purchasing choices, and although consumer groups exist, their remit only covers the consumer's relationship with the producer. Thus New Right concepts of citizenship are,

> essentially directed to promoting the individual persona and private autonomy of the individual, rather than citizenship in the sense of the relationship between the individual and the state or community. (Oliver, 1991, p.160)

Michael Peters (1994) argues that the New Right version of citizenship constructs individuals as 'homo economicus', in other words, people are defined as self-interested, rational, utility maximizers (also Dunleavy, 1991). As Peters notes, this has the effect of ignoring inequalities arising from class, ethnicity and gender differences, because it posits the individual as self-sufficient 'not defined by anything or anyone other than itself' (Young, 1990, p.228).

The 'rolling back of the frontiers of the state' and the corresponding limitations placed on state institutions in favour of action by individual citizens is reflected in an alternative New Right version of citizenship, which is not primarily linked to consumerism: the concept of the 'active citizen'. This view, favoured by Conservative politicians, focuses not on entitlements, the duties of the state towards its citizens, but rather on citizens' duties towards their communities. In 1989, Home Secretary, Douglas Hurd famously cited 'neighbourhood watch' schemes as an instance of 'active citizenship'. In 1994, Home Secretary, Michael Howard was exhorting citizens to 'walk with a purpose' in an effort to deter street crime. Thus citizens were given a key role in augmenting one of the most conservative of state functions: the maintenance of law and order. However, the 'active citizen' shares a common core with 'homo economicus' — they are both premised on the idea that citizens are individual beings who want and need only a minimal relationship with the state.

Having outlined the theoretical terrain, I will now move to an analysis of how these ideas influence practice; the next section examines community education, seeing it as a social democratic attempt to involve parents and members of surrounding localities in schools. The section looks at the problems and pitfalls of the social democratic approach and the reconstruction of community education under the New Right.

Democracy in Action or Surveillance and Control? The Statist Reform Model of Community Education

Community education is an umbrella term for a bewildering range of projects and initiatives worldwide (Poster and Kruger, 1990). However, for the purposes of this review, I propose to work with a single distinction between two main approaches to community education; the first of which I shall call the *statist reform* model and the second the *radical* model.[5] The former is underpinned by social democratic principles, and emphasizes open community access to school facilities, and closer links between the institution and the local community through the involvement and participation of local people. The radical approach is equated with adult education and community development programmes, such as those associated with Tom Lovett (Lovett, 1982; Lovett *et al.*, 1983) and Paolo Freire (Freire, 1972 and 1985). It sees education as a process through which people can identify and address social and economic issues which affect their locality. My contention is that, despite a tendency in some quarters to describe reformist strategies in radical terms, most community education initiatives currently base themselves on *statist reform* principles. The name refers to the emphasis the model places upon *statist* strategies, that is, attempts to ameliorate, improve and reform state provision. This provides a contrast with radical community education, whose advocates are more likely to emphasize *substitutional* strategies which 'concentrate on building an independent, popular educational provision' (CCCS, 1981, p.36).

The statist reform model of community education has a number of features. It concentrates on improving the access and availability of the school's resources and facilities for local residents. It is concerned to encourage closer links between the school and the surrounding population; often emphasizing the creation or regeneration of a 'community spirit' amongst all the people connected with the school (O'Hagan, 1987). This highlights the importance of building and maintaining a consensus — a sense of shared values and beliefs, and a feeling of ownership of the school organization.

However, these aims warrant critical examination on a number of grounds. First, as noted above, the social democratic definition of 'community', which is the one employed within mainstream debates on community education, is limited. Second, much community education practice can be criticized for planning educational initiatives without reference to the social and economic characteristics of the surrounding populations. Instead, community education focuses on both the alteration of those individual behaviours and attitudes which affect the school, and the formulation and implementation of apparently participatory initiatives within an unchanged hierarchical structure. If successful, these strategies may increase the legitimacy of existing ways of working, but not develop far-ranging alternatives.

The work of Eric Midwinter, an influential proponent of social democratic community education, provides illustrations of these points. Midwinter, working primarily in schools in the Liverpool Educational Priority Area (EPA) of the 1970s, was a leading figure in the development of the idea of community primary schools. Like Henry Morris[6] before him, Midwinter identified a lack of 'community' as a deficiency in the locality. His remedy, again shared by his predecessor, was its regeneration by the school; the aim being to create a sense of ownership, 'community spirit', and shared values amongst people using the community provision (Midwinter, 1972).

However, this emphasis on the commonality of views and attitudes assumes unity and consensus, and thereby overlooks the diversity inherent within urban communities, and the likelihood of disagreements and perhaps conflict between different groups with different experiences stemming from their structural locations (O'Hagan, 1987; Baron 1988 and 1989). An example is provided by Midwinter's accounts of his work in the Liverpool EPA. As Westwood (1992) notes the local residents appear to lack a social class, gender or ethnic identity, remaining instead a generalised entity, described as 'people' or 'folk'. The statist reform model of community education views conflict as abnormal and negative. Its appearance is often defined in terms of destructive, highly personal disputes, whilst the fundamental causes lie submerged and unarticulated. This process is detailed in Phil Carspecken's (1990) account of the community occupation of Croxteth School in Liverpool, and the disagreements about the future and direction of the campaign between teachers and the coordinating Action Committee. The root of the dispute was the conflict between two very different ideologies. Most teachers supported moves towards increased grassroots control of the school, while local activists wanted to court Labour Party and trade union support to reinstate a state-funded and managed school. The adoption of these viewpoints by the two opposing camps reflected their present and past experiences, and was linked to the interaction of social class and gender. However, internally, the situation was defined almost exclusively in terms of personality differences rather than variations in social positioning.

The emphasis on the importance of maintaining consensus is closely connected to the legitimizing of the schooling process — a vital function of the statist reform model of community education. By bringing the school and its 'community' together, it aims to strengthen consensus around the school's aims. It seeks to make education — 'school knowledge' (Whitty, 1985; Carspecken 1990) — more accessible to adults, through part-time classes and courses, and to children, by introducing a curriculum 'relevant' to their experiences outside school. As noted earlier, it is through these and similar mechanisms, that the statist reform model focuses on altering individual attitudes and behaviour. Interpersonal relationships between local adults and staff are expected to improve through increased contact and communication. This process will, in theory, break down parents' presumed apathy and children's resistance to the education system, as well as raising levels of achievement (Midwinter, 1972; Rennie, 1985).

However, acting as agents for the legitimization of the education system leaves community schools vulnerable to the accusation that they have, in effect, a hidden agenda of social control. Steve Baron (1989) dubs as 'surveillance' the attempts by Midwinter's Liverpool Project to collect information on the local area and residents. In particular, he criticizes Midwinter for seeking to impose a generic, liberal version of child-rearing upon the local working-class population with the purpose of making the school function more efficiently. Similarly, Will Cowburn (1986) calls much reformist community education practice a 'palliative for inner-city decay' (p.132).

Developments in the community education field are often inspired by professionals within the school or the LEA, or by outside researchers. Thus they are 'top-down', and may find it hard to gain lay confidence and enthusiasm despite the camouflage of presumed social unity. As a result, professional autonomy remains largely intact, despite spasmodic efforts accompanied by radical rhetoric, to disperse decision-making power.[7] The statist reform model has also produced particular forms of organization in community designated schools, namely, a *school-plus* model, where extra community activities and resources are 'bolted on', leaving the fundamental organization and control of the school unchanged (*ibid.*; Watts, 1990). The weakness of the 'school-plus' perspective is its tendency to result in organizational and attitudinal divisions between the compulsory schooling 'arm' of the organization and the community 'arm'. Adults entering the institution as parents, come into contact with its compulsory schooling arm which remains largely impervious to any more radical influence that might be emanating from the 'community' arm, (Martin, 1987). Within the school, professionals retain control, whilst parents may be invited in to be 'educated' into a school-approved method of interacting with their children. This leaves parents with only the choice of whether to conform or not.

> Parents were once kept out of schools so as to allow the professionals uninterrupted control; parents are now being encouraged to get involved and come into school so that they can understand why the professional exercises control in the manner he/she does. The base-line remains intact but its preservation is achieved by methods opposite to those which had been used. (Cowburn, 1986, p.18)

More radical initiatives which do seek to develop a role for lay adults as participants in the management and organization of education, remain at the level of theory, or come into existence as small-scale projects, often in non-statutory areas of education, and with limited impact on mainstream policies and projects (see Cowburn 1986; Battern, Ralph and Sears 1993 for examples). As a result community schools have had a limited impact on the state system in general, as regards formulating a more participative role for parents and other lay adults.

It is on this ground especially that radical community education projects challenge the statist reform model (Lovett, 1982). In his analysis of the 'bottom-up' takeover of Croxteth Comprehensive, Carspecken (1990) contrasts its strong effect on the activists from Croxteth's housing estates with more ineffectual 'top-down' policies.

> There was a rise in the confidence of the participants . . . the feeling that by being involved they could do something about the circum-stances of their lives. This translated into a trust of their own perceptions of educational processes so that some could challenge the experts. This growth in the desire for political and community activity along-side the growth in a critical awareness of schooling is precisely what advocates of community schooling have called for but have found so difficult to create through the policies of education authorities and educationalists. (p.181)

To summarize, the post-war ascendancy of social democratic principles has fashioned a specific model of community education — the statist reform model. It is based on a conception of 'community' that is too one-dimensional to accurately describe many urban localities. Just as the concept of 'locality-as-community' assumes shared values and beliefs between people based on a common place of residence, the statist reform model of community education makes the same assumption based on shared attendance at the school. Yet such unity cannot be taken-for-granted. Temporary agreements on specific issues may arise, but consensus is unlikely to prosper, unless differences in values and attitudes (stemming from occupational divisions, ethnicity, religion etc.) are addressed. Neither does the statist reform model challenge the con-tinuing professional dominance of the parent–teacher relationship. Thus, it cannot ameliorate lay feelings of alienation from the education system. Indeed it may even contribute to them, as the rhetoric of 'partnership' and 'ownership' risks raising expectations that are not fulfilled.

The New Right's Appropriation of Community Education

During the 1980s, concepts once acknowledged as part of the progressive, liberal vocabulary of community education were appropriated and redefined by the New Right (Allen and Martin, 1992). Martin (1992), identifying this phenomenon, suggests that schools and colleges may react by adopting particular 'attractive' elements of the community education rhetoric in an attempt to enhance their market-share. A similar point is made by Sharon Gewirtz, Stephen Ball and Richard Bowe (1995) in their discussion of the creeping incursion of private sector management techniques into public sector institutions. They assert that this forces many senior teachers to become 'bilingual', speaking both the language of education and the language of management. The language of management highlights a new benefit to developing links with 'the community'- finance. Gewirtz, Ball and Bowe quote a headteacher on this subject.

> The idea of letting and all that sort of thing has very much come to the fore. [We] have this commercial base that wasn't there four years ago ... The joy and the bliss when we got the wedding ... with the marquee, and we got loads of money for it, and I thought, what am I doing, celebrating the fact that people are going to have a wedding in the grounds? It didn't really have anything to do with what we were there for. (in press)

In his discussion of the discourse of community education, Michael Peters (1994) points not to New Right reappropriation of its values, but to their outright marginalization. Citing the example of educational reforms in New Zealand, he traces the developments in governance in secondary education. At first government reports contained commitments to establishing local community education forums and a consultative national body, the Parent Advocacy Council. However these organisations were short-lived, leading Peters to conclude that,

> given the wider context of public sector reforms [with an emphasis on consumer choice and 'effective' management rather than participation] the promise of community and devolution has been usurped by the institutionalization of neo-liberal individualistic principles. (p.71).

If, as Peters suggests, New Right discourses are essentially hostile to social democratic community education, then its future looks bleak. However, recent developments in 'communitarianism', a concept which is explored further in chapter 9, may offer the statist reform model of community education a new lease of life. Radical conceptions of community education, however, are likely to remain politically unpopular.

Conclusion

This chapter considers the uneasy relationship between school and home and the imbalances in power between parents and professionals which structure that relationship. It argues that 'space' does exist, in theory at least, for groups of non-professionals to participate in the running of state institutions. Gramsci's theory of hegemony is alluded to, in demonstrating the possibility of *collective* resistance from relatively powerless groups. However, the realization of this is subject to many constraints through established institutional practices and accepted social relations and regularities. Social democratic approaches to empowerment, participation, community and citizenship, which all contain a rhetoric of citizen participation in decision-making, are examined and found to be beset by limitations and inadequacies. Therefore, they are unlikely to result in an expansion in opportunities for lay participation, and may even lead to a reinforcement of professional power. This is exemplified, in relation to education, by the review of community education, for it is in this field that the concept of collective parental participation has found its fullest realization to date. Yet this chapter has argued that the definitions of participation, community and citizenship underlying the social democratic statist reform model are flawed, which results in a limited realization of the progressive elements of community education. However, whereas, in principle, social democratic models of participation encourage collective involvement (albeit heavily circumscribed in practice), New Right 'readings' of the concept are essentially individual. This emphasis on individualism is equally reflected in the rearticulation of the concepts of community and citizenship by the New Right.

In educational terms the New Right emphasis on individualism has resulted in the government sponsorship of parental choice and school based management. Thus in education, collective participation as enshrined in much community education rhetoric has been banished from the policy spotlight, and parents have been offered a role as consumers within a fragmented and atomised system. The next chapter analyzes how a parental role as consumer has been established and popularized by Conservative ideology. It sets this development in a historical context through briefly examining the changing economic and social context which preceded the 1980s' succession of the New Right.

Notes

1 The use of inverted commas recognizes the contested nature of the term, 'the state', and acknowledges the work of theorists who emphasize its 'erratic and disconnected' nature (Watson, 1990c, p.237). As Sophie Watson says, 'There are many different varieties of the state, spatially and historically. Each of them has its own combination of institutions, apparatuses and arenas which have their own histories, contradictions, relations and connections, internally and externally' (Watson, 1990b p.7); also Allen, 1990; Ben Tovim *et al.*, 1986 for the concept of the 'extended state').

2 The vagueness and imprecision with which the term 'empowerment' is used allows it to be appropriated and repackaged by the right, to emerge as referring to the rights of individual consumers (see Troyna and Vincent, 1995).

3 As this chapter and the next make clear, it needs to be emphasised that the New

Right is not a homogeneous group (see Dale, 1989 for various groupings who, in the 1980s, came under the New Right banner).

4 The Citizen's Charter was launched in 1991 as an attempt by the Major government to raise the standards of public services.

5 The statist reform model proposed here combines Martin's (1987) 'universal' and 'reformist' models. Martin describes the former as the secondary school/college emphasizing open access to facilities and integrated provision of resources to serve a wide age-range. The reformist model targets particular groups and areas perceived as disadvantaged. It concentrates on fostering closer links between the institution and the local population through the latter's involvement in the school. Conflating Martin's two models into a hybrid emphasizes their similarities.

6 Henry Morris was responsible for developing village community colleges in Cambridgeshire in the 1930s.

7 Jeffs further refines this point by asserting that community schools are often dominated not simply by teachers at all levels, but exclusively by senior management. He argues that the current model for the community college, which claims descent from those established by Henry Morris, encourages the headteacher's post to become that 'of a warden, not only of the school but of the community itself' (Jeffs, 1992, p.21).

Chapter 2

The Changing Role of 'The Parent' in State Education

Introduction

This chapter provides a historical framework in which to locate the study of current parent–teacher relationships. First, it briefly traces the development of views concerning parents' roles in relation to state education. These developments, from the 1960s to the present day, are embedded within their particular social, political and economic contexts. The 1960s is chosen as a starting point because this decade witnessed the switching of emphasis by policy-makers' from secondary schooling to primary and early childhood education, (Silver, 1990; David, 1993). The second part of the chapter concentrates on the education policies of the 1980s and early 1990s, and analyzes their presentation of 'appropriate' parental roles.

Social Democracy and the State Education System

The immediate post-war period was one of optimism regarding education. Expansion of the state system was expected to lead both to economic growth *and* greater social equality; yet the disparity between these aims was not widely recognized or acknowledged (CCCS, 1981). The education service was largely under the control of a homogeneous elite consisting of (white, male) local chief education officers, officials from the Department of Education and Science (DES), and some leaders of the teachers' associations. These parties assumed the existence of a core of shared values and beliefs pertaining to education (Dale, 1989; Ozga and Gewirtz, 1990). Therefore, politics — certainly party politics — was seen as having no part to play in the management of the education system. However, this climate of 'benevolent paternalism' (CCCS, 1981) left most of the population without voice or immediate means with which to influence educational provision.

This was a period of increasing influence for public sector professionals which also had specific benefits for the teaching profession. By the 1960s, the decentralized nature of the education system had allowed teachers to accumulate a certain amount of autonomy; or at least the appearance of autonomy. Gerald

Grace suggests that although the notion of autonomy is somewhat illusory, it is 'celebrated in the rhetoric of the occupational group; is strong in the consciousness of many teachers; and is seen to be the glorious culmination of the long struggles waged by teacher groups against "obnoxious interference"' (Grace, 1978, p.98). Teachers may be controlled from above, as Grace suggests, by exam boards and universities; they may be controlled from within by a conservative occupational culture and by professional training, but they are not controlled from below, and below was where parents were in the educational hierarchy. Many teachers viewed parents as inconvenient distractions from their real task of teaching the children behind closed classroom doors.

However the 1960s also witnessed the growth of public disillusionment with welfare state services (Adler *et al.*, 1989). A growing lack of trust in bureaucracy was accompanied by demands for more public participation in decision-making. Politicians responded in several ways. Initiatives were introduced to create administrative systems responsive to public demands which would generate renewed confidence. Attempts were made to enhance opportunities for greater public participation in some state activities. The Skeffington Report (MoH, 1969), for example advocated more community involvement in planning. However, as we saw in chapter 1, such initiatives may prove illusory in substance. The Skeffington Report for instance was criticized for recommending that residents should be *informed* about decisions, rather than involved in *making* them (Ward, 1976). Similarly in education, much of the debate on comprehensivization was confined to educational professionals and politicians. Ken Newton's (1976) study of local government in Birmingham showed that parents were involved, if at all, through pressure groups organized by the teaching unions. Despite, or perhaps because of, this exclusivity, independent campaigning parents' groups appeared during this period. The first was the Advisory Centre for Education (ACE), a resolutely non-partisan group, which sprang from the infant consumer movement and concentrated on informing parents about education. Another survivor from this period is the Campaign for the Advancement of State Education, (CASE), a consortium of locally active groups. Neither group presented a threat to the educational status quo, as they both stressed their general support for teachers and LEAs (Beattie, 1985). In addition, their lack of resources in comparison with other interest groups rendered their influence somewhat marginal (Woods, 1988).

The Plowden Report

The 1967 Plowden Report continued the trend of advocating more public involvement in state institutions. It argued that schools had a duty to encourage parental interest in their child's education, and that children's levels of achievement would improve, as they benefitted from positive parental attitudes (CACE, 1967). Despite the Report's emphasis on the school's duty to involve parents, it saw parental willingness to conform to the school's values as the determining factor. John Bastiani describes its approach in the following way,

> If the least cooperative parent rose to the level of the most cooperative, the effect would be much larger than if the worst school rose to the level of the best, or the least prosperous parent rose to the level of the most prosperous (cited in Bastiani, 1987b, p.92; also CACE, 1967, para.129)

The Report's research reflects a social class bias, judging parental interest from how frequently teachers saw the child's parents, and the type of out-of-school activities parents conducted with the children.

> Plowden exhorted teachers to enter into 'partnerships' with parents while simultaneously conveying that the task of the teacher in disadvantaged areas was to compensate children for all the things their parents . . . did not give them, or even to counteract parental influence altogether. (Hewison, 1985, pp.45–6)

The aim was to 'convert' as many *individual* parents as possible to supporting the goals of the school. Plowden might represent the 'biggest single influence upon the study and practice of home–school relationships in Britain' (Bastiani, 1987b, p.91), but if it 'marks the time when power begins to flow back to the parents' (Partington and Wragg, 1989, p.124) that definition of power must remain limited. Plowden embodied a consensus view of home–school relationships, stretching the school's walls to include those parents who were cooperative and supportive.

The Breakdown of Consensus

Expectations of the new comprehensive system were high. It was expected to usher in a new age of increased educational opportunities for all (CCCS, 1981). Yet during the 1970s, research began to highlight the limitations of the school as an instrument for achieving greater social equality (Bernstein, 1975; Bowles and Gintis, 1976; Halsey, Heath and Ridge, 1980). This appeared to confirm the experience of many parents — that progress through the education system was far from a guarantee of enhanced life chances. Additionally, many parents perceived their inferiority in professional eyes (Sharp and Green 1975). These concerns were taken up by a group of right-wing educationists opposed to the social democratic experiment with egalitarianism. The first Black Paper, appearing only a year after the Plowden Report, called for a return to traditional educational methods, moral values, and a curriculum representing the best of 'British culture'. Although the writers may have originally appeared to be 'the dying chant of defeated elitism' (Bash and Coulby, 1989 p.5), they soon gained ground. By 1975 the Black Papers had adopted a proactive tone, proposing more parental choice through a system of educational vouchers. Their ideas were increasingly disseminated to a wider public through the media, which fostered a 'moral panic' (Cohen, 1980) over educational standards (Chitty, 1989). The reception given to the Bullock Report (DES, 1975) on language teaching (described in the Daily Mail as full of 'trendy pieties', cited in Chitty, 1989, p.64) and the media's reception of Neville Bennett's *Teaching Styles and Pupil Progress* (1976) demonstrate that less than ten years after Plowden's publication, 'progressive' education had become a 'folk-devil' (Cohen, 1980).[1] This discourse, set in the context of a declining economic situation, became very powerful despite the lack of supportive empirical evidence. As Stephen Ball (1990) notes,

> This refrain entered into the generally accepted 'what we all know about school' . . . In this way the discourse . . . constitutes an 'imposition of the real' (Baudrillard, 1988) where the opposition between things as presented and what's really going on begins to dissolve. Signs take on a life of their own. (p.25)

This was the beginning of a reconstruction of 'parent power' to serve a conservative discourse. Whereas social democracy separated 'politics' and education, the right merged left-wing politics and progressive beliefs about education, and juxtaposed them with 'good' education and parental concerns.

> The Black Paper authors . . . 'care passionately about education' (*Daily Mail*, 2 April 1975) . . . Their opponents are 'political fanatics' who had 'brought education into politics and condemned thousands of children to live below the best' (*Daily Mail*, 10 November 1976) . . . The lay actors in the drama were those imbued with common sense who were worried about falling standards — industrialists and parents fearful of reprisals about their children. (CCCS, 1981, p.211)

In the early 1970s, greater parental involvement in education had been the concern of progressive educators, including community educators (see chapter 1). However, the 'moral panics' of the 1970s, and in particular the furore at William Tyndale Junior School, altered all this. In this London school, apparently 'subversive' teachers maintained a policy of 'total children's rights'. As the children seemingly became more difficult to manage the number of complaints grew. The teachers strongly defended their professional right to determine curriculum and pedagogy, unencumbered by parental views (Gretton and Jackson, 1976; Ellis *et al.*, 1976). After a lengthy high profile struggle with the media, the government, and the relevant local authority, the Inner London Education Authority (ILEA), the staff involved were dismissed.

> The William Tyndale case . . . made a major contribution to the articulation of 'parent power', to a conservative rather than a progressive or

radical educational programme . . . There is little in the phenomenon of parent power itself . . . that would necessarily lead to it being in opposition to, rather than in association with 'teacher power' (though on this latter point the approach of the teaching profession is clearly crucial): the example of what happened at Tyndale might seem to have pushed it powerfully in the other direction. (Dale, 1989, p.146)

Tyndale's lasting effects were various. Two in particular are worth noting here. First, the impressions of 'progressive education' that parents nationwide received were filtered through the sensationalist lens of the tabloid press. Second, as the ILEA was criticized for its inaction, the affair strengthened the legitimacy of Prime Minister James Callaghan's calls for increased central control of education and increased parental involvement, thus limiting school and LEA autonomy.

As part of this new policy direction, the Taylor Committee was established to review the functioning of governing bodies. Its main recommendation was that there should be equal representation on governing bodies of parents, staff, LEA and the 'local community'. Employing a pluralist model, the Committee felt that equal participation would lead to all groups having equal influence on the decision-making process (David, 1978). The potential flaws in this assumption did not become immediately apparent however, as both main political parties accepted that LEAs should retain their dominance on governing bodies. This acknowledged that the professional and administrative interests which had controlled the education system under the social democratic consensus still exerted influence. As Taylor's recommendations journeyed through the DES and Parliament, they were further diluted, so that the final result was of little real change in the power-structure of governing bodies (Whitehead and Aggleton, 1986).

As Michael Apple (1986) notes calls for the reinstatement of formal styles of education are often the result of searching for a scapegoat on which to blame economic problems. Indeed, the continued economic downturn of the 1970s proved a powerful incentive for Callaghan's appropriation of a conservative approach to education. The new stance was evident throughout the 1976 'Great Debate', a supposedly national discussion on the future direction of state education, which endeavoured to divert parental support away from the right, without seriously altering the parameters it had set for the discussion. The Debate resulted in few concrete alterations, but the ideological change was marked.

The Failure of Social Democratic Education

By the late 1970s, the rationale of social democracy had been exposed as bankrupt. Its attempts to establish a more equitable *and* economically efficient and prosperous society were hindered by the contradictions inherent in trying to balance that equation. Policies were tentative and piecemeal, reacting to individual social problems, and formulated with little consideration for the broader political and economic contexts (George and Wilding, 1976). Consequently, social democratic policies, aiming for a consensus, often resulted in an uneasy accommodation between different interest groups. One illustration is the hesitant adoption of the principles of comprehensivization and community education (see chapter 1 concerning the latter). The Labour Party had become increasingly associated with remote bureaucracy and corporatism. Attempts in the late 1960s to change this perception of distant, but powerful, officialdom, had been half-hearted (David, 1978). In any case, the main motivation for trying to disminish the bureaucratic image was a concern with increasing the efficiency of state institutions, rather than increasing citizen involvement. As chapter 1 noted, it was this lost opportunity to increase collective public participation in the running of state institutions, including schools, that allowed the New Right to rearticulate public concerns with the remoteness of central and local services, towards a solution which promoted individual participation through increased consumer control. This individualistic stance appealed to specific social groups. The traditional view of the working class as a homogeneous grouping was no longer adequate in the face of increasing social diversity and fragmentation. It was this phenomenon of increasing heterogeneity within the electorate that the Conservative Party under Mrs Thatcher was quick to assimilate and exploit (London Edinburgh Weekend Return Group, 1980). This forms the subject of the next section.

The Move to the Right

New Right ideologies have a long history, pre-dating Thatcherism (Green, 1990). However, the 1980s were particularly notable as the Right's principles and polices were enshrined in far-reaching legislation, which is not easily amenable to change, (Hall, 1989). Whilst advocates of New Right values were marginalized during the social democratic consensus of the immediate post-war years, their ideas came to prominence as part of the conservative backlash against the 1960s progressive social movements (Isaac, 1990). Writers such as the Black Paper group and Enoch Powell contributed to the creation of 'moral panics' 'around such apparently non-political issues as race, law-and-order, permissiveness and social anarchy' (Hall, 1989, p.151). Education provided another fertile site for New Right ideas.

The growth and nature of New Right ideologies have been discussed and analyzed at length (for example, Jones, 1989; Bash and Coulby, 1989; Chitty, 1989; Ball, 1990; Apple, 1993; Lawton, 1994). For the purposes of this chapter it is enough to comment briefly on the main values underpinning New Right approaches, and the way in which they have been translated into populist discourses.

Thatcher's radical conservatism owes its pedigree to a synthesis of neo-liberalism and neo-conservatism. Neo-liberalism, as expressed by Hayek's influential text *The Road to Serfdom* (1944) is identified by its emphasis on market-led economic policies which minimize state intervention. Thus, the creation or maintenance of a 'dependency culture', stemming, for example, from an extensive welfare state, is avoided. Citizens are allocated the role of the individual consumer, and left to make whatever gains they can in acquiring social and economic status. However, unconstrained market liberalism contains the potential for social fragmentation leading to unrest and disorder. This can be countered by the promotion of neo-conservative social policies, focusing, for example, on the family, which aim to maintain and increase social cohesion (Isaac, 1990).

It is this very mix of neo-liberalism and neo-conservatism that makes New Right ideologies so potent, despite the inherent contradictions between the two (for example, neo-liberalism disapproves of state intervention, neo-conservatism sanctions it). By separating the sphere in which the two value systems operate, the resulting government is 'economically libertarian . . . but socially and morally authoritarian,' (Whitty and Menter, 1989, p.52). On the same point, Stuart Hall comments,

> Thatcherite populism is a particularly rich mix. It combines the resonant themes of organic Toryism — nation, family, duty, authority, standards and traditionalism — with aggressive themes of revived neo-liberalism — self interest, competitive individualism, anti-statism. (Hall, 1983, p.29)

Hall describes how New Right values offer an interpretation of people's lived experiences. This 'popular morality' is inclusive, covering moral, philosophical and social issues, and straddling class boundaries. It has wide appeal, viewing Britain as an 'imagined community' (Hall, 1989, p.167), and 'construct(ing) a "unity" out of difference' (*ibid.*, p.166), which overlooks both the fundamental contradictions of New Right philosophy, and differences of class, ethnicity and gender within the populace. In contrast, social democracy lacked so complete a vision.

The New Right is also multi-faceted, and incorporates several sub-groups (see Dale, 1989), a factor which is evident in education policy, and one which has contributed to the Right's wide appeal. Jones (1989) contends that several apparently disparate, social groups including disenfranchised sections of the urban white working class, many of the skilled white working class, and some middle class groups together formed a constituency which accepted the link made by right-wingers and the media between progressive education and politically motivated teachers, low attainment, and indiscipline. They were also receptive to the assertion that the supposed 'levelling-up' of achievement resulting from the comprehensive system was, in fact, a 'levelling-down' which adversely affected their own children's chances of success (Dale, 1989). Hall (1983) describes the total process thus,

When in a crisis the traditional alignments are disrupted [as happened with the breakdown of the social democratic consensus], it is possible on the very ground of this break, to construct the people into a populist political subject: with, not against, the power block. (p.30)

This has happened in education with successive Conservative governments claiming to speak for parents, and juxtaposing their interests with those of education professionals. Thus 'parent power' has been rearticulated and redefined, away from the idea of parent-as-participant towards the model of parent-as-consumer. The next section examines such events in relation to education in more detail.

The New Right's Education Project — The Parent as Consumer

Education Policy in the 1980s

Although the first Thatcher government (1979–1983) implemented radical initiatives in housing and finance, in particular those which limited local government control, the first Conservative *Education Act (1980)* lacked a pervasive ideological framework. However, the Act did introduce the Assisted Places Scheme (state funding to allow pupils, whose parents could not afford the fees to attend private schools), and in doing so, sent out a powerful message about the deficiencies of the state system compared to the private sector, (Whitty and Menter, 1989). It also acknowledged the ideals of consumerism by slightly strengthening parents' rights of appeal against LEAs.

The *1986 Education Act* however, embodied many familiar New Right themes, a concern with 'standards' (which implies moral, not simply educational concerns, such as discipline and order), 'excellence' and 'choice' (Brown, 1990). Professional control of the curriculum was decreased in favour of governing body influence (Deem, 1989; Jones, 1989). Furthermore, parent and teacher representation on governing bodies was strengthened and LEA representation reduced. By removing power from political appointees the Act ostensibly contributes to the 'neutralizing' of education, separating it from 'politics'. As the Thatcher governments were engaged in a project to shift values and attitudes to the right, politicians expected the 'depoliticized' views of parents and other lay people to be highly conservative; a restraining influence upon progressive teachers and local authorities (Jones, 1989; Golby and Brigley, 1988). However, there is little evidence to suggest that this has been the case. To date, many governors appear to be concerned to offer teachers their largely unqualified support (Deem, Brehony and Heath, 1995).

Nevertheless, there have been instances of conflict, and these have revealed the uncertainty which surrounds governor powers and responsibilities, as they are enacted in relation to other agencies. Thus confusion over respective roles has led to sometimes fierce disputes between heads and governors (for example, Stratford School), and governing bodies and the LEA (Kingsmead Primary School, Hackney).[2] This general uncertainty allows several different ideas about the role of governors to co-exist simultaneously, if uneasily. On this point, Ball (1994a) identifies three broad models of school governance, placing emphasis on the tension which can exist in individual sites between competing values.

> The 'professional' discourse is rooted in a history of public sector/ welfare state paternalism. This trades upon the maintenance of a high level of practitioner autonomy and limited citizen or consumer participation in policy or decision-making . . . The 'business' discourse is a counter-discourse, which is articulated through neo-liberal economics and New Right politics. It asserts a financial management/ effectiveness perspective as well as a small business mentality. . . . The empowerment discourse is also a counter discourse. It stands in antagonistic relationship to both of the others but is represented primarily in rhetoric rather than in practice. Its historical status is one of irritant and unrealized hope. (p.92)

By 1987, conditions were such that radical reforms of the school system could be executed. Margaret Thatcher's government had been elected with a large majority for a third term. The left, at both local and national level, was in disarray, and the teachers' unions were subdued by their long period of industrial action in the mid-1980s. The profession's criticism of government proposals was therefore somewhat muted, fragmented, and in any case, largely ignored (Haviland, 1988).

With the introduction of the National Curriculum, Local Management of Schools (LMS), open enrolment, grant-maintained status (GMS) and City Technology Colleges (CTCs), the themes of the *1988 Education Reform Act* can be identified as follows: a neo-conservative wish to reintroduce traditional pedagogies and a 'British' curriculum, coupled with a neo-liberal desire to introduce a market-oriented, diversified system of education with less (local) state control. The 'market' in education is not, of course, a free market, but a 'quasi-market' (Le Grand, 1991). Education remains both compulsory for all children and freely provided by the state.

The key rationale for the 1988 Act's extensive changes was to enhance consumer control. This was a priority for three main reasons. First, as noted earlier, the strengthening of individual rights in the face of an apparently unresponsive state bureaucracy is a key principle in New Right ideology in respect of all areas of social welfare provision (Butcher *et al.*, 1990). Second, the introduction of market forces also serves the additional purpose of stripping local authorities of many of their powers. Some commentators have suggested that this motivation was at least as powerful as central government concern with remedying individual grievances (Adler *et al.*, 1989; Whitty and

Edwards, 1993). During the 1980s, a group of mainly urban, left-wing councils promoted collectivist policies and high-profile equal opportunities campaigns which brought them into bitter conflict with central government (Lansley *et al.*, 1989; Gyford *et al.*, 1989). In response, the New Right conceived of a model for local government that would considerably limit its powers. Councils would be concerned solely with the provision of basic services and not the dissemination of particular political ideologies; the local state was there to administer, not to govern (Loveland, 1991 and 1996). This is an example of a neo-liberal strand of New Right discourse — the desire for a smaller, more 'efficient' local government sector — connecting with the neo-conservative theme, of 'equiphobia', which Kate Myers has defined as a marked distrust of equal opportunities initiatives (Myers, 1990).

The third reason for the 1988 Act's emphasis on enhancing consumer control was to affect a corresponding diminution in 'producer capture'. This term describes the belief that those who are involved in producing a particular service will try to maintain exclusive control over that process. Dunleavy outlines this view in relation to other related groups of welfare state professionals. He dubs them,

> 'poverty professionals' (such as social workers, lawyers, and middle class cause groups demanding more welfare spending) [who] shape policy implementation so as to maximise their own role in the process and to perpetuate and increase . . . dependence upon them. (Dunleavy, 1991, p.39)

However, it is arguable that consumerism in education has not affected 'producer capture' to the extent that other aspects of the reform package, such as the National Curriculum, and local management, have. The National Curriculum was seen by the Conservative government as a way of diluting professional control of pedagogies and curriculum content. Through close prescription regarding the content of the curriculum, teachers are directed towards particular teaching methods, and retain far less autonomy with which to develop their own courses (although see Bowe, Ball and Gold, 1992, for an account of how schools are, in some cases, managing to reinterpret the demands of the legislation. For further discussion, see Hatcher and Troyna (1994) and Ball (1994b)). In addition, financial constraints loom large for most schools. As budgets are largely dependent on pupil numbers, even over-subscribed schools are aware of the need to maintain their market share. With this, as a major concern, the role of many senior teachers has become one of managing, not education, but an educational institution (Ball, 1994a).

Roger Dale argues for the recognition of another influential discourse which could be broadly described as part of the New Right panoply. In addition to neo-liberalism and neo-conservatism he identifies 'new institutional economics' (Hood, 1990). The term describes a package of reforms which pull together several strands within New Right discourse, and which seek to radically alter public sector administration (Dale, 1994; see also Boston *et al.*, 1991; Dunleavy, 1991). Under 'new institutional economics', education loses its special status, its separateness from relatively less complex and value-laden state provision, and becomes another function to be administered in the same way as buildings or recreational facilities. Dale (1994) refers to this process as '*mainstreaming*', and emphasizes the way in which it threatens the status of education as a 'public good' (p.28). The focus of his comments are developments in New Zealand, and he cautions against too-easy extrapolation from one country to another. Despite this important caveat however, it is my contention that the effect of 'mainstreaming' can be also discerned in the UK, albeit filtered through the unique characteristics of the British educational system. (This issue is discussed at more length in Troyna and Vincent, 1995.)

Education Policies in the 1990s

In comparison with Margaret Thatcher, his predecessor for the premiership, it may seem that in some areas John Major brought a more pragmatic approach to Government policy-making (witness the abandonment of the poll tax, and the rapid changes of economic and European policy). However, the general direction of education policy remains constant.

This can be illustrated with reference to the rising number of quangos in education. These include the Office for Standards in Education (to coordinate the privatized system of school inspections introduced by the *1992 Education (Schools) Act*), the Funding Agency for Schools (to oversee grant-maintained schools) the Higher Education Funding Councils, the Further Education Funding Council (for the funding of universities and sixth-form colleges respectively) and the Training Agency (for vocational education). Quangos are non-elected bodies whose members are appointed by ministers, in this case, the Secretary of State for Education and Employment. They offer a striking example of the way in which the role of directly-elected local authorities has been superseded).[3] For example, the Funding Agency for Schools (FAS) established by the *1993 Education Act*, and responsible for the funding of GM (grant maintained) schools, is accountable to the Secretary of State, but not directly accountable to the electorate. Its members do not hold ward surgeries, they cannot be petitioned and its meetings cannot be attended; all ways in which voters can make their views known to local councils. Despite this, in localities where over 75 per cent of pupils are in GM schools, the FAS has sole responsibility for planning to ensure that there are sufficient school places. It is also worth emphasizing that the FAS is a funding body. Unlike most LEAs, it is not concerned with promoting or disseminating a particular 'vision' of education.

Therefore, it can be seen that some of the primary intentions and effects of the 1988 ERA are also apparent in later legislation. These include the implementation of a more 'rule-bound culture', which has the affect of limiting the autonomy of teachers (at least in relation to the curriculum), and the ability of local education officers to exercise discretion in decision-making. Thus, in some respects, 'producer capture' appears diminished. The question remains, whether 'consumer control' has been enhanced as a consequence?

Parents and the Education System in the 1990s

This section briefly explores, first, parental involvement in governing bodies, grant maintained schools and CTCs, and second, parental choice policies, in order to determine whether parents' involvement and participation has increased in response to discourse of consumerism.

Parent governors

The main question here is to what extent can parent governors act as representatives of the parent body? As individual governors derive their power from being part of an integral whole, it is difficult to see how parent governors can take on this role. Even within the governing body they may find it difficult to act as a spokesperson for the wider parent body. Deem, Brehony and Heath (1995) suggest that members of a governing body can be divided into two groups, those who operate at the core and those who remain at the periphery, with parent governors being disproportionately represented in the latter grouping. The forum for governor–parent contact, the annual parents meeting, is notorious for often being organized in a dull, unimaginative way that does not inspire discussion, and attracts low attendance, although there are some signs suggesting that these events may be becoming more high-profile, better-organized, and more attractive to parents (Martin *et al.*, 1995).

Grant maintained schools

Grant maintained status for schools was presented by the government as a mechanism for increasing school diversity, despite the fact that these schools are required to teach the National Curriculum. Given this apparent contradiction, Fitz, Halpin and Power (1993), in their study of grant maintained schools, asked whether opting out of local authority control has led to the formation of distinctive school identities, and whether the school experience, including parental relationships with schools, shows signs of change. They conclude that the introduction of GM status has had little significant effect upon parental perceptions of the availability of choice of school in a locality. Nor did the degree of school responsiveness to its pupils' families increase with GM status. This was because, rather than engage in consultation exercises, the schools in their study tended to make their own judgments about parental priorities. In addition, the amount of parental involvement, once the child was at the school, remained comparable with levels in LEA-maintained schools (the reasons for this will be further explored in chapter 3).

CTCs

In their study of CTCs, Whitty, Edwards and Gewirtz (1993) found a disjunction similar to that identified by Fitz, Halpin and Power, between parents' actual views and priorities and those that the government expected them to hold. In the aftermath of the 1988 ERA, the government presented CTCs as a major component of the new product diversity within the education market. Their brief was to become inner-city beacons of excellence, developing innovative styles of schooling. Indeed as the researchers point out, the high number of applications to the small number of CTCs would seem to suggest a widespread demand for a new style of education. However, when parents were questioned about the appeal of CTCs, the high-tech environment and ethos were subordinated to other concerns. CTCs were seen as selective schools with additional resourcing and traditional values and styles of discipline (Whitty and Edwards, 1993).

Therefore, neither increasing the responsibilities of governing bodies, nor introducing new types of institutions appears to have resulted in identifiable shifts in parents' relationships with their children's schools. This section continues by considering policies supporting parental choice of school. These measures are presented as capable of directly augmenting 'parent power'.

Parental choice

The criticisms of parental choice — that, despite the rhetoric, these policies offer parents limited choices, and moreover, ones which are not open to all — are well-known by now. However, it is worth rehearsing the main arguments here. Parental choice policies overlook the ways in which individuals differ markedly in their ownership of social and economic resources; differences which profoundly affect their ability to compete in the educational market place. However, a careful reading of the 1992 White Paper, *Choice and Diversity*, suggests that only 'deserving' parents are eligible for the role of consumer. It starts by claiming that 'parents know best the needs of their children, certainly better than education theorists or administrators, better even than our mostly excellent teachers' (DfE, 1992, para.1.6). That this 'reality' (para.1.7) does not apply to all parents is apparent later. Teachers are described as struggling to imbue children with moral codes and values, and being hampered by 'the indifference of parents or the surrounding community' (para.1.26). These 'irresponsible' parents are apparently working class and poor, as they live in 'our inner cities or large housing estates' (para.1.26).

Even those parents who are in a position to evaluate fully all available choices, will be constrained on several levels by those supposed choices. First, as noted earlier, the philosophy of individualism denies the effect of class, ethnicity and gender stratifications, and instead maintains that everyone has an equal chance to succeed, and responsibility for that success (or failure) is their own. Other forces that limit the choices available to people are also ignored. For instance, the Parents' Charter claims to offer parents the information they need to influence their child's education (DES, 1991, p.1; DfE, 1994), but the overall control of the system is not open to question. In metaphorical terms, the government has opened the 'shop', however dilapidated it may be, and so any complaints about the quality of the 'products' must be due either to shop assistants' inefficiency or consumer carelessness when making choices (Vincent, 1992). Second, many parents' will feel that to safeguard their children's future, they must act as 'rational consumers demanding a product in line with the requirements of the enterprise culture' (Jonathan, 1990, p.118). In so doing, they may make choices regarding the style of education that their child receives, that they would not otherwise have wished to make. Indeed, the study of primary school parents' reactions to recent changes conducted by Hughes and his colleagues (1994) suggest that parents are reluctant to see themselves as consumers, feeling that this was an inappropriate way to approach the education system. Third, individual choices, may, in aggregate, have adverse consequences both for their child and others. For example, a parent, aware of the additional funding that a CTC commands may feel it is in her child's best interests to apply for a place, even though she may be concerned about the imbalance in funding between CTCs and 'ordinary' schools (Bash and Coulby, 1989). Thus her application suggests approval for the existence and philosophy of CTCs in particular, and of the right to choose in general (see also Ball, 1990). It may be argued that the sum of such individual choices does not always benefit society overall. A few children may attain a place at a well-resourced CTC, but many attend under-funded schools — ever vulnerable to cuts in the level of staffing and resources (Jonathan, 1990). The logic of open enrolment itself suggests that it will eventually lead to less not more choice, if some schools close due to waxing and waning of public approval. Moreover, a school trapped into a downward spiral of falling rolls, low morale, and fewer resources can offer less and less to its existing pupils. Ranson (1988) comments that choice of school cannot be treated like other consumer choices. 'If I purchase a chocolate bar . . . my 'purchase' has no effect upon the product . . . but my preference for a school, privately expressed together with the unwitting choices of others will transform the product' (p.15). A school with a relatively low class size for instance, may see a dramatic increase in the pupil–teacher ratios if it becomes popular. Hirsch refers to this situation as resulting from a 'tyranny of small decisions' (cited in Adler *et al.*, 1989, p.221). Such reliance on 'neutral' market forces could result in fundamental changes to the appearance of the state education system, (for instance moves towards racial segregation in schools, see Vincent, 1992). Gutmann (1987) and Jonathan (1990) argue that the state has some duties of 'trusteeship' towards all children, as a vulnerable group. Thus their education should not be left solely in their parents' hands, regardless of how effective those parents are as participants in a race already structured so as to be unequal. Chubb and Moe (1990) present an opposing view. They argue strongly for the end to direct democratic control of American schools, which they claim causes bureaucracy and inertia, thereby inhibiting the fundamental reforms essential for improvement. Parental choice and professional autonomy are seen as the key to change. These mechanisms will result in greater differentiation between schools, and therefore greater motivation and commitment from students, parents and teachers to 'their' supposedly freely-chosen school. Chubb and Moe's position minimizes the structural limitations imposed on individuals by class, ethnicity and gender variables which constrain parents' ability to operate within such a system. They also recommend what I would argue is an essentially false distinction between education and politics, presenting the two as entirely separate spheres.

> Direct democratic control stimulates a political struggle over the right to impose higher order values on the schools through public author- ity, and this in turn promotes bureaucracy — which is both a crucial means of ensuring that these higher-order values are actually imple- mented at school level (by personnel who may not agree with them) and a crucial means of insulating them from subversion by oppos- ing groups and officials who may gain hold of public authority in the future. (*ibid.*, p.167)

As earlier sections of this chapter have suggested, reliance on the market is not a value-free philosophy, any more than professionalism, school autonomy or parental choice are neutral ideas. The values on which these philosophies rest may be submerged, but this does not detract from their powerfulness.

Flew (1987) also argues in support of opening up the market to allow parents' unlimited choice of school. He differentiates between political power and economic power, maintaining that parents need only the latter not the former.

> The political power conferred by a right to vote constitutes in many cases an extremely unsatisfactory substitute for the economic power provided by the right of exit and transfer. (p.101)

Similarly Chubb and Moe (1990) contend that parents, having chosen a school, should then be encouraged to withdraw, offering teachers simply their passive support. 'Schools tend to prosper when outsiders trust them and leave them alone' (p.164; also Tooley, 1992). In contrast, Adler *et al.*, (1989) employ Hirschman's concepts of '*Exit, Voice or Loyalty*' (1970) to argue that dissatis- fied 'customers' have an alternative to 'exit', which is to use their 'voice'; that is to stay and work together to change the present situation (see chapter 1). This is a collective rather than individual response and as such it faces direct political opposition from the New Right. As Westoby (1989) comments,

> Making 'exit' easier may well atrophy 'voice'; voice may be loudest, and perhaps of greatest effect when monopoly conditions prevail, and customers are securely 'locked in'. (p.71)

Westoby also notes Hirschman's proposition that the results of 'exit' are more certain than those of 'voice'. The publication of school 'league tables' aims to increase the certainties of exit for the individual parent, making that a more attractive option than the uncertainties inherent in collective action.

During the 1990s, several researchers conducting studies on aspects of the reforms introduced by recent legislation, have used their empirical data to argue that the effect of these policies has been to promote, not a diverse range of institutions, all with equal-status, but rather local school hierarchies (what Phil Woods and his colleagues term 'local competitive arenas', Woods, 1994a). Segregation on the grounds of social class (often linked to residential segregation) has been a constant feature of the post-war education system, and hierarchies within local secondary school systems certainly existed prior to the 1988 legislation. Now however, they appear to be solidifying, with an increasing division between popular, oversubscribed schools, and unpopular, undersubscribed schools. In response to their need to maintain market share (and thus a healthy budget, every pupil being worth an identifiable sum of money under LMS) there is a temptation for schools to 'price' pupils. Children with disabilities, those experiencing difficulties in learning, or those who are disaffected are more expensive for a school, requiring a higher input of resources and with less guarantee of a sufficient output in terms of exam results (Vincent *et al.*, 1995).

So where does all this leave parents? A recent research study on parental choice of secondary school (Gewirtz, Ball and Bowe 1995) identified three ideal-type groups of parents, and illustrated their differing relationships to, and conceptions of, choosing a school. All groups were found to be influenced as much, if not more so, by their own and their child's affective responses to a school, as by exam results. However it is the first group, the *privileged/skilled choosers* who have the inclination and the necessary social, economic and cultural capital with which to engage in the choice process. Of the other two groups, the second, *semi-skilled choosers* operate more on the margins of the choice process, whilst the third group the *disconnected*, disregard or are unaware of many of the priorities they are required to hold in order to operate as an effective consumer of education. Gewirtz, Ball and Bowe suggest that they substitute alternative values, for instance, placing priority on having their children educated locally. The researchers argue that choice policies simply reflect already-existing structural inequalities.

> There were significant processes of differentiation and choice prior to 1988. Some skilful and resourceful parents were always able to 'work the system' . . . But post 1988, the stratagems of competitive advantage

are now ideologically endorsed and practically facilitated by open enrolment, the deregulation of recruitment and parental choice . . . Class selection is revalorized by the market . . . There are clear indications here of class, 'race' and gender dimensions to choice. That is despite some commonalities, the meanings (and implications) of choice vary distinctively between classes . . . Where most recent analyses of class differentiation in education have stressed the work of selection and allocation done by schools and teachers, here selection and allocation is produced by the actions of families . . . Education is subtly repositioned as a private good. (Ball, Bowe and Gewirtz, 1994)

Similarly Whitty, Edwards and Gewirtz (1993) whose research on CTCs was referred to earlier conclude,

In education, the so-called comprehensive system was never as homogeneous as the concept of mass produced welfare suggests. Indeed it was always a system differentiated by class and ability. What may be different in the new era is an intensification of these differences and a celebration of them in a new rhetoric of legitimation, involving choice, specialization and diversity to replace the previous language of common and comprehensive schooling. (p.170)

Donald Hirsch, in his report on school choice for the Organization of Economic Cooperation and Development (OECD) notes that,

In the market for schools, where successful suppliers are not in a position to multiply their product easily or indefinitely, there will always be a danger of 'choice' creating a hierarchy of supply with the most popular schools rationing places. (Hirsch, in press)

Hirsch recommends encouraging diversity between schools, thus allowing parents to make different but equal choices (also Walford, 1992; Adler, 1993; Walker and Crump, 1995). There have, indeed, been attempts to control choice and modify its destabilising potential. For example some American choice schemes are regulated (Witte, 1993). However attaining a system of 'different but equal' institutions (the original description of the tripartite system) is far from easy when one takes into consideration, first, the absence of innovation in the CTC and GM sectors to date, and second, the degree to which children's experiences of the education system are stratified by social class. Such a system would require a government willing to intervene in the market with the precise aim of ameliorating segregation, a goal which would run counter to the aims voiced by successive governments since 1979. In the absence of this political will, parental choice policies will continue, not only to reflect, but also to intensify, inequalities based on social class.

Conclusion

This chapter has concentrated on the relationship between the central state and a particular group of citizens, parents. The relationship is presented as primarily determined by the central state's view of parents' contribution to the fulfilment of its main concerns; that is, to maintain hegemony and service the economy. This does not mean that concessions have not been made when necessary to legitimate the actions of the state and maintain the 'active consent' of the majority of parents, the abolition of the tripartite system is a case in point. Indeed, this is part of a larger pattern whereby the particular 'needs' the education system has fulfilled have changed over the past 100 years. Keypoints in this process can be identified. The 'need' in the post-war education system was to increase the productivity of the workforce, and to accommodate demands for increased social equality. The 'need' for a shift in emphasis towards vocational education in the mid-1970s, and increased teacher accountability was occasioned, first, by employers' complaints about the irrelevance of education to the world of work; and second, by alleged parental concern, underwritten by the media, concerning 'excessive' teacher autonomy. During the 1980s and 1990s, the education system has been given a new agenda which offers parents a seemingly powerful role. 'Parents-as-consumers' is the mechanism through which disparate elements of Conservative ideology — individualism, freedom, consumer choice, morality, discipline and order — are bound together in the education system.

Philip Brown (1990) makes a similar point with his concept of 'waves' of education reform.

> The 'first wave' involved the development of elementary state education for the 'lower orders'. This schooling of the working class was primarily concerned with the inculcation of basic information and knowledge seen to be appropriate for their predetermined (ascribed) place in society. The 'second wave' can be characterized as one involving a shift in educational ideology and policy from that based upon social ascription to one based upon 'age, aptitude and ability' . . . In a meritocratic system of education all must be given an equal opportunity of gaining access to jobs concomitant with their abilities. However, the *meritocracy* never promised equality, only that inequalities would be distributed more fairly . . .
>
> The 'third wave' can be characterized in terms of the rise of the ideology of parentocracy. This involves a major programme of educational privatization under the slogans of 'parental choice', 'educational standards', and 'the market' . . . In the educational parentocracy, selection will be determined by the free play of market forces, and because the State is no longer responsible for overseeing selection, inequalities in educational outcome . . . cannot be blamed on the State. (pp.66–7, 69 and 80)

Brown's 'waves' summarize the educational apparatus and discourses through which the central state *seeks* to fulfil changing 'needs' (this is not to suggest, of course, that it will be completely successful in so-doing). The ways in which particular 'needs' are defined and altered provides an illustration of Foucault's emphasis on the subjectivity, the 'regime-relativity' of truth which suggests that a society will generate those 'truths' which best support its power structure at a particular moment (Gutting, 1989, p.276).[4]

To conclude: the legislation and related policies of the late 1980s and early 1990s have given parents power as individual consumers which some parents, mainly members of the professional middle-class, are able to exploit. What parents have not been offered is the collective political power to influence the decision-making which determines the organization of their children's education. The next chapter examines, in further detail, the possible roles on offer to them.

Notes

1   Despite Bennett's own protestations, his report was simplistically presented in the media as claiming that 'traditional' methods of teaching were more effective than 'progressive' ones. A similar reaction greeted the Alexander report on primary education in 1991 (Alexander, 1992).

Cohen (1980) describes 'moral panics' around particular 'folk devils' in the following terms:

> Society appears to be subject every now and then to periods of moral panic. A condition, episode, person or group emerges to become defined as a threat to societal values and interests; its nature is presented in a stylized and stereotypical fashion by the mass media . . . socially accredited experts pronounce their diagnoses, and solutions [and] ways of coping are evolved or (more often) resorted to. (p.9)

2   The dispute at Stratford, an East London grant-maintained school, was complicated, but centred on the respective roles of headteacher and governors in making staff appointments. The governing body had been racked by internal dispute since the school opted out of LEA control, but things reached crisis point in 1992, when amidst accusations of racism, corruption and assault, the Chair of Governors suspended the Headteacher, alleging 'gross professional misconduct'. The Headteacher was later reinstated and the DfE placed two of its own appointees on the governing body. In an LEA-maintained school, the LEA could be expected to mediate in such a dispute, but as Stratford is a GM school that route was not available to teachers or governors.

In 1994, in Hackney, London, the Headteacher of Kingsmead Primary was viciously pilloried in the tabloid press for deciding against taking a group of children to see a ballet of 'Romeo and Juliet'. She had several reasons for her decision, but the one that was trumpeted across the front page was a comment that the play depicted solely heterosexual love. Allegations concerning her relationship with a former governor of the school followed. The LEA recommended to the governing body that the Head should be suspended. However, the governors, mindful of the key role she played in raising levels of achievement at the school, and the existence of parental support for her, refused.

3 In what was known as 'clause zero' of the 1993 Education Bill (now clause one of the Act), only the Secretary of State and schools are named as responsible for promoting and delivering the education services. In contrast to the comparable section (s.1) of the 1944 Education Act, local authorities are not mentioned. For a discussion of the constitutional implications of the concentration of so much power in central government, see Loveland (1996).

4 This does not mean, however, that 'truths' in opposition to a regime are unable to emerge, although there may be state-sponsored attempts to suppress them (Gutting, 1989).

Chapter 3

Parental Involvement: The Present Day

Introduction

Since the Plowden Report (CACE, 1967), parental involvement in education appears largely accepted as part of professional 'good practice'. Many initiatives — such as home-reading schemes, parent helpers in the classroom, parent–teacher consultations, curriculum evenings and so on — have been enacted nationwide, and articles on new projects regularly appear in the education press. However, that same press also features dissenting voices; parents declaring that they need to be informed about their children's day-to-day classroom experiences, alternate with teachers bemoaning parental apathy and amorality. Zita Lysaght (1993) suggests that parent involvement is not such an established feature of the education system as rhetoric would suggest.

> The issue of parental involvement/partnership in education as in other professions is highly charged . . . Traditionally, change has been endorsed in theory and resisted in practice. (p.197)

This chapter examines that assertion through an analysis of the different forms of parental involvement and participation, the mechanisms through which they work, and the underlying values that structure different approaches.

Parental Roles

The accompanying diagram (figure 1) outlines the roles currently on offer to parents with children in state schools. Four main possibilities are identified, although it is important to emphasise that these are all ideal types. The four are *the parent as supporter/learner, the parent as consumer, the independent parent,* and *the parent as participant.*[1] The first option is preferred by many professionals. The recent influence of the New Right on the education system seeks to modify the dominance of the supporter/learner model by introducing the concept of parent-as-consumer. Independent parent describes the role which I suggest many parents actually play, whilst parent-as-participant is seen

Figure 1: Parental roles in state education

Parents' role	Supporter/learner	Consumer	Independent	Participant
Function	To support professionals and adopt their concerns and approaches	To encourage school accountability and high standards	To maintain minimal contact with the school	To be involved in governance of the school as well as the education of own child
Mechanisms	– Curriculum support via professionally-run schemes – Attending school educational events – Supporting/organising school social and fund-raising events	– Choosing a school using 'league tables' and provisions for open enrolment – Receiving information as detailed in the Parents' Charter	Little home–school communication or interaction Parent may provide alternative forms of education eg supplementary classes	– Parent governors – Statutorily-based parents' groups – Membership of local/national educational pressure groups
Focus	For educational issues-individual child/children For extra-curricular activities and fundraising — whole class or school	For educational issues-individual child/children Limited involvement in management issues — for example, voting for GMS status	Individual child/children	Potential focus on all aspects of education on range of levels: – individual child – whole school – local and national educational issues

as less common in actuality, but potentially a very powerful strategy for future development.

The Supporter-Learner Model

This section argues that, as illustrated by the diagram, many current strategies in home school relations are directed by professionals, and place parents in the broad supporter/learner category. Their function is to support the professionals by assimilating their values and behaviour. Thus parents may be required to support a range of school events (Bridges, 1987; Bastiani, 1988b), and act as teacher aides in the classroom or at home. The supporter-learner model can be sub-divided into four foci: parents in the classroom, parents and the curriculum; accreditation schemes, and home–school contracts.

Parents in the classroom

A parental role within the classroom represents considerable changes in professional attitudes since the almost total exclusion common in the 1960s (Tizard *et al.*, 1981). However, such arrangements are often fairly ad hoc and left to an individual teacher's discretion (Jowett *et al.*, 1991). Parental involvement in the classroom usually has two main aims. First, to allow the teacher freedom from mundane practical tasks, and second, to make the parents more aware of the opportunities and constraints offered by the classroom environment. Thus parents become familiar with the rationale behind the teacher's working methods, and able to appreciate the difficulties and complexities of the job. However, traditionally teaching is an autonomous task, and having parents in the classroom is not welcomed by all teachers, as the following quotation explains.

> The principal issue for teachers . . . relates to their status as professionals . . . Several [teachers] were clear that whilst help was acceptable with secretarial and office work, and in providing extra help on trips, they did not want parents in the classroom or having any part in the planning and implementing of the curriculum. (Mayall, 1990, p.51; also Atkin, Bastiani and Goode, 1988)

Parents and the curriculum

During the 1980s, the involvement of parents in teaching basic curriculum areas became more common (Edwards and Redfern, 1988). Initiatives vary in emphasis. Some aim to educate parents and make them more familiar with the teacher's methods, in the hope that the parents' will copy school activities at home (Smith, 1988), while others involve parents in a more direct educator role (for example, Merttens and Vass, 1993). This latter group include home-reading and home-maths projects, and mark a significant development in parent–teacher relationships. They acknowledge that parents are 'the child's first teacher' and offer a continuation of this role throughout compulsory schooling (at least at primary level). Hewison (1985) concludes that the most important factor about these interventions is that, unlike earlier compensatory programmes, parental involvement in curriculum support,

> is based on an analysis of what parents can do for their children, not what they cannot. Compared to the 'supportive home' analyses, this leads to a very different understanding of the relationship between teachers and parents — a changed understanding which is shared by teachers, parents and children alike. (p.53)

However, acting as classroom aides will not necessarily increase parents' understanding of teachers' methods, nor alter traditional demarcations which locate parents as 'passive supporters' (*ibid.*; also Smith, 1988; Tizard *et al.*, 1981).

The difficulties inherent in changing these fixed roles is illustrated by an intervention planned by Barbara Tizard and her colleagues (Tizard *et al.*, 1981). The project focused on activities designed to encourage parents to visit the school and learn more about teachers' methods. Parents' meetings, toy and book library sessions, and 'open' sessions in the classroom were introduced. However, after discussing the project with parents, Tizard comments on the lack of *effective* parent–teacher communication, and the need for staff to make their aims and teaching methods explicit to parents. A year after the intervention, the researchers found that most teachers had dropped the structured parental activities, whilst retaining the opportunities for social contact. Tizard notes that the staff were concerned to gain parental recognition of, and trust in, their professionalism so that they could teach without external constraints. She continues, 'the price that teachers pay for parental belief in professionalism may therefore be an apathetic even hostile parent body', (p.105). Although this study took place several years ago, a more recent study undertaken by Sandra Jowett and her colleagues (1991), and involving a range of primary and secondary schools identified similar teacher attitudes and priorities.

The assumption of a link between parental involvement and achievement has led to more structured programmes, involving reading (for example, PACT[2]; see also Jones and Rowley, 1990; Tizard *et al.*, 1982; Hannon and Jackson, 1987; Hewison and Tizard, 1980; Siders and Sledjeski, 1978), maths (for example, Merttens and Vass, 1987 and 1993), and general curricular programmes (for example, Dye, 1989; Loughrey, 1991). These schemes involve direct participation in the education process, as parents supervise their child carrying out a particular task, sometimes at school, but more often at home.

Parental involvement in curriculum intervention programmes can be advantageous in 'demystifying' school for parents, although a constant dialogue with teachers is necessary to ensure that this process is happening. At their best such programmes can show parents how and why teachers work, rather than concentrating on what parents themselves should not do. Teachers are encouraged to become more open in discussing their pedagogy (Dye, 1989; Loughrey, 1991). Curriculum intervention programmes can also establish a mechanism for communication between parent and teacher, which encourages a more interactive relationship. This is claimed by the IMPACT (Inventing Maths for Parents Children and Teachers) team who pioneered home-maths projects.[3]

> An interventionist project of this nature is bound to structurally alter the institutional base from which it runs. Until recently parents were generally involved in school if at all, as either fund-raisers or as un-paid primary helpers . . . [But] children learn first and foremost from their parents . . . IMPACT deals with this in a quite immediate and specific fashion. (Merttens and Vass, 1987, p.24)

However, it is arguable that many curriculum intervention schemes seek to make the home function like the school. Parents are encouraged to structure their interactions with their children in ways that the school considers 'good practice'. There are, of course, variations in the way particular projects are implemented, and these are symptomatic of the school's view of its pupils' parents. (A parent–teacher discussion about reading, for example, can vary from a lecture with lists of rigid 'do's and don't's', to an individual or small group discussion which gives parents the opportunity to air their concerns.) Whilst offering parents curriculum guidelines can be extremely helpful, many schools present parents with fixed models of 'good practice', and insist on their compliance (Jowett *et al.*, 1991). This ignores the fact that professionals are often divided on preferred teaching methods. Parental criticism may be seen as a threat or an embarrassment, and opportunities for it to arise are minimized accordingly (see Hannon and Jackson, 1987; and Brito and Waller, 1993, for examples). Such rigidity also causes parents to respond by continu-ing to work with their children as they feel best, without recourse to the teacher (see Sharp and Green, 1975, and chapter 6 of this book). Fixed models of 'good practice' as presented by schools contain culturally-bound assump-tions about 'good' parenting. As mentioned earlier, the rigidity of such ideals can lead to parents feeling guilty and inadequate, and to professionals devel-oping negative views of those who do not adopt such standards. Burgess and his colleagues (1991) note that,

> Staff engaged in the education of young children often attempt to change aspects of parents' behaviour. This devaluation of working class culture through initiatives which are aimed 'to teach mothers how to get it right' (Finch, 1984b, p.15) gives professionals a

dominance at odds with shared partnerships between parent and teacher. (p.105)

Miriam David adds that much of this pressure on parents to act as educator in relation to their children impacts, in practice, upon mothers adding quite considerably to their childcare responsibilities, an issue that will be further explored in chapter 5 (David, 1993; also Walkerdine and Lucey, 1989). Another related criticism of curriculum intervention schemes is that, although they present an apparent climate of openness, yet the involvement they offer can be carefully limited by the professionals (Burgess *et al.*, 1991). The researchers involved with IMPACT have themselves identified this problem. One team member comments that parents are, in effect, 'being asked to act as agents of the teacher within the home, carrying out teacher-set activities and delivering the products back to school', (Brown, 1993, p.209). The IMPACT parents' booklets implicitly present a model of a 'good parent' as one who acts in accordance with the following series of imperatives — '"Be a GOOD LISTENER!". "ENJOY working together!" "Why not sit down on the rug and have FUN together — make it a FAMILY time!"', (*ibid.*, pp.206–7). In the IMPACT diaries, which particularly solicit parental comments, the possible forms of dialogue are constrained through the parent–teacher relationship where expertise clearly remains with the professionals. For instance, parents may not question how the teachers teach (also Brito and Waller, 1993).

Curriculum intervention programmes represent a considerable broadening of the parental role from the confines of acting as audience and fundraiser. Parents are now active rather than passive, as professional recognition and support is given to their efforts to educate their own children. However, teacher discourse still emphasizes professional superiority, seeing parents as supporters, albeit active supporters. Torkington (1986) comments on this fundamental weakness in curriculum-centred parental involvement (such as the schemes mentioned above) and school centred parental involvement (such as fundraising), by contrasting them with a third, parent-centred approach.

The rationale for the two previous approaches is that . . . schools are helped towards their objectives by parental involvement. The rationale for the parent-centred approach is that parents' knowledge of their individual children is far greater than that of a teacher, and that the teacher's knowledge and skills about children and learning in general should merely complement and build on the specific knowledge that parents hold — both these aspects are equal and essential for learning to take place . . . Curriculum-centred and the school-centred approaches can be employed by teachers without them ever examining their own attitudes and values, without them ever accepting the need to learn the skills of working with adults . . . and without looking at the implications of working with parents for their own professionalism. (pp.14 and 16)

Accreditation

One of the most recent developments in parental involvement has been the formal recognition of parents' work with children. This can vary from the presentation of school certificates to parents through to their gaining credit as part of a more formal programme of learning through a further education institution. Projects are therefore diverse both in their scope and their goals. John Bastiani (1994) makes this observation when he notes,

> The involvement of schools in this work also varies enormously in the extent to which experience *as parents*, both in the home and school settings, is the focus or whether the real agenda is parents' own learning and development as adults. (p.1)

As Bastiani notes, such accreditation can be of benefit to individual parents in terms of their personal and career development. But accreditation will not necessarily facilitate a more participative education system. The school remains unchanged, offering the parents knowledge, skills and perhaps space for developing initiatives of their own in their work with the children. There is nothing, however, to guarantee or even suggest that the learning process can be a two way one.

Home–School Contracts — 'Promises of good behaviour'? (Sallis, 1991)

Home–school contracts have been the focus of attention and support since the early 1990s (Labour Party, 1989 and 1991; Association of London Authorities, 1991; Macbeth, 1984, 1989 and 1995; Jones *et al.*, 1992). Macbeth (1989) proposed a minimum twelve point programme for home–school relationships, stressing the obligations of both parties. The school would provide a range of structures to support and encourage home–school contacts. The parents' obligations would be to respond to these initiatives and attend meetings when required. An examination of sample contracts reveals that parental obligations are often specific and concrete, whereas school commitments are more general. One example reads as follows,

> To provide a school service suited as far as possible to your child's needs and to your wishes, so far as is compatible with the provision of suitable instruction and the avoidance of unreasonable public expenditure. (handout, adapted from Macbeth, 1989; see also Macbeth, 1995)

Contracts have been criticized on various grounds. First, they 'veer towards "support for the professionals who know best" rather than equality between equally informed partners' (Tomlinson, 1991, p.13). Second, even if such a professionally-dominated contract remains as a model, the school must at least have made attempts to improve communication with parents, 'before it could even think of tying them (parents), however loosely, to promises of good behaviour', (Sallis, 1991, p.7). Third, and most fundamental, is the socio-economic bias inherent in contracts. Many of the commitments the school requires from parents are easier for relatively affluent parents to comply with — somewhere quiet for homework for example. Attending parents' meetings is easier for those with transport, money for child-care and such like. Macbeth is quite explicit that contracts are about obligations — those of the school as well as parents' — and that parents should not have the 'right' to opt-out. However, for many parents fulfilling such contracts would constitute a severe burden.

> The fear is that the emphasis will shift to lecturing parents on inad-
> equacies they may be unable to remedy, and that those feelings of
> inadequacy will only be increased. Even suitable clothes for the
> weather, rationed television, not going to school late or too early . . .
> might seem things a school shouldn't pressurise parents about if it
> doesn't really understand their problems. Homes with such problems
> need all that a school can give children — even without return. Don't
> dismiss the possibility that close co-operation with the school could
> become just another social privilege. (*ibid.*)

Macbeth suggests that the school can help parents fulfil their obligations, by for example, providing home-work space, or a creche. However, this type of response fails to consider the possibility that some parents may resist the imposition of middle class educational values, and the corresponding assump-tion that the home should automatically support the school. A parent might not see the need to ration television, might find school meetings an uncom-fortable, tedious experience, and might not value and support all the school rules.

Despite suggestions by the proponents of contracts that schools should consult with parents on the substance of their agreement, this process might extend no further than an unrepresentative group of school-supportive parents. The contract may then be presented to others with no allowance for discussion or alteration (Tomlinson, 1991). Of course, schools differ. Teachers at a middle school in Somerset, describing the development of a contract at their school, appear willing to negotiate if parents are unhappy about parts of the contract (White and Smith, 1993). Gewirtz, Ball and Bowe (1995), however, refer to a school where the contract is used to regulate parent and child behaviour.

> (A) practice which may be interpreted as constituting informal selec-
> tion is the home–school 'contract' which parents and children are
> required to sign before they are offered a place. These are becoming
> increasingly common in schools but vary in the nature, specificity and
> quantity of expectations stipulated. The Matineau [School] contract
> is particularly demanding of parents. They have to agree to ensure

attendance and punctuality, encourage and support their daughter with her work, supervise her homework, attend parents' evenings and school functions in which their daughter is involved, keep her in the correct uniform, provide her with a well-stocked pencil case, a calculator, dictionary and recorder, pay for the replacement of damaged or lost books and support the policies of the school. The agreement includes a warning (in bold print): 'Failure to keep this agreement may result in disciplinary action. Serious cases may be taken to the governors'. (in press)

These two examples illustrate that a contract will not transform home–school relations; indeed, it is more likely to reify the existing power-balance. Schools that have little parental involvement are likely to produce a contract featuring their idea of what parents want from the school and what the school wants from parents. A pre-existing and continuing dialogue with as many parents as possible is a prerequisite if a contract is to be more than a professionally-written 'paper policy'. Tomlinson (1991) comments that,

> Formalized contracts must be only part of a structure which gives parents more legal and participatory rights and have definite obligations to involve themselves in their children's schooling, and in which teachers are educated to regard working with parents as part of their professional duty. (p.14)

Practitioners and researchers agree that a 'contract' would have no enforceable legal basis. Quite apart from the ethical implications, the potential number of contested areas would be enormous. The language of sample contracts illustrates their aspirational nature, making enforcement extremely difficult. How could it be proved that a school had not 'valued [a child] as an individual' or that a parent had not 'helped my child to learn that he/she is part of a community both in and out of school' (*ibid.*, pp.13 and 15)? Furthermore, who would oversee the contract's implementation? Tomlinson suggests that contracts could be 'binding in honour only', perhaps with recourse to a local Ombudsman or to a new national body if either side thought the agreement had been wilfully broken (*ibid.*, p.16).

However, the fundamental flaw in the concept of home–school contracts remains. They propose a 'partnership', 'mutual obligations' between school and parent. Yet the power balance between the two is so weighted on the school's side that it is arguable that it is the school's duty to work towards gaining parental support without placing impositions on parents. Certainly, an automatic readiness from parents to recognise their new 'obligations' cannot be assumed. Historically, the control of the curriculum, the management and organization of the school have all been carefully guarded by professionals. Parents need to be given more rights to participate in their children's education before they are asked to fulfil their obligations as defined by the school.

The issue of parental rights is central to the policies of John Major's Conservative Government. The next section examines its assertion that it will ensure the recognition of these rights.

Parents As Consumers

The Parents' Charter — 'rights . . . responsibilities and choices' (DES, 1991, p.i)

The Parents' Charter (1991, updated 1994) claims to provide government guidelines to regulate home–school relations in the 1990s. When it first appeared, there was also speculation that it was intended to enhance parents' positions in the education system with the specific expectation that they would support the government's attempts to return to a more formal style of education. The Charter allocates parents the status of consumers, which sits uneasily with their more traditional role as supporters/learners. The Parents' Charter is part of the Citizen's Charter, the government's initiative to encourage national competitiveness and improve the standard of public services (DfE, 1994).

The core of the Charter is the promise of 'five key documents' which will enable parents to monitor their child's progress, and to compare all local schools. These include individual reports of the National Curriculum test results, regular reports from an independent inspectorate, performance tables for all local schools, a school handbook; and an annual report from the school's governors. Much of this information was already available to parents in many schools.

The next section of the Charter, headlined 'A School Place for Your Child' (*ibid.*)[4] sets out the different types of school from which parents can apparently choose. 'Self-governing' (grant maintained) schools, city technology colleges, technology colleges, voluntary schools, selective schools and independent fee-paying schools are all mentioned alongside the majority, the latter being distinguished as 'local council' schools (*ibid.*, pp.10–11). The term 'comprehensive' is conspicuous by its absence; indeed selection has become far more acceptable. The 1991 Charter stated, 'a school cannot make its decision on the basis of your child's academic ability unless it is a selective grammar school' (p.9). By 1994, however, this had disappeared, and selective schools are now included in the general list of institutions.

The Charter also gives parents direction in acting as responsible consumers. On this point, Bowe, Gewirtz and Ball (1994) note,

> In the Charter, the rights of individuals to choose and the responsibility that rests upon parents to undertake their choosing in an effective way is given considerable emphasis . . . choice is powerfully promoted as a personal matter, a question of individual parents taking responsibility for their children's educational future. (p.67)

Parents are not, however, guaranteed a clearly defined or influential role once their children are at a school. Whilst, the Charter details parents' consumer rights of 'entry' and 'exit' from a school, and their right to information from the chosen school, their rights to respond to that information and enter into a dialogue with the institution are less clear. As Roger Hancock (1993) argues,

> The main thrust of central government's interpretation of parental involvement has been to stress parents' rights to information about school performance and children's progress. Clearly, schools need to give such information but an over-concentration on this has served to set up a climate of 'information-giving' from schools to parents; a one-way accountability exercise in which parents passively listen to what schools are doing rather than engage with teachers to support and influence the content of education. (p.17)

This is borne out by the section of the Charter stating 'You have a right to a good education for your child,' (1994, p.15). However, it remains the case that parents have no 'right' to challenge the government's view that the National Curriculum constitutes a major part of a 'good' education. The Charter continues by talking about how parents can influence their child's school. The possibility of becoming a parent governor is mentioned briefly, as are annual parents' meetings. However, the most space is given over to the third 'right': voting on grant-maintained status, an option favoured by the Conservative government (DfE, 1994, pp.18–19). However, in this scenario, the parents' 'voice' lasts only for a moment, the involvement does not continue after the ballot, and research indicates that they are usually enacting the wishes of the headteacher and governing body (Fitz, Halpin and Power, 1993).

Therefore the possibility of parental participation in the daily life of the school is marginalized (Hughes, Wikeley and Nash, 1994). Although parents can elect parent governors, this position involves only a tiny minority of the parent body, and, as noted in chapter two, governors in general, are encouraged to see themselves as integral parts of the governing body, rather than representatives of particular interest groups (Hatcher, Troyna and Gewirtz, 1993; Deem, Brehony and Heath, 1995).

It is clear that the expectation embedded in the Parents' Charter is that parents are to be concerned only with their individual child's progress, rather than, say, the conditions his/her class works in. The Charter does not tackle such questions as minimum guarantees of books, materials or teacher–pupil ratios. Parental duties include providing a good example for their children (particularly where behaviour is concerned), seeing that their child gets to school on time, attending school events, supporting the school's policy on homework and behaviour, and giving their older children space to do their homework (1994, pp.25–6). Otherwise, they may trespass into daily school life only on specific occasions, to allow them to learn from the professionals how to help their individual child (also Chubb and Moe, 1990). An alternative to the

DfE's Charter was provided by the Campaign for State Education (CASE), who launched its Classroom Charter on the same day as the 1994 Parents' Charter. Alongside CASE's demands for increased resources was the right to establish a parents' association, something for which headteachers and governing bodies can currently refuse permission.

In summary, the Parents' Charter is helpful in clearly specifying what information parents should receive from schools, and thus ending any irregularities in what schools actually provide — although the quality and the tone of the information can still vary greatly. The Charter also highlights the concept of parents' rights in relation to schooling; embedding the idea in the collective mind of the teaching profession and the wider public. However, information and participation are not concepts that can be elided, nor does more of the former necessarily lead to the latter. The Parents' Charter does nothing to support those parents who for various reasons find it difficult to approach the school. Nor does it create a more equal relationship between teachers and parents. The two 'factions' are still kept apart. Indeed, such a division is crucial, if parents are to act in accordance with government wishes, and constrain any 'progressive' impulses that might emanate from educational professionals (Johnson, 1991; Dale, 1989).

Independent Parents

This term describes parents who have minimal contact with the school. For some this might be a deliberate decision, whilst others are non-participants through circumstance. The first category includes parents who have become disaffected with the school, and developed their own 'oppositional logic' (see p.5). They might feel that their child is unfairly treated because of his/her ethnicity, religion, behaviour or personality. Such a perception leaves parents with several choices. They can confront the staff, and as a result may themselves be labelled as a 'difficult' parent; they may transfer the child to another school; or they may decide to minimise contact with the school. This is characterized as 'active non-participation' by Pugh and De'Ath (1989).

Alternatively, 'passive non-participation' describes a parent who may wish to have more contact with the school, but is prevented from so doing for various reasons. She may not be fluent in English, but there are no interpreters present at school events, nor does it send home translated notes. She may work long hours. She may have small children and no child care. Or she may simply be under a degree of financial or emotional stress that precludes involvement. School-inspired events may not meet parents' concerns or interests, and a rational decision over the allocation of their time may therefore exclude such meetings (Showstack-Sasson, 1983).

Some parents may choose to supplement their child's formal education without reference to the teacher. This may be because they disagree with the teachers' pedagogy (Sharp and Green, 1975), or lack faith in the school's standards. A coherent and widespread form of additional provision — supplementary schools — has developed as a result. Such schools were originally established by African/Caribbean communities to compensate for the perceived inadequacies of the state system as the founder of a black supplementary school commented,

> Without exception we said that Racism was the major reason why our children were failing in school. We complained, we advocated . . . but with little avail. That did not deter us . . . we began to set up alternative supplementary education institutions rooted in our community. (Jones, 1986, p.2; see also Coard, 1971; Tomlinson, 1984)

Supplementary classes now serve various communities, concentrating on religious teaching, the children's home language or culture, and/or a reinforcement of the 'basics' to ensure that children are progressing at an appropriate rate. The relationship between parents and teachers is often more friendly, open and informative than in mainstream schools (John, 1992; Jones, 1986). In addition, community provision has a function beyond remedying the deficiencies of the mainstream.

> The supplementary education movement was seen, not as reactive but as pro-active, and to be about positive education. It aimed to project positive images of black people, black achievement, black history, in a society where a person's worth was thought to be determined by the colour of their skin. (John, 1992)

Parents-as-Participants

It is clear that the *formal* inclusion of parents in the existing systems of representative democracy is patchy and uneven. A 1994 report from the Research and Information on State Education Trust (RISE) shows that out of the seventy-seven responding local authorities in the UK, only twenty-two had parent representation on the education committee. Over half of those were London boroughs maintaining or copying the systems established by the Inner London Education Authority. Thirteen authorities (four of which are in Scotland and five in London) have consultative parents' organisations (O'Connor, 1994, pp.6–7). RISE also concluded that less than half of the local authorities have any representative organization for governors of *any* sort. Even where there are systems for formal parental representation in place, problems still remain, notably the need to try and ensure that the various associations attract as wide a membership as possible, the difficulties of representing such a sprawling, diverse group as 'parents', and the risk of representatives and groups being marginalized by local authority officers, teachers, and politicians. Being seen (or 'consulted') but not heard is a problem faced by many parents endeavouring to assert themselves in relation to the education system (see chapter 1).

RISE argue that other countries offer examples of ways in which representative structures have been established to communicate parents' views to schools and government at various levels, including the national level (*ibid.*, pp.25–8). However, as the problems mentioned here are associated with simply 'tacking on' parental representation to existing systems of governance, a more radical approach, operating at several different levels, is necessary in order to develop a new participative dimension to home–school relations. As Beattie (1985) points out, many current initiatives in the supporter/learner category could be defined as parent activity. That is,

> Associational activity organised by or for parents whose children attend school. Its purposes may be quite diverse, but its main defining element is negative: it has no official or legal status in the eyes of the state, and therefore in the eyes of schools which are state institutions. (p.243)

Some commentators (for example, Sallis, 1987; Tomlinson, 1991) have suggested that legislation is necessary to raise the status of potential parental contributions. Sally Tomlinson, proposing statutorily-based HSAs (Home–School Associations), argues that such groups have a better chance of survival if supported within a structure that gives them legitimacy. Thus she suggests that HSAs would be open to parents, teachers, governors and older pupils, and would discuss educational issues rather than the more peripheral and mundane matters that often dominate parent groups (Moore, 1990). They would be funded by a government grant, and be statutorily consulted about educational decisions at local and, through representatives, at national level (Tomlinson, 1991, p.16). However, the effectiveness of legislative change cannot be assumed. The last part of Beattie's statement, quoted earlier, suggests a direct causal link between recognition by 'the state' and automatic recognition by schools, (the context suggests that by 'the state' Beattie is referring to the legal system and to Parliament). However, as much legislation is of an enabling, rather than an enforcing nature, a direct causal link between legislation and practice cannot be assumed (Ball, 1994a).

Tomlinson (1991) and Macbeth (1989 and 1995) also advocate class associations whereby parents and teachers have regular group meetings about the curriculum and organisation of learning. School and class meetings could be supplemented with regular individual teacher-parent consultations concerning individual children's progress. Thus parents would have opportunities to participate at each level — the individual child, the class and the school. Such changes would involve great alterations in current relationships between teacher and parent. Several schools in a recent Royal Society of Arts (RSA) project have attempted innovations along these lines (although establishing whole school parents' groups seems to be less popular). Progress is slow, as individual schools endeavour to implement reforms that run counter to the dominant tenor of home–school relations (Jones *et al.*, 1992). Indeed, in recognition of this, one school adopted a snail as its logo for its development of a home–school contract (White and Smith, 1993). Although unlikely to be wholly transformative, legislation could promote reform. It is also important to have structures and networks outside individual schools to support parents, and the role of parents' centres is considered further in later chapters. Another development is the networking of parents' groups from different parts of the country. One result of this was a conference, *Parents Talking About Education*, held in 1993, which was organized by parents' groups from around the country in order to give parents a channel through which to express their views and concerns to education professionals (Parents Talking About Education Steering Group, 1994).

However, changes in both structures and relationships are necessary if there is to be any discernible increase in participative processes in schools. Yeatman (1990), writing about the democratisation of institutions, comments,

Democratization . . . would involve the replacement of the hierarchical (vertical) principle of managerial/professional authority by non-hierarchical (lateral) principal of reciprocal exchange between differently positioned and skilled participants and contributors. (p.24)

Many writers in this area advocate attempts to achieve lateral home–school relations (for example, Stacey, 1991; Atkin, Bastiani and Goode, 1988). Yet the dominance of the supporter-learner model persists.

Conclusion

This chapter has argued that the exercise of collective parental 'voice' in relation to the state education system is a rare phenomenon. Indeed, with the exception of parental ballots on grant maintained status, the only available and widespread avenues for collective parental involvement at school level are attendance at Annual Parents' Meetings (APMs), and school-based Parent–Teacher Associations. However, the 'voice' of parents through both these mechanisms is muted. APMs are often poorly-attended (Martin *et al.*, 1995), and the activities of Parents' Associations tend to be focused on arranging fundraising and social events. Therefore, parents are not encouraged to comment upon the operation of the school as an educational institution. Even the opportunities for the exercise of individual 'voice' are dependent, to some extent, upon local circumstances.

Four possible roles, currently open to parents with children in state schools, are identified: *the parent as supporter/learner; the parent as consumer; the parent as independent, and the parent as participant* (see also David, 1993). The first model relies on parents assimilating professional values and behaviour.

Alterations in this model during the last thirty years allow parents the opportunity to collaborate with the school in helping their children with reading or maths. However, the model still renders parents passive in their relationship with the school, as they carry out those functions which the school prescribes. Home–school contracts, a recent development, have the potential to be appropriated by the school, and used not as mechanisms for creating a home–school dialogue but for regulating the behaviour of pupils and their families.

The second model, parent-as-consumer, where parents apparently mould the school system through the indirect means of parental choice of schools, is the one preferred by the Conservative government. However, an examination of one of the key documents in this area, the Parents' Charter, suggests that the aim of this model is to coopt parents into a role as supporters of government-directed changes. Under these circumstances I suggest that a sizeable proportion of parents reject the first two models and adopt the third, *parent as independent*. Thus, either as a result of a deliberate decision or due to circumstance, these parents have minimal contact with the school. This reaction is illustrated in later chapters. The fourth model, *parent as participant*, is the least common, and also the only option to offer opportunities for the exercise of individual and collective voice.

Later chapters of this book set out to test the accuracy of these ideal type models against an analysis of lived parent–teacher relationships. However, before this question can be considered further, it is necessary to introduce the schools and the local education authority.

Notes

1 See chapter 2, for some parallels with Ball's (1994a) model of school governance.
2 PACT (Parents And Children and Teachers) was one of the first home-reading schemes and spawned several imitators. The child regularly takes a book home to read with an adult. A record card provides a means of communication between home and school.
3 IMPACT involves the school sending home maths games and activities for children and their parents to work on together.
4 In the original version of the Charter this section was entitled, 'The Right to Choose'. Presumably because so many parents experienced problems getting their children into the school of their choice, it has become necessary to down play this 'right'.

Chapter 4

City Schools

Introduction

This chapter introduces the borough of 'City', its council and education authority and, in particular, the two main case study schools, Hill Street and Low Road primary schools. The section on the schools also includes an outline of current forms of parental involvement, and a consideration of relationships between the teaching staff in both schools. The latter, in particular, is seen as a key element in creating the ethos of each institution. The chapter ends with a brief section describing and analyzing aspects of the research process at each school site.

The Locality

'City' is a small, inner city borough with a largely working class population, although in the last fifteen to twenty years gentrification has bought middle class residents into several areas within the borough.

City's popular image is of an area with multiple social and economic problems. Media portrayals concentrate on the dramatic and negative facets of life in the locality, frequently presenting it as depressed and forlorn; the archetypal inner city, fostering a myriad of social and economic ills. Although this is by no means a complete picture of the borough, statistical evidence does corroborate the extent of the difficulties faced by some residents. High levels of unemployment and low standards in housing[1] are the two main problems for City's residents. The borough has a predominantly young (under 35) population, which is ethnically diverse.

City Council

City has a long history of being a Labour controlled area, and during the 1980s was one of a group of new urban left councils committed to collectivist policies and high profile equal opportunity policies (Lansley *et al.*, 1989). The new urban left councils experienced common problems. The tabloid press quickly labelled the councils 'loony', and a number of notorious stories began to circulate

about their policies and activities. These included tales about Labour councillors banning things as diverse as the nursery rhyme 'Baa, Baa, Black Sheep',
black refuse bags, and the phrase 'black coffee' on the grounds that they were
racist (Lansley *et al.*, 1988; Jenkins, 1987). Needless to say these stories were
either entirely false or heavily distorted. However, it seems undeniable that
such accounts did sway public opinion concerning the Labour left councils.
Notwithstanding this, the opposition which proved fatal for the councils was
that of central government, as the Thatcher governments of the 1980s regis-
tered their suspicion of an autonomous, politically active local state. Thus,
throughout the decade, central government successfully exerted its control by
curbing local state spending (Lansley *et al.*, 1989). By the late 1980s, a combination of all these factors — media hostility, splits amongst Labour activists,
the lack of support for Labour left councils from the national party and, above
all, the determination of the Conservative government to impose its will —
led to a change in climate in most of the councils concerned, including City.
The 'new realism' stressed service delivery, efficiency and accountability (*ibid.*;
Jones, 1989; Epstein, 1993). During the early 1990s, City Council experienced
several blows to its attempts to establish a reputation as efficient and effective.
The first was accusations of fraud and corruption made against officers in a
particular department, and the second, recurrent and public splits within the
ruling Labour group. As a result, councillors acknowledged a loss of faith in
the Council amongst its electorate.

However, despite evidence of political and administrative incompetence
and malpractice, the borough's difficulties and shortcomings must be placed
within a local and national context. City Council provides services for an inner
city area; one which suffers from unemployment, poverty and a crumbling
housing stock. Furthermore, central government's intolerance of political
pluralism and the subsequent financial constraints has had a demoralizing
effect upon many local authorities. As John Gyford *et al.* (1989) comment,

> In such circumstances, it is hardly surprising if crisis management
> becomes the norm . . . long term planning appears futile and sheer
> survival replaces a commitment to service delivery and innovation.
> (p.95)

City Local Education Authority

'At Least We'll Get This Right'[2]

Until April 1990 education services in City were managed by the Inner London
Education Authority (ILEA). At first, City, like most of the other London Labour
boroughs, displayed little enthusiasm for the transfer of responsibilities for
education. However, when it became clear that the government was going to
proceed with the abolition of the ILEA the boroughs' reluctance dissipated

somewhat. In fact, relationships between them were marked by an element of competition, rather than cooperation.

Each borough was required to produce an Education Development Plan (EDP) a year before transfer was to take place. City's EDP was produced after what was acknowledged as a very widespread consultation exercise with different groups within the borough. Its themes included equal opportunities, under-5s education, special needs, the educational needs of black and ethnic minority populations and parental involvement.

However, almost immediately, the new LEA was beset by a number of local problems. Chief amongst these was instances of administrative shortcomings, fierce acrimony between the LEA and the teacher trade unions, especially the local branch of the National Union of Teachers' (NUT), and a severe teacher recruitment and retention problem. However, the point that was made in mitigation of the Council as a whole is also relevant here; namely, that the LEA's ability to address these difficulties was constrained by national factors. These included the decrease in the amount of central government money given to the Council in general, and the Education Directorate in particular; difficulties involved in collecting the unpopular poll tax; the radical changes to the school system caused by the 1988 ERA; and the widespread teacher shortage. Limited finances had a profound effect upon education policy and planning. For instance, in order for City's budget to remain within cash limits, increases in the percentage spent on staffing (which were necessary to attract more staff) had to be balanced by cuts in grants to youth and community groups. Initiatives in the EDP, such as cutting pupil–teacher ratios, were postponed due to regular budget difficulties. Even the instances of maladministration were often exacerbated by understaffing. Thus the LEA faced the fundamental difficulty of trying to deliver sketchily-resourced services in an area of economic deprivation.

Recruitment drives which were then frozen (for financial reasons), a lack of permanent and supply teachers, and dilapidated buildings did nothing to raise the morale of City's teachers, or administrators, nor increase parental confidence in the LEA. The primary concern of senior officers and members was to maintain as much of the service as possible within existing financial limits. They were criticized, by the teachers' unions amongst others, for not contesting those limits with central government. However, as mentioned earlier, the Labour Left no longer saw such action as appropriate. This stance affected the type of relationship the LEA attempted to develop with parents. For example, plans to involve parents more closely in the management and organization of the education service through the newly-established City Education Forum (see chapter 8) appeared to be designed to give parents information, and win their support for Directorate decisions, rather than mobilize parents to campaign on City's behalf against central government restrictions.

The early 1990s saw local government services slowly emerge from over a decade during which relationships with central government had been marked by intense financial pressure and ideological hostility. In these circumstances,

City sometimes gave the appearance of being trapped in a downward spiral caused by the need to undertake constant exercises in damage limitation. Its first two years were largely marked by crisis management rather than innovation and forward planning. Stability of funding which could have ameliorated this situation was not forthcoming; instead, as the government's transition grant expired, City was forced to continue trying to maintain a service within ever tighter cash restrictions.

Schools and Localities: Hill St and Low Rd Primary Schools

Collecting Data

During the 1990/91 school year, I spent five weeks in each of two City primary schools, Hill St and Low Rd. During that time I interviewed ninety-five parents (including parent governors), thirty-one teachers, and the Chair of each governing body (please see the appendix for further details). I revisited both schools briefly towards the end of the school year to trace the development of particular initiatives and situations, spoke informally to some teachers and re-interviewed a small group of parents. During my time at the schools I helped in classrooms, attended some staff meetings, spent most lunchtimes in the staffroom, and attended a governors' meeting at each school. I made contact with parents through two routes. In each school I attached myself to two classes, one infant and one junior and spent several sessions working with the teacher and children. I then wrote to parents of the children in these four classes explaining my project and asking them to take part. However, my second strategy was the more successful, depending as it did on immediate, personal contact with parents. At the beginning of my time in each school I was in the playground as parents collected and delivered their children. I spoke to as many parents as possible, and handed out leaflets (translated into the relevant languages) which also explained the purposes of the project. Fruitful though this was, it caused me some initial anxiety as it involved 'cold selling' myself and the project. I also contacted community groups and several individuals who agreed to act as interpreters. With their help I interviewed parents from all major ethnic groups in the schools.

Hill St School

Hill St Primary School was a squat, brick building, occupying a large concrete site. The main playground displayed recent attempts at beautification with small trees, raised flowerbeds and benches. However, the building itself needed decoration and repair. Inside, there was no central area or reception to provide a focus. Each storey had a main artery, a long, somewhat gloomy, corridor that ran the length of the building. Classrooms, relatively well-sized and well-lit areas, were spaced out along the corridors. The staff had tried to ease the building's severity with plants and attractive displays of children's work, but deficiencies in design and maintenance remained. The school had over 300 children (including a nursery class) and the roll was rising. Over half the children had English as their second language, and, in addition to English, another eighteen different languages were spoken by pupils. The largest group spoke Gujerati. Many of these children were Muslim and their families were well established in the area. By contrast, the second most common language was Turkish, spoken by children who were recent arrivals. In 1990/91, nearly half the children received free school meals, and 41 per cent of families had no wage earner at home (the borough averages were 50 per cent and 35 per cent respectively). The majority of parents who were employed had semi or unskilled manual jobs.

The teaching staff were predominantly white. The school had fifteen full-time teachers, their length of time at the school varied from teachers in their first year to those who had over ten years' service. The Head, a white woman, Jane Horton, had been in post two years.

Low Rd School

Low Rd Primary School was a Victorian building. Spacious, but now increasingly shabby, such three-decker buildings can be seen in many inner city areas, physically dominating the surrounding houses. Indeed, Victorian public buildings were designed to emphasize the might of education (schools), health (hospitals), or the law (prisons) (Grace, 1978). However, the view of Low Road School from the street was largely obscured by blocks of council flats. Access to the main entrance was down an alleyway. It was a large building, set, like Hill St, in concrete-clad grounds with a small grass area in the playground. The interior was remodelled in the 1970s, and had plenty of space for extra-curricular activities. Attractive displays of children's work brightened the corridors. The school also housed a self-contained nursery, and a class for children with learning difficulties. The school was large with over 400 children. In 1990/91, nearly 70 per cent of the children were eligible for free school meals and over half came from families with no wage earner. Nearly a third of the school's population were of Bangladeshi origin. Over 40 per cent of the children spoke English as a second language, with Sylheti, a Bangladeshi dialect, being the most common. The Head had an explicit open-access policy, so Low Road received children whose behaviour had proved too disruptive for other schools. Again, the teaching staff, especially the permanent staff were predominantly white. When fully-staffed the school had nineteen full-time teachers, but during the research period there were severe staff shortages. Five teachers were new to the school. The Headteacher, a white woman, Jennifer Court, had been in post for six years.

Forms of Parental Involvement

Hill St

Ostensibly there appeared to be many opportunities for parents to involve themselves with Hill St. However, closer examination suggests that some structures were ineffective, whilst others like Hill St's parent group operated only within a particular sphere, and involved just a small group of parents.

Hill St's *Parents' Association* (PA) concentrated on organizing fundraising and social events. Internal disputes had reduced the core membership to about four or five individuals, who, undaunted, continued to arrange fundraising events. Relations between some teachers and the PA soured after disputes as to how the proceeds from a bazaar should be spent, and this resulted in the association finally disbanding, its members feeling that their time and effort were not valued.

The marginal status of the PA in particular, and parents in general, is further evident when the *Parents' Room* is considered. It contained old furniture and discarded reading scheme books. The walls were decorated with out-of-date notices, and health education posters. Fieldnotes, recording my first sight of the room, conclude with '. . . seems like a junk room'. The only parents who visited the room were PA members and the parent governors. The school used the room for 'left-over' activities as well as 'left-over' furniture. Children not attending school assemblies spent the time in there, Urdu and Gujerati classes taken by outside teachers were held there, as were detentions. One teacher commented, 'Who wants to go in there at the moment? I wouldn't. The kids are taken in there as a punishment!' Ms Horton felt that parents should raise money to refurbish the room as 'that way they'll use it'. As there was no sign of parents feeling any sense of ownership towards the room, this seemed unlikely to happen.

Hill St had three *parent governors* (one white woman and two white men). All three visited the school frequently, and at the head's suggestion held regular surgeries so that parents could voice their comments, questions, or complaints to a governor and another parent.

> [Holding the surgeries] . . . was Jane's idea. It was a good idea . . . it was more to take the pressure off her because obviously every day there are several parents outside her office waiting to see her, and she does have a lot to do . . . and it was to give us a little more contact with the parents. But they're not interested. (female parent governor)

Certainly, the response rate was low, something all three parent governors explained with reference to parental uninterest. However, there is a number of other possible reasons. The first was that about a third of the forty-five Hill St parents who took part in this study (and at least one of the teachers) did not know who the governors were. The second was the uncertainty and confusion surrounding the status and role of a parent governor. This was acknowledged by the governors; as one of them said, 'if people have a problem, they go to the top. They don't go to the oily rag, they go to the mechanic'. However, the Head described the governors as the school's link with the parent body;

> It just hasn't got across yet [to parents] that [they] have a big say in how the school runs and that [the parent governors] are their repres- entatives for putting their point of view forward. (Jane Horton)

On the other hand, she also viewed the parent governors as potential aides, saying 'the ideal thing would be to involve them in admissions. That would then be taken away from the secretary and myself and given to parent gov- ernors.' The two roles are not obviously complementary.

For most parents, contact with the school was through *parent evenings*. There were three main types: 'meet-your-teacher' (MYT) evenings at the beginning of term (to inform parents of the topics children would study that term); an annual parents' evening in July when parents were offered indi- vidual appointments; and occasional curriculum workshops. The individual appointment sessions attracted a much larger response from parents than the initial MYT evenings. For many parents who attended both, the distinction between talking about the curriculum, and their particular child's progress was irrelevant, and they saw little difference between the two events.

Forms of parental involvement: Low Rd

There was no parents' room at Low Rd, no parents' association, nor any regular parent–teacher meetings. The lack of home–school contract had been peri- odically discussed by staff, but little action taken. The two years prior to the research period had been particularly unstable with regard to staffing; and survival, in terms of getting through the day, had been the staff's main con- cern. Their lack of enthusiasm for closer contact with parents was illustrated by the organization of the autumn term *parents' evening*. Whilst I was in the school, the Headteacher, Jennifer Court, reminded the staff that they had pre- viously made a commitment to invite parents into school to discuss the chil- dren's work. As staff were unused to planning such meetings, she left them to choose their own arrangements. Many of these appeared to have been organized to suit the teacher rather than the parents. For instance, one infant teacher held a coffee morning at 9.45am. As school started at 9am, this meant that parents were expected to bring their children to school, go home, and reappear forty- five minutes later. This time also excluded working parents. Thus, although teachers voiced support for regular parents' evenings in interview, some dis- played so little interest in planning their own meetings that their actions belied their words. Certainly, it had taken the head's insistence to ensure that all the staff arranged meetings. During the previous year only one teacher had done so voluntarily.

Low Rd's *parent governors* had a lower profile than those at Hill St, reflecting the lower level of home–school contact generally. Over three-quarters of parent-respondents and five teachers had little idea who they were. In fact there were two governors in post, and two vacancies. One governor, an African/Caribbean woman, had been involved in pressing the Education Directorate to ameliorate the school's teacher shortage. Although she felt that she had helped to hasten the acquisition of a teacher, she shared with her counterparts at Hill St an appreciation of the limits on her power.

> They say we have more power now, but I don't really think so. I don't think you can go over certain heads, you haven't the authority to demand that things happen as a parent governor.

Both parent governors wanted more home–school contact. The governor just quoted, suggested that, given encouragement, parents would attend school events if they were arranged. The other governor, a white woman, shared the viewpoint of the Hill St parent governors, maintaining that many Low Rd parents were simply not interested in their children's education. Thus she made little effort to establish contact with other parents.

Staff Relationships: Hill St and Low Rd

One factor influential upon the ethos of a school, and the way it presents itself to 'outsiders' is the relationships between staff members.[3] Ball (1987) describes the task of headship as achieving control of the organization, while at the same time encouraging commitment. The way a head endeavours to resolve this contradiction shapes his/her headship style, and Ball identifies four ideal-type categories:

> *Interpersonal* heads rely primarily on personal relationships and face-to-face contact to fulfil their role. In contrast, *managerial* heads have major recourse to committees, memoranda and formal procedures. The *adversarial* tends to relish argument and confrontation to maintain control. Whereas the *authoritarian* avoids and stifles argument in favour of dictat. (*ibid.*, p.87)

Hill St's Headteacher, Ms Horton, had a 'managerial' style. Whilst generally admiring of her organizational ability, several teachers also commented that she tended to dominate decision-making procedures. She maintained control with formal management techniques which emphasized documentation, such as the weekly timetables staff were required to submit for her comments. Such practices tend to emphasize the gap between Headteacher and staff. Indeed, several teachers commented that they had no clear idea of the Headteacher's priorities for the school. The Head's style also distanced her from parents. A number of parents participating in the research specifically commented that Ms Horton, was always 'busy' — too busy to talk to them. One parent governor expressed concern about this.

> You don't see Jane. Sports Day, the parents were invited along, Jane wasn't there. And people are starting to think, 'what does she do?' ... People don't [come to us if there's a problem], you see, so it builds up, and every now and again you get an explosion ... We were spoilt, one Head we had, Ms Dateon, she did something, ... didn't seem much at the time, she was in the playground ... in the morning and ... when the kids came out. She saw every parent who brought the kids in, and that had a great effect on the parents. (parent governor, male)[4]

Divisions were also noticeable amongst the Hill St staff body. The question of teaching styles was contentious, and there were noticeable differences in classroom organization and styles between those who adhered to a child-centred pedagogy and those whose approach was more formal.[5] However, conflicts about the values and aims held by different people were infrequently articulated in any formal debate, which meant that the staff had not negotiated a joint agenda regarding the school's prevailing pedagogy and ethos (see Bastiani, 1989). This made it harder for them to operate as a team, a factor which contributed to the way in which relationships with parents were forged. Individual teachers developed relationships with individual parents, but there was little enthusiasm for initiatives that required a whole-school approach.

The style of *Low Rd's* Headteacher, Ms Court, corresponded most closely to that of an 'interpersonal' head.

> There is an emphasis on personal interaction, face-to-face contact between the head and his or her staff. There is a preference for individual negotiation and compromises. (Ball, 1987, p.88)

Ball argues that the style of an interpersonal head can mask the operation of power. Issues are discussed informally on an individual basis rather than in the public arena of a staff meeting. One Low Rd teacher commented on this situation.

> It's very much the Head and Deputy [involved in decision-making] and [the Head] keeps a lot of information to herself in terms of power. It's a contradiction really. She gets on with people, but in terms of the school she keeps things to herself. I don't think people do feel involved in decision-making. We'd have to be pretty forceful to get into that really. (white, female teacher)

Unlike Hill St's Headteacher, Ms Court encouraged parents to come and see her, something which several parents commented on appreciatively. This was part principle, to 'create a spirit of willingness . . . [it] is important that people feel they can come and see me', and part pragmatism, to divert any parental anger and criticism away from staff. The Headteacher knew that some teachers felt that close, and often personal contact, with parents was not part of a head's job. She defended her position thus;

> I do know a lot about what goes on, and I talk to the children and the parents a lot, but an inspector came in at one point and I got a tight feeling of anger because I felt the message was coming across that I would prefer to be a social worker rather than a teacher. That is not true at all. It is important to have a sense of other dimensions. But unless a parent is in acute distress, I do not do social work . . . I would resist very strongly [the idea] that I'm doing an awful lot of things I shouldn't be.

Despite differences between individuals, Hill St did have relatively stable and consistent staffing. In contrast, staffing discontinuities hindered Low Rd's teachers in their attempts to form a coherent body. However, the permanent members of Low Rd's staff shared a common child-centred approach to education (for example, they supported developmental approaches to teaching basic literacy). In common with Hill St teachers, they allocated parental involvement a low priority, and while individual teachers established and maintained good relationships with individual parents, there was no sign of any whole school attempts to progress beyond this.

   Finally, it must be emphasized that teachers at both schools worked under considerable pressure, as a result of the combined force of the changes resulting from the 1988 ERA, organizational upheavals following the transfer of education from the ILEA, and a marked teacher shortage. Most Hill St staff were involved in after-school or lunchtime activities, and had a lengthy working-day. One young female teacher commented,

> For me, my job here is to teach the class, and I'm in charge of art, so something has to give. I was keeping my head just above water, but then the Head spoke to me about some other things she wants me to do, and I got that feeling of 'oh, I can't cope' coming over me again. That's the first time I've felt it this term [a month into the term]. For [job] satisfaction you need to get half of you out of the water . . . A lot of it [the workload] has been crisis management [and therefore low on job satisfaction].

At Low Rd, working in an understaffed environment with several children who displayed disruptive behaviours, placed considerable strain on some teachers.

> I was nearly at the end, ready to throw in the towel. I went to [an exhibition], and seeing all those normal looking people, beautifully

dressed, I just freaked. I felt I was mentally ill, I was crumbling. It was as if there was a glass wall between me and all these normal people. (senior teacher, female)

The Research Process

A Note on Researcher-respondent Relationships

An interviewer needs to develop a rapport with respondents to encourage them to feel comfortable, relaxed, and able to talk freely! However, there are dangers here. Maurice Punch (1986) suggests that researchers often dissemble, unconsciously or semi-consciously, in order to gain access to the field and gather data. This might mean, for example, that the more controversial implications of a research project are 'played down' with potential respondents, or that an interviewer appears to agree with respondents' views when in fact she does not share them. Punch concludes that this results in elements of covert research in a supposedly overt research project.

In response to this scenario, qualitative researchers have, in recent years, turned their attention to researcher-respondent relationships and the way in which these shape the outcome of the research process (for example Walford, 1991; Halpin and Troyna, 1994). Various dimensions such as social class, age, or professional status may be influential in determining the relationship. Gender and ethnicity have attracted much academic comment, and it is worth identifying the main issues here.

Many women researchers, informed by a feminist perspective, have attempted to remedy the marginalization and exploitation of the presentation of women in social research. They have sought to do this by giving the experience of women centre-stage, in a manner that aims for the emancipation, or at least, non-exploitation of the respondents. To this end, feminist methodologies emphasized the development of non-hierarchical, reciprocal relationships between women researchers and respondents (Stanley and Wise, 1983). Feminist writers have, therefore, focused on the close bond they felt it was possible to form with their female respondents (Oakley, 1981; Finch, 1984a). This bond arises from a shared experience of being female in a patriarchal society which so often denies female experiences. Thus, these researchers rejected the impersonal stance taken by many interviewers towards their 'subjects', and instead, attempted to develop more equal and intimate associations.

As Sarah Neal (1995) comments, if women have been rendered invisible in much social science research, then the opposite is true of black communities. There the focus of white researchers has been on black people themselves, serving to render problematic individuals and groups, rather than critically analyzing oppressive institutional power structures. Such research has resulted in a conservative anthropological stance. The ethnocentric approach of some studies has been criticized as ignoring the effects of structural racism on researcher-respondent relationships (Lawrence, 1982). This model has been exposed for its paternalistic arrogance which validates researchers visiting a community, gaining information and analyzing 'their' data without further references to that community (Bourne, 1980). These critiques focused in particular on dissemination, claiming that the results of the research often encouraged a pathological view of black communities.

However, acknowledging the justification of the criticisms in relation to both gender and 'race', does not mean automatically advocating the matching of researchers and researched. Even if this were desirable, it is not always practical, especially in fields involving a variety of social factors. Nor does a shared experience of say, gender, negate other potential differences, perhaps of ethnicity or social class, of occupational status, religion or age (Ball, 1992). Since each individual is constructed within various social discourses, the process of trying to separate out particular elements can be an artificial one (Hewitt, 1992). Thus it would appear more fruitful for a researcher to engage in reflexivity, in an attempt to acknowledge particular identifications or tensions in his/her relationships with respondents. The limitations of space only allow me to make a brief attempt at this here.

Neal (1995) makes the important point that criticisms of researcher-respondent relationships which focus on the former's ability to exploit the latter assume that the researcher is in a more powerful position than the researched. Writing from a similar position to my own, as a relatively young, low status woman researcher, Neal describes her struggle to maintain her own position throughout interviews with people (mostly male) holding powerful posts in universities and trade unions. Interviewees in my own project spanned a wider social range than those in Neal's study, and included working class parents, headteachers, trade union representatives and the Director and councillors of City Education Authority. To some degree, therefore, I occupied a shifting position in terms of researcher 'power', depending on the social positioning of the respondent. At first I responded to this diversity by following the advice given by Lynda Measor, that when interviewing, 'it is important to "come over" as very sweet and trustworthy, but ultimately rather bland', (1985, p.62). However, I had reservations about adopting such a gendered stereotypical persona, and in any case with individuals I interviewed more than once, it was hard to maintain such a characterless facade.

The majority of my respondents, especially parents from Hill St and Low Rd, *were* unused to being interviewed, and I was concerned to develop a relationship and setting in which they could discuss issues of importance to them. Semi-structured interviews have a considerable advantage in helping to avoid hierarchical researcher-respondent relationships. They allow respondents to introduce and develop themes, thereby giving them some control over the shape of the interview. They also allow a more natural, conversational style to pervade the encounter. Other common strategies which I employed were to offer all my respondents guarantees of anonymity, and to leave the choice of interview setting to them. Some respondents preferred to talk to me at home, others at school or their place of work. I took full notes rather than tape-recorded interviews if the respondents preferred. On two or three occasions, I spoke to parents who were under such stress that I abandoned my interview schedule to discuss whatever topics they chose.

Most of the respondents in my study were women. It is certainly arguable that the shared experience of being female caused an initial positive feeling in my relationship with mothers, and that some of them may have felt uneasy discussing their children and home lives with a male researcher. However, other disjunctions remained. Being a white middle class woman without family responsibilities (as I was) suggests a different range of experiences to those of, say, a black working class woman with children.

I had previously worked as a primary school teacher in the area, a fact that certainly helped my access to schools and provided an initial topic of conversation with staff. Since I shared with many teachers (although by no means all) a similar profile in terms of social class, ethnicity, gender and professional status, I was constantly aware of the need to ensure sufficient detachment to prevent me from uncritically accepting a professional view-point. This process was eased by the obvious differences within the teaching body in the case study schools, concerning pedagogy and definitions of professionalism.

Conclusion

This chapter has introduced the borough of City, its council and the case study schools. It emphasizes that the problems besetting City Council and its education authority cannot be considered in isolation from the wider context of central government hostility to local government. Similarly, the local and nationally-derived pressures operating on teachers in the case study schools produce a working environment which allows them to feel that it is both necessary (if they are to fulfil their many other responsibilities), and acceptable to accord parental involvement a low priority. However, it is worth restating here that parental involvement has never been a priority for the majority of the teaching profession (see chapters 2 and 3).

This chapter continued by describing and analyzing the two case study schools, the forms of involvement on offer to parents, and the relationships between the staff. The latter is seen as a key component of the ethos of each school and the way in which it presents itself to 'outsiders'.

The chapter ends with a short section on the research process which seeks to avoid 'editing [myself, as the researcher] out of the text' (Gitlin *et al.*, 1989). Such an inclusion avoids researchers presenting research as a neutral process and themselves as spectators, making no value judgments, and with no past or present to affect either choice of research topic, methods or approach to the field. Although this brief section does not do justice to all possible issues, it does highlight some important considerations with regard to researcher-respondent relationships.

The next chapter takes up the themes of gender, ethnicity and social class, this time examining them in relation to teacher-parent relationships.

Notes

1 This includes both the council and private rented sector, although the 1990s have witnessed several large scale initiatives aimed at improving the public housing stock.

2 A Conservative councillor suggested that this was the view of the Labour group as the Council took control of local education services.

3 References to 'staff' refer to teaching staff. At both schools, I did interview at least one member of the ancillary staff who had children at the schools. However, as they preferred to position themselves as parents, rather than as staff members, I have included their views with those of other parents. Relationships between ancillary staff and teachers at Hill St seemed especially distant. Ancillary staff, for instance, rarely used the staffroom.

4 Interestingly, two teachers suggested that Ms Dateon felt her playground stint to be an effective way, not of developing closer relationships with parents, but instead, maintaining a high profile stance, clearly in control of her school.

5 The teaching styles mentioned here are merely generic categories, used to give some idea of the variety of pedagogies. I use 'child-centred' to suggest an approach which emphasizes development through discovery on the part of the pupil. In contrast, more formal, traditional styles emphasize teacher-centred didactism.

Chapter 5

Researching Home–school Relations: A Critical Approach

Introduction

This chapter gives further consideration to the way in which relationships between parents and teachers, homes and schools are presented in the literature. The first section of this chapter argues that much of the home–school debate lacks a critical approach, and advances three illustrations to support this. The typology given in the previous chapter is expressed in terms of 'parents', and lacks detailed references to class, gender or ethnic-based differences. Therefore the second task of this chapter is to rectify that omission, by highlighting, with reference to Hill St and Low Rd, some of the salient ways in which ethnicity, class and gender affect home–school relationships. The chapter concludes by suggesting that a focus on structural dimensions, such as social class, is an integral part of an analytical approach to researching and debating home–school relations.

Problematizing Home–School Relationships

A Closer Look at the Literature

Before focussing on class, ethnicity and gender, three illustrations can be advanced to illustrate and support the contention that discussions around home–school issues are often perfunctory and superficial. The first example is the reliance on consensual language, such as 'partnership', 'dialogue', 'involvement', 'sharing', which feature strongly in the home–school literature, thus editing tension and conflict out of the relationship. As will become clear in chapters 7 and 8, such terms encourage easy agreement, but may also serve to obscure difficulties in interpretation and emphasis. These differences may not be articulated, but can nevertheless result in increasing tensions, capable of significantly disrupting an initiative. Consensual words and phrases, although vague and lacking specificity, can also be powerful in constructing norms for home–school relations (see p.3 above). The terms suggest a warm 'community-spirit'; if this is not achieved both teacher and parents are vulnerable to feelings of disillusionment and inadequacy, and the initiatives may lapse. However, in the recounting of projects, a cheery, unfailingly positive tone seems *de rigeur*, which means that pitfalls, problems or failures get edited out of the 'story' being told. This manner of dissemination means that it is difficult to get beneath the rhetoric and critically assess projects. Thus an article in the Royal Society of Arts' (RSA) 'Parents in a Learning Society' newsletter purports to evaluate home–school activities in fifteen schools in East London (Wolfendale, 1994). This, admittedly short, article categorizes parental responses into six groups. All the categories and illustrative quotes from parents are positive. Yet even the most successful project surely runs into some problems, fails to reach some groups, tries, perhaps successfully, to broaden its scope. All these considerations are absent. Similarly, Lysaght (1993) writes of a project in a socially disadvantaged area of Limerick City in Eire. One of the project's aims is to attain 'the representation of parents at all levels of management to ensure their involvement in decision-making procedures' (p.203). There is scant mention of any potential or actual problems in achieving this goal. Dissemination in this manner fails to inform or aid others trying to develop practice in this area, and instead cloaks the possibility or actuality of conflict, non-participation, apathy or hostility with a rosy glow. This is being addressed to some extent by the increasing degree of contact between small, local projects. These include developments under the banner of the RSA, the Intercultural Education project, the European Research Network about Parents in Education (ERNAPE), and the National Home School Development Group amongst others (see Bastiani, 1993).

The second factor illustrating the occasionally superficial nature of home–school discussions is the assumption of a positive correlation between parental involvement and children's educational achievement (for example, Epstein, 1994; Jowett *et al.*, 1991; Stacey, 1991; Lareau, 1989; ILEA Research and Statistics, 1985). On closer examination, the exact relationship is unclear. What kind of involvement triggers such improvement, and how is that improvement defined? There are two main claims in this area. Some projects argue that their results reveal a quantifiable increase after a period of close parental intervention in the curriculum (Epstein and Herrick, 1991; Dye, 1989; Hewison and Tizard, 1980). Others claim a more general improvement. For instance, frequent, positive home–school contact is assumed to result in the child feeling happier in the classroom, and thus achieving a higher standard (Stacey, 1991; Edwards and Redfern, 1988). With reference to the first group, Peter Hannon (1989) examines several home-reading initiatives and the evidence supporting their claim for higher achievement. He identifies several problems with reading tests. Do they test recognizable reading behaviour, or do they ask the child to decode out-of-context words? Are they prone to cultural bias? Other variables can also affect results, such as levels of existing parental involvement, and the attitudes of staff (*ibid.*; Boland and Simons, 1987). For instance, Dye's study (1989) claims that basic skills tests showed the increased achievement levels attained by her 'experiment' group. Yet as the intervention was only for a short period, it could also be claimed that the parents and teachers could maintain maximum enthusiasm for this limited time, thereby provoking temporary rises in test scores. Hannon (1989) concludes, 'we know . . . that in some circumstances, parental involvement improves scores, whereas in other circumstances there may be virtually no improvement' (p.39). He adds that at least there does not appear to be any evidence that parental involvement decreases achievement levels! Awareness of such problems leads advocates to make more general assertions concerning the value of parental involvement for children's learning. In theory, positive parent–teacher relationships will result in trust and congruence between home and school, which will then help the children progress further and faster. However, as chapter 3 noted, improvements in parent and teachers' social relationships do not necessarily increase the amount of interaction over educational issues (Smith, 1988; Tizard *et al.*, 1981). Second, increasing the congruence of home and school often means in practice that the home is required to change to match the school, a task which many parents will be unable or unwilling to undertake. Therefore, conclusive evidence of the direct link between parental improvement and achievement is difficult to obtain because of the many variables involved (David, 1993).

A third illustration of the home–school debate's somewhat superficial nature is its vulnerability to trends (Torkington, 1986). This results in one particular innovation being seen as sufficient to 'solve' the 'problem' of home–school relationships. One such example, particularly prevalent in City in the mid-1980s, was the establishment of parents' rooms in primary schools.[1] A more recent example is home–school contracts (see chapter 3). As single strategies however, such initiatives can have only limited and temporary effects.

Social Class, Ethnicity, and Gender in Home–school Relations

As chapters 2 and 3 suggest, over the last fifty years, educationists' approaches to home–school relationships have undergone considerable change both in style and emphasis. Parental roles, once confined to ensuring that children attended school, have expanded to include the provision of ancillary help within the school, and even a role as educator in conjunction with teaching staff. Once the potential of parental influence upon the child's attitudes, behaviour, and perhaps abilities, entered the professional consciousness, educators sought to induct parents into school norms (see the *Haddow Report*, Consultative Committee, 1931, and the *Plowden Report*, CACE, 1967). Ideas of 'appropriate' parental behaviour were, of course, influenced by dominant social discourses concerning social class, gender and ethnicity. The *Plowden Report*, for instance, is pervaded by middle-class conceptions of ideal parent-child interaction. Hewison (1985) comments,

> Parents were seen as essentially passive 'supporters' of the activities of schools: a 'supportive' home provided a child with appropriate language skills, an appropriate interest in books and learning, and even

> appropriate role models . . . children from supportive homes arrived
> at school well-equipped to learn from their teachers; children from
> 'unsupportive' homes provided teachers with much less satisfactory
> educational raw material. (p.45)

'Norms' of child development evolved from the experiences of middle and
upper class children in the late 1800s and early 1900s. Yet it was against this
'norm' that working class children were also measured and often found lacking
(Steedman, 1985). Therefore, mothers (the term 'parent', despite its gender
neutrality, often applies primarily to women) required careful guidance to ensure that they exercised their influence in pursuit of the correct goals (David,
1933). As teachers are predominantly white, middle-class individuals (Musgrave,
1979), their relationships with working class parents are shaped by an imbalance
of structural power (in class terms at least). Teachers also have recourse to
their professional identity, which may enable them to remain dominant in a
relationship with parents with whom they share a social class position.[2] New
teachers are introduced to particular values, attitudes, and language, as part of
their socialization into the profession. Values and attitudes are also refined
locally, through staffroom conversation which reflects both the school's general ethos on home–school relations, and the reputations of particular families. Many parents lack access to an equivalent forum. Andrew Brown (1993)
comments;

> Through actual interactions, spoken or written, an image of 'what
> parents are' is built up within teacher discourse. This acts to build up
> a 'normalizing' image of parents and parenting practice, which in turn
> provides . . . a standard against which to judge 'actual' parents. This
> is however, at a high level of generality, although the inscribed qual-
> ities might be highly specific . . . Placed in relation to this 'general',
> 'normal' or even 'natural' parent, are specific groups of parents who
> may diverge in some way. (p.197)

One identifiable, through heterogeneous group of parents who may be seen
to diverge from the norm are ethnic minority families, particularly non-white
groups. Research has consistently found evidence of stereotypical and negative attitudes towards black pupils, (Tomlinson, 1984; Wright, 1987 and 1992;
Mac an Ghaill, 1988; Gee, 1989; Gillborn, 1990 and 1995). The same attitudes
extend to their families. When Barabara Tizard and her colleagues (1988)
asked white teachers about their experience of black parents, 70 per cent
mentioned a negative attribute in reply (see also Townsend and Brittan, 1972;
Smith, 1988; Howard and Hollingsworth, 1985).[3] Heidi Mirza (1992) argues that
the neo-conservative discourse of 'dysfunctional' families, often applied to
African/Caribbean families, emphasizes 'family composition' (for example, one-
parent families) over 'family disposition' (for example, attitudes and values).
Unsurprisingly, black groups and individuals often respond with disillusionment

and suspicion of the white-dominated education system. Participants at an ACER (Afro-Caribbean Educational Resource Centre) conference in the late 1980s revealed considerable wariness of home visiting, for instance. One is reported as asking, 'are they coming with a set of values and assumptions that imply our way of life is inferior?' (1986, p.17). Indeed the tone employed by 1960s compensatory initiatives lingers on. A project described by Macleod (1985), attempted to 'involve' South Asian parents in their young children's education. Home–school liaison teachers (HSLTs), (mainly monolingual), visited parents at home to 'explain school policy and practice' (p.2). Macleod illustrates the 'problem' of 'parents who fail to conform' (*ibid.*, p.14), by describing a mother who did the ironing throughout the HSLT's visit.

> She showed no sign that she had even the remotest understanding of the value of the . . . intervention programme — or indeed any motivation to understand what was going on. (*ibid.*, p.30)

Macleod continues, not by suggesting any reasons for this reaction — perhaps the woman resented the invasion of her privacy by someone intent on showing her how to interact with her child — but by warning the HSLTs to guard against being treated like childminders (for examples of similar attitudes amongst education professionals, see Mac an Ghaill, 1988; Mirza, 1992). However, Tizard, Mortimore and Burchell (1988) and Tomlinson and Hutchinson (1991; also Tomlinson, 1992) also writing about the involvement of ethnic minority parents, comment on the isolation of schools and teachers from the surrounding locality and its residents. Teachers may spend little time in the area, other than when they are inside the school building. They may be unaware of locally-based groups or provision, such as supplementary schools, although, to parents, these may be important sources of education for their children. Such isolation does not help foster teachers' awareness of cultures, religions or languages other than their own (Tomlinson and Hutchinson, 1991). Nor does it foster close parent–teacher links, leaving minority parents, who may have been educated in different, and often more formal school systems, disenchanted with what can, in contrast, appear as the lax atmosphere characterizing many British primary schools. In schools which are fundamentally monocultural, in terms of curriculum, staffing and ethos, racial prejudice may go unremarked. While equal opportunity policies may be fairly widespread now, in many settings these remain 'paper policies', making little difference to practice (Troyna, 1993; Gillborn, 1995). Certainly, parents are rarely involved in the planning of such policies and may not even know of their existence. Tizard, Mortimore and Burchell conclude that, faced with this situation, it is hardly surprising that many minority parents view their children's school with a mixture of wariness, bemusement and anger.

Much literature on home–school relations speaks routinely of 'parents.'[4] Yet particularly in primary schools the overwhelming majority of parents, involved with the school, are women. The use of 'parents' can be seen as an advance from the once-common and overtly paternalistic 'mums'. As Newman (1983) comments,

> 'Mum' is a demeaning word, implying warmth and emotion, but no imagination or thought. It deprives the person referred to of her individuality, turning her into a homely stereotype. (p.245)

This is illustrated by this 1976 quotation, from a community education coordinator, describing the effects of opening a Parents' Room.

> A fundamental change is taking place in the parents' daily routine: the placid plod to school to deliver and collect the little ones is now one of purpose . . . The chat is no longer confined to the gossip 'tit-bit' of the day, but is more concerned with the school programme. Rearranged and streamlined washdays are a necessity if mum is to fit herself into a group. (quoted in Rawling, 1988, p.66)

'Parent' at least includes the possibility of male involvement. However, Bob Burgess and colleagues noted in their recent study, that the slippage from 'parents' to 'mums' persisted and was common amongst nursery educators (Burgess *et al.*, 1991; also David, 1990). Furthermore, gender divisions were reinforced as women helpers were assigned tasks traditionally designated as 'female' occupations, such as sewing and cooking.

In recent years, feminist researchers have highlighted the way in which mothers, especially in the early stages of their child's education, are subject to considerable pressures to conform to an idealized image of 'good mothering'. State education has long been seen as a potential remedy for the inadequacies of working-class mothers (David, 1993; Griffith and Smith, 1987). Specific practices, (notably a child-centred approach), are normalized through the agencies of (often female) teachers and healthcare 'experts', as well as the media. As many 'school-approved' activities stem from the cultural practices and values of a specific socio-economic group, (the white middle class), white working class women, or women from ethnic minorities are presented with an image of 'good mothering', which for various economic, cultural or ideological reasons they may be unable or unwilling to fulfil (Duxbury, 1987; Walkerdine, 1985; Finch, 1984b). For example, Valerie Walkerdine (1985) suggests child-centred approaches are less likely to be adopted by those in an economically insecure position. Failure to maintain the correct image can cause feelings of guilt or inadequacy; if the woman rejects or is unaware of the ideal, she risks being branded by professionals as a 'bad mother'. As Urwin (1985) comments,

> To the emphasis on mothers as central to the completion of infants' emotional needs, which we have come to associate with the normative appropriations of psychoanalysis, such as Bowlby's work, we

now have an orthodoxy which stresses mothers' contributions to infants' intellectual and social development as well. (p.196)

Walkerdine and Lucey (1989) further develop these ideas by 'unpacking' the concept of the 'sensitive mother'. This requires women to educate their pre-school children in two ways; first, by giving them experience of early number and language ideas by turning household tasks into 'learning experiences', and second, by teaching them social skills. Walkerdine and Lucey argue that the 'sensitive mother' ideal oppresses women who ascribe to it. Their study suggests that these mothers made little time for themselves because of the pressure of constantly interacting in a 'sensitive' way with their child. Again failure to match the image could provoke severe guilt. Similarly Griffith and Smith (1987) argue that once a child is school-aged, her mother has little opportunity, and less power to intervene in the classroom. Yet if a problem arises concerning the child, the likelihood is that the mother, rather than the teacher or any other family member, will assume responsibility for the child's 'deficiency'.

This brief overview has examined the three dimensions of class, ethnicity and gender and their relationship with home–school issues. The following section examines the 'workings out' of these elements as they affect teacher–parent relationships in the two case study schools. Although class, gender and ethnicity are considered in turn, the illustrations given also seek to highlight the different ways in which these dimensions articulate, both with each other, and with other elements, such as sexuality, to give rise to particular experiences and perceptions which cannot completely be explained by focusing on one alone (Hewitt, 1992).

Hill St and Low Rd: Class, Gender, Ethnicity

Class: The Experiences of Working Class Parents

Perceptions of social class distinctions between parents and teachers were particularly noticeable at *Low Rd School*. Although there were many individual exceptions, relationships between parents and teachers were often marked by wariness and in a few occasions, outright hostility. It may be thought that the degree of mutual suspicion which existed suggests that this school is atypical in this respect. However, I would argue that relationships pushed to the limit more easily reveal their underlying assumptions.

Although incidents of physical and verbal abuse were not the determining characteristic of most teacher–parent contacts, there had been a period at the end of the 1980s when there had been a marked increase in such assaults. The legacy of this time was discernible in the attitudes of the present staff. For many teachers, the working class parents of Low Rd were distinguished by their 'otherness', and were perceived as a potential threat, both to teachers personally and to the smooth-running of the school. In a 1988 letter to an LEA officer, the Headteacher, Ms Court stated,

> Parents are most often around in the early mornings, lunchtime, and at the end of the day. I find that it's vital to be around at these times, to act as a litmus paper. A lot is averted or defused in this way . . . Gradually effective relationships build and small pieces of grit don't become boulders . . . The families we are taking into school are without doubt getting more difficult and we are certainly vulnerable to our 'open admissions' policy . . . The commitment, caring and creativity of the staff is unrivalled. Yet the pathology is all around — in the bloodstream of the place. . . . Is harassment [of staff] increasing and if so why? Is it happening more at Low Road or is it general? What are the features of the area that make this an outcome?[5]

The last line of this quotation focuses on the undeniable pressures upon some families. However, such an emphasis risks ignoring the school's contribution to parent–teacher relationships. Schools are not neutral institutions, and whilst their effects are undoubtedly more minor than poor housing, or high unemployment rates, they are nevertheless discernible. The period 1988–90, coinciding with the rise in the harassment of staff was a time of disruption at Low Rd with high levels of teacher turnover and inexperienced staff. The degree to which such organizational disarray affects the standards of learning and behaviour within schools is often not appreciated by those not in daily contact with them. By contrast, the research period of 1990–91, saw a decline in such incidents, coinciding with a clarification of expected standards of behaviour from the children and more stable staffing. However, teachers retained the feeling that they were in the front line battling against unreasonable, potentially violent families.

> Some of the staff feel threatened by just having parents in the classroom and if you saw the way some of them just come in and let off steam, you'd understand it! (white, female teacher)

It is arguable that the underlying cause of parents' aggressive behaviour lies in their structural location within society. Ms Court had attempted to strengthen the school's links with social services, housing departments, police and health service. This is explained by the school's need to know what is going on in other areas of the children and parents' lives in order to understand conflicts that might surface at school; an approach which is common in schools in areas of economic deprivation and has been influenced by the ideology of reformist community education (see chapter 1). The rationale is that the school should no longer appear remote from other concerns in everyday life, nor blind to outside influences affecting the children's enthusiasm and willingness to learn.

However, this type of contact with other agencies operates over the heads of local families (see also Baron, 1989). The school appears to form part of a 'wall' made up of the 'caring professions', backed-up by the police, and designed to 'manage' the local population. The families themselves remain 'cases' or 'clients' and have no entry into the power structure of such institutions. The amount of blank walls some parents met with in an attempt to run their lives was guaranteed to induce a severe sense of frustration. The following quotation gives some sense of this, although the respondent emphasized that she felt herself to be in a more secure financial and personal position than many.

> It's a poor area, housing conditions are bad, it's not just education, there are other social problems. You try and keep the children settled and calm but look at the bad housing, the unemployment. I'm not trying to make excuses for the kids not learning, but parents do try to keep them on a steady keel and present some form of normalcy. My husband was unemployed for almost two years. That's not just a one-off thing, here it's almost normal . . . There's just too many factors. What can you do? . . . I said to the councillor, 'Look at this place, it's not centrally heated, we can't even get our repairs done.' This is just basic living, we're not asking for a swimming pool in the back garden.
> (African/Caribbean mother, Low Rd)

This sense of having to battle to improve or just to protect one's position and belongings, increases the likelihood of conflicts between parents and teachers starting because the parent is defending his/her child, often on non-educational matters. This individualistic focus did not mean that parents thought their own children were incapable of doing wrong; indeed, several respondents acknowledged how difficult it was for the school, and sometimes themselves, to manage the child. However, they often perceived the school's criticism of their children as an implicit criticism of their parenting ability, and in self-defence would turn the complaints back against the school. One mother finally responded to what she perceived as constant disparagement of her child with the words: 'You deal with it, you're the teacher. You never say nothing good about him.' For many parents the school was another institution seeking to exert control over their families, but over which they apparently had no control. The school made demands of them (send your children to school regularly and punctually, make sure their behaviour is good, read to them at home and so on), but there seemed to be no effective channel through which parents could present their demands. Anger grew from frustration; but it also served another function, motivating parents into tackling those who worked in the school, who understood how it operated, and who could (seemingly) determine their children's future (see also Grace, 1978; Carspecken, 1990). The teachers, however, perceived the situation quite differently, feeling themselves vulnerable as potential victims of parents' often misdirected anger. Experience of a very few abusive parents had contributed to some teachers' seeing parents' lifestyles and personalities as abnormal, which helped to legit-imize their exclusion from school.

However, some teachers at Low Rd, especially the (all female) senior management team (SMT), stressed the severe social and economic pressures which prevented parents becoming more closely involved with the school.

> The parents are all interested, if it's your child, you're interested. It's either pressure of work, or they think you're the teacher they'll let you get on with it, or possibly language differences. A couple of children in the class, their families have got so many pressures, home pressures, emotional pressures, social pressures, they're just glad that someone's looking after the children during the day. (white, female teacher)

It should be remembered, however, that Low Rd parents were not offered many opportunities to display their interest in their child's education or the school. When I asked one woman if there had been school social events for parents, she laughed,

> *Ms. Castle*: People do that way out [in the suburbs]. This is [City], they wouldn't do that here.
>
> *CV*: Is that because the teachers wouldn't do it, or the parents wouldn't be interested?
>
> *Ms C*: (pause) I don't know. If they did discos even for the kids . . . we could come in and help. They could give something a try.

Ms Castle had regular contact with the school, concerning her son's behaviour. She was aware that home–school communication on issues other than discip-line was limited, and disliked this minimal relationship. However, she accepted it as the norm for an inner-city school. She discerned quite clearly the social class differences that characterized the two 'sides'. However, she was unaware that she, and parents like her, were seen by the teachers as responsible for this situation through their apparent lack of support for the school.

Even within the locality, class-related differences were perceived by teachers. Low Rd was in a poor part of City, an area the staff saw as inhabited by deprived working class residents, unwilling or unable to take an interest in schooling. One teacher compared Low Rd to a school in 'Crossways', an area with pockets of middle class residents, (Hill St. was located on the fringes of this area).

> You can go up to Crossways, I spent four terms there, there's much more parental involvement. Sometimes when the transport was bad [due to rail strikes], I'd be doing the register for four classes in the hall when the teachers hadn't made it on time, and immediately you'd have a group of parents saying, 'what can we do to help?' I knew you

could put three parents in a room, tell the children to read and they'd be fine. There were always parents around. Here I wouldn't do that. (white, female teacher, SMT)

Gender: The Experiences of Mothers

The negative views held by many of the *Low Rd* teachers of their pupils' parents were also gendered, and did not impact equally upon the children's mothers and fathers. An example of this is the casual derogatory comments both male and female teachers made about the sexual morality of particular women.

Her children have all got different fathers, she's not 'Mrs.' at all!

Some of these kids don't even know where their mum spends the night, if you see what I mean.

Oh, he's terrible [the child] and she's awful! . . . Of course, she's not the mother really, she's his dad's girlfriend.

Two mothers who met at a battered women's refuge and now shared a flat commented, 'We tell everyone we are sisters, otherwise they'll think we're gay . . . they don't like us round here anyway.' The implication of such remarks is that women who do not live within a traditional nuclear family are inadequate as mothers; they are deemed so for disrupting conventional notions of sexual morality. Such condemnations have a long history of being manipulated to control women's sexual and moral behaviour (Macintyre, 1985). Similar constraints do not apply to men. However, not all women are subject to the same degree of prurience. Middle class women (with the possible exception of lesbian mothers) are less likely to have their ability to be a parent measured in terms of who they are having a relationship with. With limits on welfare state spending, unorthodox families who cannot provide for themselves economically are seen as likely to be suffering moral poverty too (Isaac, 1990). Such value systems are pervasive. In the playground, insults about a mother's sexuality ('Your mum's a slag') are understood by children as one of the severest types of verbal attack. Strong norms delineate the limits of acceptable sexual behaviour (Cowie and Lees, 1981; Stanworth, 1981), and girls can be made aware at an early age of the need to behave modestly. One white Low Rd mother told me her 9-year-old daughter had been described on her school report as 'flirtatious'. Her mother had challenged the teacher over this saying that her daughter may be a 'tomboy' and often played with boys, but she did not 'flirt'. However, she did not challenge the intrinsic appropriateness of the concept to describe a child, rather its application to her own daughter. Neither did she ask for the offending item to be removed, nor did the teacher offer to remove it. Here gender, sexuality and class discrimination interact. For the working class women of the Low Road area, sexual behaviour is one characteristic that contributes towards the picture of them as the 'undeserving poor' (Golding and Middleton, 1982). Such comments were not made about mothers at Hill St. It is arguable that Low Road mothers, because of the greater degree of poverty in the area, were seen as living less 'normal' lifestyles than their Hill St counterparts. Golding & Middleton (*ibid.*) conclude that explanations for poverty that focus on individuals' failings — 'blaming the victim' — are widespread and co-exist with a persistent belief in the existence of an irresponsible welfare 'scrounger' figure (also Taylor-Gooby, 1985). The prevalence of such ideas within society has the potential to affect all its members, including teachers. Certainly, more casual comments made by some teachers — for instance, 'The parents were all in the pubs, instead of doing PACT' [the home-reading scheme] — suggested that they employed such stereotypes.

Ethnicity: The Experiences of Black and Bilingual Parents

On paper, Hill St and Low Rd both had anti-racist policies. In practice, however, the two schools reacted to particular racial incidents rather than proactively trying to create an environment in which racism was deemed unacceptable (see Troyna and Carrington, 1990; Gillborn, 1993). Low Rd provides an example of this point. While there were instances of stereotyping and ethnocentric remarks made to me by white parents at both schools, it was at Low Rd that a significant minority of white parents and children made overtly racist comments, particularly directed towards children or adults of Bangladeshi-origin. The primary complaint of these racist parents (16 per cent of the Low Rd parent-respondents) was that the school favoured the 'Pakis', although no-one was able to give any example of this phenomenon. This was unsurprising given that little or no provision existed which was specifically directed to the Bangladeshi population. It might be argued that there is little a school can do to affect parents' attitudes and behaviour. However, Low Rd made few overt attempts to encourage a climate throughout the school, which might mitigate such behaviour on the part of the children, and clearly publicize its non-racist stance to their parents. Indeed, as becomes clear in the following section, the school neglected the experiences and concerns of Bangladeshi families and other minority groups; a neglect which, in effect, compounded the overt racism shown by some parents.

Parent–teacher communication: Bangladeshi parents at Low Rd

The families of approximately one-third of Low Rd's pupils came from Bangladesh. Speaking mainly through Shajna, the interpreter, the parents who took part in this study felt very strongly that the school's ethos was shaped by teachers with whom they shared no common ground, be it in terms of ethnicity, social class, language or religious belief. As evidence, they argued that Low Rd had only one Bengali-speaking member of staff, made no provision for Bengali classes, and had no books in Bengali, (teachers claimed the school did actually have a few dual-language books and was ordering more). Several factors combined to make communication between home and school particularly difficult for Bangladeshi parents. The one Bengali/Sylheti speaking teacher, Ms Ali, was a class teacher, and therefore, despite her best efforts, not always available to see parents. This problem was compounded by the absence of any regular parent–teacher meetings at Low Rd. As noted earlier, there was wide-spread parental support for specific invitations to visit the school. Planned parent–teacher meetings with interpreters present were particularly important for those Bangladeshi parents who were monolingual, and found themselves faced with monolingual teachers. Since the primary mode of teacher-parent communication at Low Rd was informal, unscheduled conversations, Bangla-deshi parents frequently resorted to using their children as interpreters. This often proved unsatisfactory, particularly as the children themselves were usu-ally the subject of discussion. As Ms Ali was the only person able to tran-slate notes home, she tended to concentrate on individual letters, and the more general notes often went out in English only. Given this situation, it is unsurprising that all of the Bangladeshi parents interviewed during field-work, felt, first of all, that they had no reliable and easily accessible source of information on the progress of their individual child, and second, that they were precluded from knowing about general, organizational develop-ments at Low Rd.

This linguistic isolation was mirrored in the parents' perception of Low Road's attitude towards religion. Little attention seemed to be given to Islam; even obvious opportunities to do so, for example by celebrating Id-ul-Fitr, the festival which marks the end of Ramadan, had not been taken (a similar criticism was made by Muslim parents at Hill St). Later in the year, Low Rd appointed a second Bengali/Sylheti speaker to the staff. This teacher considered that Bangladeshi culture and Islam should be afforded a more visible role in school life. He found that other teachers were not opposed to such developments, (they encouraged him as he organized a celebration of Id, for example). Such inaction, he commented, was in itself an action, symbolizing the marginalisation of Bangladeshi families at Low Rd.

Community-school relations: South Asian Muslim parents and Turkish-speaking parents at Hill St

It was not only at Low Rd where ethnic minority parents suggested that they felt the school was unaware of, and uninterested in, their concerns and opin-ions. At Hill St, many black and bilingual parent-respondents revealed a sim-ilar sense of alienation. The combined impact of the incidents and events to which they referred indicates the level of institutional neglect of issues related to ethnicity. This section adds further weight to this point by first examining relations between Hill St School and two Islamic community associations run by South Asian Muslims.

Hill St School had instituted twice-weekly, separate assemblies for Muslim children. The initiative had been prompted by a Muslim governor, and was supported by a nearby mosque. The Muslim parents who participated in this study all welcomed the development, which, however, proved short-lived. The assemblies were soon reduced to a weekly basis; the school apparently found, as one teacher put it, that the logistical requirements for more frequent assemblies were 'intrusive'.

This was not the sole initiative that Hill St undertook, as one member of its staff expended considerable time and energy in building links with local community groups, particularly the two nearby Islamic associations. But the school, as a corporate body, had no clear view of the type of liaison it wished to establish. The issue, in fact, was not discussed, as visiting the centres was seen as an end in itself. Thus the community groups were used as resource centres, places that could provide translations, information and teachers for language lessons. Pressure of work on all those involved meant that such contact remained limited and infrequent. Thus opportunities to establish a more interactive, pervasive link between Hill St School and the community centres were lost.

This is exemplified by the school's arrangements for the Gujerati and Urdu lessons which were offered to South Asian children during the school day. Teachers for these lessons were found through one of the local Islamic community associations. In several respects, however, the programme seemed half-hearted. The lessons were conducted in the shabby room, which was nominally the Parents' Room. There was no attempt to integrate these teachers into the main staff body; when they finished their lessons, they left the premises, having had little chance to make contact with other teachers or children (see also Macdonald *et al.*, 1989, for similar examples).

Families recently arrived in England are particularly likely to perceive institutions as remote and distant, unless the institution actively endeavours to present itself otherwise. One of the most recent groups of arrivals in City were Turkish-speaking families. Hill St had a part-time Turkish-speaking teacher, Dideem, who was funded by a local community group to work with children from eight or nine families. All the families had been in England for less than two years (although the issue was not explored, it is likely that most of these families were Kurdish refugees). Through Dideem, I spoke to five parents. On arrival, many had had no information on schools, housing, or jobs, and were almost totally reliant on other community members. They stressed the importance of education for their children, but found the English education system informal and unstructured, compared to Turkey's (see Sonyel, 1987). This contributed to their difficulty in gaining information; there was no timetable, no homework, and the children claimed they mostly did maths and drawing, (ie simple activities for teachers to arrange for bilingual beginners). The parents wanted opportunities to talk to the teachers, to ask about teaching methods and school routines, and how they could help their children at home. In previous years, and on her own initiative, Dideem had arranged meetings to try and answer these questions. However, the teachers tended to perceive her as a resource, someone to interpret and translate for them. This was important work, but Dideem was able and willing to establish coherent links with Turkish-speaking parents, rather than simply acting as a link between individual teachers and parents.

Discipline and behaviour: Bangladeshi parents at Low Rd and African/ Caribbean parents at Hill St

Bangladeshi parents at Low Rd shared a general parental concern with questions of discipline and behaviour, and this was a frequent topic in interviews. With Shajna interpreting (and contributing her own expereinces), we also discussed racial abuse and harassment. Parents had divergent opinions on the issue of racist behaviour at school. Some felt that bullying and name-calling were directed at Bangladeshi children more than at other groups. Others considered that there was a generally high level of indiscipline at Low Rd which involved all children. (It should be noted that children may not always tell their parents about racist incidents; Troyna and Hatcher, 1992.)

Nevertheless, the Bangladeshi parents all agreed that teachers rarely followed up incidents or complaints from children. This criticism was in fact voiced by parent-respondents from all ethnic groups. Low Rd did have a policy for dealing with fighting and name-calling, and all such episodes should have been recorded and the headteacher notified. My limited contact with the children meant that I was unable to ascertain how effectively the system worked. However, the fact that the parents seemed largely unaware of this procedure suggests that senior management needed to make a greater effort to clarify and publicize the school's policy, to all staff, parents and children.

Issues of discipline and behaviour are particularly controversial in respect of the disproportionately high rate of exclusions of African/Caribbean children, especially boys. Several studies have explored the interaction between teachers and black children in an attempt to explore the factors which lead to this situation. David Gillborn (1990), for example, focuses on what he terms 'the myth of an Afro-Caribbean challenge to authority' (p.19). Gillborn argues that much conflict is triggered by teachers' expectations that African/Caribbean boys will engage in disruptive or challenging behaviour, and also by their ethnocentric interpretations of these pupils' preferred clothes, their manner of speech, or even the ways in which they walk (*ibid.*, see also Wright 1987 and 1992; Mac an Ghaill, 1988).[6] Four of the ten Hill St African/Caribbean mothers who took part in this study commented on this syndrome. They felt that they had witnessed examples of their children being labelled as 'trouble-makers', as this mother describes.

> They think I think he wears a halo, but I know what kind of kid he can be . . . [But] the child who came to school was not the child who came home . . . Sometimes he's treated quite rightly, sometimes it's

just the name of the child, regardless of who did what. If he's involved, he's the culprit . . . He's got a name that goes with him from class to class.

A similar dislocation between school and home was described by another African/Caribbean woman, Ms Abrahams. At face-value, the episode appeared to be relatively minor; yet the divergent ways in which it was perceived by the school and the mother concerned lent it considerable significance in shaping her attitude towards Hill St School. Ms Abrahams felt that her son's teacher, Ms Field, concentrated on criticizing her son's behaviour, and did not pay enough attention to his academic performance. She believed the teacher adopted a negative attitude to her son, and described an incident when she felt Ms Field had humiliated him by 'calling him like a dog'.[7] Ms Abrahams had subsequently insisted that her son be moved to another class. The incident had also fostered a sense of mistrust among other black parents. This is clear in the following account of events. The speaker, Ms Watson, uses 'we' to refer to a small group of African/Caribbean mothers who were friends. It also emphasizes their separateness from the school.

> The teacher — when we first heard of it, we thought it was just a one-off thing and it was the child — but we found she was picking on the black children in her group. There was an incident where she . . . said [to the child] that this is the way she'd treat her dog. And other little things we felt were wrong, were racist basically . . . It was specifically aimed at the black kids, if we thought it was the white kids as well we wouldn't have made too much fuss . . . We tried to put that over to the head but she said the teacher said she didn't do it that way [ie talk to the child in a way that was offensive] . . . she [the head] doesn't pay much attention to what you are saying . . . I don't feel comfortable around that teacher now. I don't have much contact with her now . . . [But] I think apart from that particular teacher and the head . . . all the others have done their best to be aware of all the different cultures and teach in the class to suit everyone and get all the kids involved. That teacher is just one, they're not all like that. (African/Caribbean mother, Hill St)

The teacher and the child clearly held very different views of the incidents concerned. But in this context, the question of 'truth' is not the most important consideration. Regardless of what actually occurred between the child and the teacher, the parents were dissatisfied with the school's response to an issue which held considerable importance for them. Neither Ms Abrahams nor Ms Watson had adopted a pervasively negative view of the school; indeed, they were both at pains to focus their comments on the particular teacher concerned. However, from that point onwards, they maintained a conscious distance between themselves and the teachers.

Incidents such as these are not atypical. They may, in isolation, be considered insignificant by the school authorities, and therefore not fully investigated. They may only rarely have such formal consequences as a complaint to the school's governing body. But from a parent's perspective, they may contribute to rapidly cooling home–school relations.

Many black and minority ethnic parents at Low Rd and Hill St harboured an appreciable sense of disaffection with their children's apparently insular, ethnocentric schools. But it cannot be assumed that a particular view of, or approach to, a school can be 'read off' from membership of a particular ethnic group. Although most parent respondents also shared the same gender and class groups, other factors played a integral part in structuring their attitudes. These included such matters as their previous familiarity with the English primary education system, their perceptions of their children's progress, and also their religious affiliation. Similarly, many white working class parents who took part in the study also argued that the schools neglected their particular needs and concerns. As McCarthy (1990), has suggested it is oversimplistic to conclude that the reactions and relations of actors in any school context can be explained simply in terms of ethnicity.

Conclusion

This chapter locates the home–school debate as an illustration of Miriam David's assertion that,

> a particular framework has been used by policy-makers and social scientists alike to inform and interpret social and educational reforms. This framework has tended to ignore, or not make explicit, questions of gender or race. However despite both the gender-neutral and race-neutral language, reforms and research have been constructed around gender and racial divisions. (David, 1993, p.207)

The chapter has supplied empirical examples of the ways in which home–school relationships are framed by the effects of social class, gender and ethnicity. Omitting these, and other structural dimensions, from the debate can result in uncritical and superficial discussions, which assume consensus over key issues such as appropriate teacher–pupil relationships, curriculum issues, or modes of parental involvement. However, a closer analysis of home–school relations may reveal differences and divisions between different social groups concerning all these issues. Understanding this situation is vital if simplistic strategies are to be avoided. The next chapter of this book focuses in more depth on structures, events and relationships in the two case study schools to provide a more detailed picture of the complexities contributing to relationships between home and school.

Notes

1 Parents' rooms evolved from a recognition that many parents were uncomfortable in schools and that their non-professional status was underlined by their lack of space. Some schools went to great lengths to make their rooms welcoming, but the existence of a room alone is insufficient to encourage parental presence unless it is part of a coherent programme.

2 This point is disputed by Lareau (1989), who found that teachers often had to struggle to maintain their position with the middle class parents in her study.

3 One may, of course, challenge, on ethical grounds, the practice of asking questions which invite respondents to employ stereotypes (Troyna and Carrington, 1989).

4 It is interesting to note that the term 'carer', which includes guardians who are not biologically related to the child, is rarely used.

5 Ms Court was concerned that I should be aware of incidents where parents had been abusive, and gave me copies of her notes and correspondence on such events. No such information was offered at Hill St.

6 In the detention book at Hill St, most entries were for fighting and swearing. However, one child was given a detention for 'walking insolently' and another for 'attitude problems' (see Gillborn, 1990).

7 After an incident between two children, Ms Field apparently called the boy over to her, suggesting by her words and her tone of voice that he was a dog. Ms Field told Ms Abrahams that she was joking with the child in an attempt to defuse the situation. I report primarily Ms Abrahams' interpretation of events, because Ms Field was unwilling to discuss the subject with me in any detail.

Chapter 6

Parents and Teachers: 'Mutual Enemies'?

Introduction

This chapter focusses on parent–teacher relationships at Hill St and Low Rd schools. In so doing, it explores the appropriateness of Waller's (1932) designation of teachers and parents as 'mutual enemies'. The chapter starts by outlining the teachers' conceptions of a 'good parent' — a standard against which parents are judged, and often found wanting. The next section concentrates on two areas: the curriculum and discipline, which highlight particular aspects of parent–teacher relationships and parental interaction with the schools. Finally, the chapter ends with a typology of parental roles, similar to that outlined in chapter 3, but adapted to account for the specifics — the particular harmonies and tensions — of Hill St and Low Rd.

The 'Good Parent'

In 1975, Sharp and Green carried out a study of the dynamics operating within three primary classrooms organised along child-centred lines. After interviewing teachers and parents they formulated the concept of a 'good parent', identifying the degree to which the parent conformed to this ideal as a key element in shaping the relationships between home and school (also Jowett *et al.*, 1991). Meighan (1986) summarizes the role of the 'good parent' as follows:

> Parents are expected to avoid either being interfering, by questioning school critically or admitting to direct teaching at home, or neglectful by not providing required clothing and skills of neatness and tidiness. The good parent defers to the school and the professional claims of its teachers. (pp.61–2)

As Meighan implies, the ideal of a 'good parent', as defined by teachers, contains particular social values and attitudes, and this became apparent during interviews with Hill St and Low Rd teachers. For instance, working class City parents, (or at least a particular sub-group of City parents, this being a distinction which is returned to later in this chapter), are not *expected* to be interested in education.

> *White, male teacher:* In City, I don't think parents value school. School is a place to send their kids. Not all parents have great expectations of their kids. The ones that do and that are worried do make an effort to come [to school]. The ones who don't come, I'm assuming, don't come either because they are busy or because school was just something they had to get through. At 16, they go and be a brickie or whatever. I don't deny that there are people who would come if they could but really can't because they don't have the time.

> *CV:* So there is a difference between parents who have a practical reason for not coming, and those who . . .

> *Teacher:* Just don't bother, yes.

The concept is also highly gendered. As the previous chapter made clear, the word 'parent' is commonly used to refer to mothers, and this was the case at Hill St and Low Rd.

Hill St and Low Rd teachers shared a substantially common view on what made a 'good parent', although there were minor differences between the schools.[1] Casual questions to me, such as, 'Have you found out how apathetic the parents are yet?' were regarded as unremarkable and acceptable. Parental interest was equated with parental presence, which, in both schools, was generally low. However, teachers did make exceptions to this general picture, and all had positive relationships with some individual parents.

The notion of the 'good parent' is worth considering in more detail, and this section examines it from the perspectives of both teachers and parents in the two City schools. The concept derives some of its potency from being inclusive, and extending to cover relationships between the parent and child, as well as the parent and the school.

Hill St School: Teachers' Ideal

Parent and child

A fundamental part of being a 'good parent' is to have an overtly positive attitude towards the school, and encourage the same in the child. First, the 'good parent' would ensure that the child developed a 'sensible attitude to school: that it's a place of learning and one does expect certain types of behaviour to happen,' (white, female teacher, Hill St). Second, the 'good parent' interacts with his/her child in a way that will prepare them for school.

> Lots of parents are quite ignorant of what we are trying to do . . . You can tell who talks to their child, some children just aren't used to listening and talking at all . . . for me, it's automatic that if you've got a young child, if you're going shopping, to say 'shall we have a big one or a little one?' or when they're getting dressed, 'do you want your blue socks or your yellow ones?' (white, female teacher)

This quotation illustrates how one particular style of communication with one's child is seen as the ideal, and set above all other forms (see also Tizard and Hughes, 1984). As noted earlier, the ability to be, and to demonstrably be, a 'sensitive' mother (with all that implies in terms of social class resources) is a major part of being a 'good parent'.

Parent and school

The 'good' parent also behaves in a particular way in school. A Hill St teacher expands on this concept;

> It's a good idea [to have a parents' discussion group], but you're only as good as the calibre of parents. If the parents are not able to cope with the situation then the whole system breaks down. [It's] a very good idea when you have parents who are very sensible and can see how to do things. But if you don't have that and you leave them in that situation then you have all the chaotic results [*reference to the personal disputes within the PA*]. It would need to be done very gently, and you would have to have a training system. (white, female teacher)

With regard to parental involvement in the classroom or with the educational minutiae of the child's day, the 'good parent' has a well-defined, if rather narrow role as helper. Several teachers disliked having parents in the classroom as 'you can feel watched, spied upon. I feel I can't raise my voice', (white, female teacher, Hill St). Another teacher commented,

> There's a tendency [amongst teachers] to feel that if parents come in and do things other than reading, and so on, well, I suppose it is a mystique amongst teachers, and if it breaks down, parents might be encouraged to say, 'Well, shouldn't you do so and so?' Whether that's a good thing or a bad thing, I don't know. (African/Caribbean female teacher, Hill St)

Thus parental help in school was carefully controlled. Parents were often directed towards a class where they did not have children (making the situation more nerve-wracking for them) or towards a more general support job, such as repairing or classifying library books. The jobs that mothers were asked to do around the school often revolved round domestic tasks traditionally associated with women, such as sewing or cooking. The teachers were also enthusiastic about parents acting as a resource, coming in to talk to the children on a subject on which they had expertise. In this way, parents would assume the status of a visitor and pose little threat to the teacher's more permanent position. Overall, the role of parent as helper was limited by the staff, in order to maintain rigid boundaries between the professional and the lay person. This would prevent parents attaining 'insider' status as this mother of a new child wished to do,

> I could get more of a first hand feel for things . . . if I actually have a chance to go in [to help] and become part of the staffroom, you're accepted as part of the school. That would be my aim eventually, so that they know I'm friendly. (white mother, Hill St)

All the Hill St teachers qualified Sharp and Green's 'good parent' definition in one important respect. The teachers in Sharp and Green's study (1975) disapproved of parents helping their children at home, feeling that parents could not replicate the school's child-centred approach. However, the Hill St teachers said they welcomed parents working at home with their children, although some expressed doubts about whether parents used the 'right' teaching method. They also seemed unaware of the many parents, particularly of infant children who saw themselves as conducting educational activities at home with their children. The staff were also united in their opposition to parents being involved in decision-making, particularly where the curriculum was concerned. Two reasons were given for this: first, that parents were not in possession of the necessary expertise, and second, there was a feeling that parental involvement in decision-making would sink any initiative in a myriad of conflicting opinions.

Hill St: Parents' Reality

However, few parents, even those who were highly supportive of the school, managed to remain within the confines of this role. Those who displayed much seemingly ideal behaviour could still, without knowing it, step beyond the boundaries of 'appropriate' parental behaviour by being 'a fussy mum' or 'very difficult when they don't get their own way'.

The PA members fell outside the Headteacher's definition of a 'good parent', partly because of the arguments that had taken place between PA members themselves, and partly because all the current members were white, which the Head felt prevented other parents from becoming involved. Her solution was not to expand, but to reconstitute, the parents' group;

The other thing I inherited when I came here is the ongoing, fishwives thing . . . the petty power struggles . . . With some parents [I'm] waiting for their kids to leave and attracting at the same time more parents in, particularly from the ethnic minorities. It's not a healthy situation [at the moment]. To me it's like a boil that will hopefully come to a head, burst and disperse. Meanwhile you're trying to get some nice strong roots coming in.

Thus the PA's acrimonious demise did not overly concern Ms Horton, the headteacher. She intended to encourage other more 'suitable' parents to the group. However, professional interference in selecting parents is likely to result in adherence to the 'good parent' ideal, a stereotype of the deferential, but interested parent, based fundamentally on the teaching profession's values and priorities. This is already a tendency in the selection of parent governors, many are persuaded to stand by teachers (Pascal, 1988 and 1989; Deem, Brehony and Heath, 1995). Thus at Hill St, the definition of a 'good parent' is informed by the teachers' social class and occupational perspectives, which serve to limit parents to a role both supporting and subordinate.

Low Rd

Teachers at *Low Rd* worked with a more tentative definition of a 'good parent' than their counterparts at Hill St. Low Rd provided fewer opportunities for parents to respond to invitations to visit the school. Thus, the staff had little evidence on which to equate parental interest with parental presence. However, teachers apparently assumed that parents, whether due to apathy or practical problems, would not turn out to visit the school in large numbers. In accordance with these beliefs, the autumn term open sessions were organized half-heartedly, and thus did receive a fairly poor response. For Low Rd teachers, the 'good parent' was someone who came in informally to talk to the teacher, showed interest in the child's progress, and whose support could be relied upon if the child was disciplined. Staff had adopted this more nebulous definition in response to the type of parent they felt the school had, and what they perceived as realistic to expect in a socially disadvantaged area. It is worth repeating that not all staff adopted a uniformly negative view of all parents. Some of the more established teachers, especially the senior management team, had built up informal contacts with particular families, and commented on their friendly, mutually-supportive relationships with individual parents. However, this included only a small proportion of the children in their care.

To summarize, staff at both schools did hold an ideal of a 'good parent', although their definitions, particularly at Low Rd, were less fixed than those identified by Sharp and Green. However, one main theme runs through all three variations: a 'good parent' should adopt the role of *supporter/learner* in matters connected to both the children's behaviour and their work. Whilst other research has shown that this desire for parental support is equally important for teachers working in middle class areas (Miles and Gold, 1981; Lareau, 1989), the teachers at Hill St and Low Rd also displayed a tendency to employ a reified and deficit model of working class culture which shaped their opinions of the parent body.

Parent–teacher Relationships

Forty per cent of the ninety-five parents I spoke to found visiting the schools intimidating. They may not have known their way around, nor have met the individuals they had come to see. They may have been reminded of their own dislike of school. Parents from all class and ethnic groups mentioned these reactions. Some working class parent-respondents perceived the social class and occupational divisions between themselves and the teachers (see Lareau, 1989). Several mentioned that the teachers talked down to them, as if they were children themselves. 'I hate it! I think, don't talk to me!' (white mother, Hill St). Others related incidents when they felt they had been firmly put in their (subordinate) places.

> On his first day, I was in the class with him, and he did a picture. I told him to write his name on it, I thought that's what you did at school. [*The child wrote his name in capital letters as his mother had taught him.*] The teacher said to me, 'Oh no, we don't like that.' They like them to go to school with nothing. (white mother, Low Rd)

Another woman resisted showing deference to the professionals' status.

> I tend to treat the teacher, not as the teacher, but as someone to talk to. I've always been on first name terms with the teacher. I don't like saying 'miss' because I find it makes you inferior as if they are better than you. (white mother, Hill St)

At each school there were particular teachers that parents praised for their friendly manner. However, although a positive relationship with a teacher may make it easier for a parent to approach him or her, it does not necessarily mean the parent will receive more detailed or exact information about the child's progress. Often parents did not know what questions to ask, and occasionally, teachers assumed knowledge and information that parents did not have. This last is an issue we shall return to, as this chapter goes on to consider two areas which highlighted the nature of parent–teacher relationships. The first is parents' experience of the curriculum; the second concerns the differing views on discipline, held by some parents and teachers.

Parents and the Curriculum

Parents at both schools felt they were kept relatively well-informed on organizational matters via letters home. However, it was where curriculum content or teaching methods were concerned, that misunderstandings could arise. At both schools, parents received much of their curriculum information 'third hand' through their children. Fifty-six parents said that they saw increased involvement with the curriculum as a priority (see also Hughes, Wikeley and Nash, 1994, for similar points. They also argue that the implementation of the National Curriculum has made little impact upon parents' knowledge). Parents' interest was mainly directed towards finding out more about what the children were taught and how. Only a dozen parents expressed interest in commenting on curriculum policies; the majority, especially at Low Rd where some parents and teachers had very little contact with each other, simply wanted to find out how things were currently organized.

> *Ms Castle*: Even to get involved to find out how they teach reading, visit them during the day, sit in the class for half hour or so [would be good]. I know the kids will show off, kids are all the same.
>
> *CV*: Do any parents help in the classrooms that you know of?
>
> *Ms C*: No, I've never heard of people doing that at all.
>
> *Ms Lind*: I think that would be quite interesting, because you only know from your kid's point of view what goes on. (white mothers, Low Rd)

Another parent said,

> The school should let you get involved . . . I would like to know more about the teaching, I want to know why they do the things they do. (African/Caribbean mother, Low Rd)

Nearly all Low Rd parents felt that the teachers should arrange regular open evenings. The school operated an 'open door' system, and the freedom to 'drop-in' was appreciated by some parents. However, this was a minority view as 'open door' systems alone only attract those parents sufficiently sure of themselves within the school setting to initiate discussions on their child's progress. Ideally, they also need to be familiar enough with a primary school regime to ask detailed questions, otherwise, the teacher, unaware that the parent was coming, met vague questions with vague answers. Most parents wanted specific invitations to visit school.

> In [my daughter's] nursery the teachers were sort of like friends, if
> you had a problem, you could go to them. Here a couple of things
> happened and I wasn't sure that I could go to the teacher, and you
> don't know them. I used to take her to the door and wait outside, so
> at least I used to see them. Now she goes up[stairs] on her own and
> unless you're called up, you don't even get to see them. (white mother,
> Low Rd)

As chapter 5 noted, invitations were especially important to a group of Bangladeshi women who pointed out that a language barrier prevented them from
chatting informally to classteachers. Individual appointments sessions were
the most popular option with parents as these offered privacy, and allowed
them to ask questions without feeling as if they were 'interfering'. As a result
of the generally low level of teacher-parent contact, many parents made links
for themselves. For instance, Ms Hamina at Hill St, unaware of the educational
justifications for sand and water play, commented that it was a good idea
to have a class sandtray as City children rarely visited the seaside, (Tizard *et
al.*, 1981, recorded similar misunderstandings). Two mothers of children due
to transfer to secondary school related tales their children had told them of
extreme bullying in the prospective schools. Having taught in City, I recognized the stories as ones that circulated annually amongst year 6 children
there, and doubtless throughout the country. However, both women lacked
other sources of information other than the general impression conveyed by
the poor public image that these particular City secondary schools possessed.
In several cases, even when parents received information directly from teachers, there was still misunderstanding and confusion. Teachers (and researchers) possess much 'taken-for-granted' educational knowledge which many
parents do not share (*ibid.*, pp.65–6; Smith, 1988). To give just one example,
a parent who asked about maths teaching in her granddaughter's class did
not recognize the name 'Scottish maths' as referring to a commercial scheme
(Scottish Primary Maths) but interpreted it as maths from Scotland. Even
parent governors were not necessarily apprised of curriculum policies. One
commented,

> I found out the other day that we were [teaching reading by] doing
> the 'real book' method. I just thought we were reading books! I knew
> they weren't Janet and John which I did [at school]. I've never heard
> of that in my life! (white, male parent governor, Hill St)

Generally, newer approaches in primary education were unfamiliar to parents.
Staff at Hill St had recently stopped using a highly structured reading scheme,
and some teachers there complained of parents' traditional views of learning
— 'some parents force their children to sit and learn the alphabet, that's awful!'
However, the staff had not made a systematic attempt to inform, explain or
defend developments in their teaching methods. Likewise Low Rd's infant

classes operated a developmental approach to reading and writing. But there had been no coherent effort to justify this approach to parents. Thus, many had only a partial idea of its rationale, and felt that children's writing should be more strictly corrected or wanted them to learn the alphabet by rote. Such a process takes time and regular contact; one meeting to explain 'progressive' methods could cause more misunderstandings than it resolves. Not all parents will be convinced, of course, by a teacher's explanations, although most parent-respondents were concerned only that a method of teaching, any method, seemed to work for their child (also Hughes, Wikeley and Nash, 1994). Teachers who believe strongly in employing 'progressive' methods to teach basic skills are missing their opportunity to present their case to parents. Indeed, teachers in City occasionally appeared reluctant to give detailed information, perhaps because, as this mother suggests, they wish to maintain the boundary between professional expertise and lay ignorance.

> I went to [visit local] schools to see what kinds of [reading] methods were in vogue . . . It wasn't easy to find that sort of thing out . . . Most treated it as 'this is something we deal with'. Very negative really. I don't think they grudge you the time to listen to your questions, but they don't really think that's your role . . . One head was telling me about the high standards of reading and writing they have there — above average. Well, that's very interesting, but I wasn't worried about my child being behind anyway. They didn't tell me anything in much detail. Perhaps they thought I didn't really want to know. (white mother, Hill St)

Hill St and Low Rd teachers were keen for parents to help their children at home. Some, however, insisted that parents copy their particular methods, which they presented as the only 'right' way of proceeding.

> A few pointers to parents could be helpful, like the little booklet that has been prepared for Bookworm [the home-reading scheme], saying how to read with your child . . . like for example it's extremely important to know the alphabet in order, but also to know the sounds. 'CAT' — it's not phonetic to say 'see-ae-tee' as the sounds. That kind of train-ing I think is what the parents have to have. (white, female teacher, Hill St)

However, there were teachers in Hill St who would disagree with the primacy this teacher accorded to learning the alphabet. This clash of teaching styles meant that staff occasionally contradicted each other, thus further confusing parents. Many parents would have welcomed guidance on the school's approach to basic maths for example, but it appears counter-productive for teachers to condemn the use of particular methods, (perhaps stressing mental maths rather than practical maths). Certainly some parents knew that staff would disapprove of the type of activities they carried out with their children, and therefore were reticent about their efforts. Whilst parents at both schools were involved in this kind of intervention, in nearly all cases they acted independently of the teachers. One mother at Low Rd conducted an intensive reading programme, buying a batch of second-hand, structured reading scheme books, and reading with her son every night for six months. Several parents at Low Rd commented that having a series of supply teachers had left gaps in their children's education, which they tried to fill. One mother said sharply, 'I wonder sometimes if I'm teaching her more than what the school is'. Some ethnic and religious minority parents sent their children to local supplementary schools, which concentrated variously on religion, home languages and cultures, and basic education. Despite the economic deprivation which characterized the area, two Low Rd parents had employed private tutors to help their children with reading. They expressed considerable embarrassment over this, feeling it was something they could not divulge to the classteachers.

Two groups of parents appeared to have more frequent and productive contact with teachers than was the norm. One group was the parent governors, particularly those at Hill St. They were in a privileged position, insofar as they saw teachers regularly and felt personally at ease with them. They could use their position to attain information about their children, as this governor recognized:

CV: Are you keeping in touch with how your children are getting on?

Mr Sidney: Um . . . yes . . . but only I think because we ask . . . and it's my position. I meet teachers in the staffroom and things like that. For a true answer to that you'd need to ask someone who wasn't a parent governor, someone who didn't even come in and help. (white parent governor, Hill St)

The second group comprised parents of children with recognized special educational needs. At both schools, parent-respondents whose children had been referred for statutory assessment said that they felt fully involved in the process.[2] One woman commented that her son's referral to the educational psychologist enabled her to air her views on her child's school experience.

That's the only way to get to say [what I think] really. You can't just go up to a school and say 'we think this and that'. Know what I mean? It's only because we got the opportunity to say it that we did. [So if there hadn't been that situation] it would never have got said. (white mother, Low Rd)

Another Low Rd mother commented that 'if your children are well-behaved, you don't get to go up the school'. This worked both ways; one parent suspected she would have been far less involved in her daughter's schooling 'if Anna had been normal'.

The teachers in the class for children with learning difficulties at Low Rd, had closer relationships with parents than was common in the rest of the school. There was a system of home books where staff and parents could write messages. All parents wrote occasionally, and some regularly. Parents could also ring teachers directly, and were encouraged to visit during the school day (all had done so at least once). These parents were amongst the few who felt confident enough to question staff on curriculum content and teaching methods.

> We've had some almost arguments. One mum and dad came in and said, 'This education system is awful, you're just messing around.' . . . But at least it's out in the open and there is still a dialogue, although it's clear they think we've the wrong idea about Ricky. (white, female teacher)

The children's experience of difficulties in learning had caused these parents to be formally involved with their education, which in turn legitimated their questioning.

Most other parents, however, felt powerless in their dealings with teachers. Nearly 30 per cent of parent respondents complained of feeling 'fobbed off' with reassuring general comments. This is illustrated by a teacher's description of his appointments with parents:

> I have a piece of paper which is my assessment, and I read it to them, and they look it over, and I try to explain what I meant by all that, and try and have a conversation to allay any worries, because they are always worried. (white, male teacher, Hill St)

Most parents were reliant on the teacher's judgements of their child's progress (see also Tomlinson and Hutchison, 1991). Ten described, often bitterly, how they had found out that their child's achievement was below average, long after the teachers had presumably identified the problem (see also Dhasmana, 1994). One mother, concerned about her child's progress, summed up parental opinion by saying,

> [The teachers] will soon approach you if the child is playing up . . . they should approach you over their education . . . They shouldn't say, 'Oh, he'll be alright in a year's time, two years time', because sometimes they're not. (white mother, Hill St)

Parents were generally unsure of what questions to ask to elicit more detail, and some commented that teachers focused on the child's behaviour rather than academic achievement.

They always say she's a good girl . . . but I think she needs pushing with her work. I have spoken to her teacher about it . . . but if you go up there and say anything, you always get the impression that they are busy and that you are a nuisance. Although they're very kind. (white mother, Hill St)

It's almost impossible to get a feel for what's going on. I really wanted to know more anecdotal detailed stuff, like how my son gets on with the other kids. I think if you don't know much about primary education the information is pretty unhelpful, well it doesn't really give you anything to latch onto. It's vague and reassuring, but in a way you don't want reassurance, you want to know the worst things that happen . . . not what the intentions are. (white mother and student teacher, Hill St)

The combination of professional control and parental awareness of their lack of knowledge about the curriculum was apparent in both schools. This made it harder for parents to communicate their own knowledge about the child.

Teachers can be the dominant partner because they have information parents don't have . . . But parents also have lots of information about the children. They may read better at home where they don't feel pressurised, they may know lots of things the school doesn't even have on the curriculum. I think the problem is getting those bits of your child into the school picture. (white mother, Hill St)

Parent–teacher conferencing was designed to overcome this (ILEA, 1989). One woman described the system at a neighbouring school.

I got a letter to see the teacher, I thought he'd been in trouble, but what it was, was every parent in the class had a time to go and talk to the teacher for half-an-hour. [We talked about] what he liked doing, does he have any problems? . . . That was a good thing . . . They don't have anything like that here. (white mother, Low Rd)

In fact, Ms Court, the Headteacher at Low Rd, had an explicit preference for conferencing over either ad-hoc parent–teacher meetings, or the traditional open evening which she saw as the school putting on annual display.

What often happens is that teachers feel they know the parent and relate to the parent, but when you look at what they are actually relating about, it tends to be lost coats or bullying or help on an outing. If the meeting is about how the classroom is to be organized or how the curriculum is to be structured, then I think you have a different style of relationship. (Ms Court)

However, the earlier description of the cursory manner in which parents' meetings at Low Rd were arranged reveals her difficulty in getting the rest of the staff to share her enthusiasm.

Parents who were unhappy about their child's progress rarely challenged the teacher, but instead would either accept the situation or make alternative arrangements. Often, parents did not feel competent to question the teacher's professional judgment directly, although they often expressed clear opinions on curriculum content and teaching in interview. One African/Caribbean father at Low Rd discussed in depth his perception of the disadvantages in developmental approaches to reading, and the advantages of phonics. However, when he spoke to his daughter's teacher about her progress, he expressed his concern in much vaguer terms, because he did not want to appear to be criticizing the teacher. Thus his specific points remained unanswered. Formalized lay intervention in curricula issues was an unfamiliar concept to most parents, which could explain why so few voiced a wish to be involved in policy-making (see p.97 above).

In some cases parents' passivity sprang from a quite different cause. Some adults saw their child's ability and readiness to learn as fixed. Their children either had 'got it up there' or not. Two white Low Rd women drew a clear distinction between one's son and the other's daughter. The little girl was 'forward' and 'brainy', whilst the older boy 'didn't like work . . . you can't get a child to learn if he doesn't want to, it's not the teacher's fault, it's John's'. Another white Low Rd mother commented '(My daughter) gets on alright here . . . she is above average, I think it all depends on the actual child. A Bangladeshi woman expressed confusion about the interaction between the effectiveness of the school and the child's 'natural' ability.

> My daughter is not good at studying. I don't know if the problem is her or the school. My [teenage] sons say it's the school . . . it's got worse [since they attended]. (translated response, Low Rd)

In his study of Croxteth Comprehensive, Carspecken (1990) also notes this phenomenon of parents' viewing children's ability as innate and divorced from their learning environment.

> Take the case of the working class parent whose child is doing poorly at school . . . their perception of their child's educational experiences could take a number of culturally shaped forms. They could blame their child for being lazy or thick . . . The real reasons for the child's negative experiences would likely be related to the difference between the culture of the school and the culture the child is growing up within . . . Working class families are more apt to interpret poor educational results in terms of personal faults . . . [rather] than to view them as a product of cultural disjunctions between school and home. (p.11)

Such explanations stem from the meritocratic philosophy informing state education. Failure is seen as the fault of individuals: usually the student's own failings (not making enough effort, not concentrating, not having a positive attitude); occasionally the teacher's (not able to keep control, or perhaps using 'ineffective', progressive teaching methods, or spending too much time on 'political' causes such as anti-racism). People are not, however, encouraged to question an education system dominated by the demands of an exam hierarchy that continues to label many young people as failures (CCCS, 1981 and 1991).

Whilst parents at both schools seldom queried teachers' judgments on educational matters, they would challenge the teachers on non-educational issues. The Head of Low Rd commented that 'lost coats and headlice' were common grievances. Likewise, a frequent criticism at Hill St was the school's recent ban on children bringing drinks to school. Where these apparently mundane welfare issues are concerned, the teacher's role is one of carer rather than educator and overlaps with that of the parent. Therefore the latter can legitimately challenge the staff's effectiveness in this role. Parental opportunities to make an active and productive contribution in other areas, especially the curriculum, are circumscribed by widespread notions of professional exclusiveness. Generally the parents in this study did not feel competent enough to challenge this status quo. Thus many of their interventions into their child's education were carried out independently from the schools, which in turn often assumed parental uninterest and apathy. During an interview, Low Rd's Headteacher spent some time discussing the charge often levelled at inner-city schools, that the teachers have low expectations of their working class pupils. This study does not reveal whether this would be an accurate criticism of the attitudes of the staff at Hill St and Low Rd towards the children. It does, however, suggest low expectations held by the schools of their parents.

Parents' Views on Discipline

Discipline is an interesting area for further consideration, as it is a topic where the pastoral and educative aspects of a teachers' role both come into play. As a result, most parents felt that discipline was not an area where professional expertise restrained them from commenting. The subject was most contentious at Low Rd, where over 60 per cent of the fifty parent respondents mentioned their concern with school discipline. Parents at Hill St did mention individual instances where they were displeased with the disciplinary procedures, but there were few disapproving comments about general standards. This is not to suggest that all the children at Hill St were impeccably behaved, nor that all the Low Rd children were out of control! Rather, at Low Rd there was a clash of values between the Head's beliefs about discipline and those of some parents. At Hill St there was no evidence to suggest that this conflict existed on any wide scale. Low Rd parents gave a variety of reasons for what they perceived as the children's poor behaviour, including the influence of the locality or parental inadequacies. However, most parents concentrated their dissatisfaction on the school and, in particular, Ms Court, the Headteacher. Frequent comments suggested that 'discipline should come from "the top", the children "ran rings round the Headteacher" who was too "soft"'. Particular complaints centred around the perception that when children behaving disruptively were sent to her, they often ended up 'playing' in her office, and that playground fights and bullying were not followed up. Ms Court believed that disruptive behaviour was often a sign of unhappiness and needed understanding rather than a more authoritarian reception. This contrasted with the more traditional view of discipline held by some parents (from all ethnic groups), and some teachers (see Foster, 1990, for similar clashes between Headteacher and staff). The disciplinarian ideal is also informed by gender stereotypes, as illustrated by one mother's description of the Head at a neighbouring school, who was male, and therefore 'naturally' more effective.

> It's like at home, who do they take more notice of? Their father. I'll say 'don't do it' a couple of times, but he says 'DON'T DO IT!' once and they'll stop . . . The headmaster there is brilliant, no mucking around. Dave had spent some of his dinner money . . . and he'd made a little fire in a bin around the back so I took him to see the headmaster. He's still on home-report and it's been five weeks now. He said to him 'Straighten your arms!' and he was like this [immediately stiffens arms]. That teacher's got the respect of all the kids in that school. (white mother, Low Rd)

Ms Court realized that her credibility problems arose from her divergence from this 'norm'.

> One of the strengths and drawbacks of pre-me Low Rd was that they [the then separate infant and junior schools] were extremely well-run schools administratively, everything had its place, including members of staff. The children were well-behaved but I thought incredibly dull. My own view was that children should become responsible for their own learning . . . and that their linguistic abilities and cultures provided them with a tremendous resource that wasn't being built on. Part of my task was to take the lid off . . . When children were referred to me I had to go through the whole business of sitting down and gaining the child's trust. Some of the staff and parents . . . had been used to a more cut and dried punitive approach . . . There was a sort of mythology around that seemed to be fairly popular, that when the children were naughty, they were patted on the head and allowed to play. That suited some people's purposes . . . Yes, that's still a problem . . . [but] I feel supported in my philosophy now by the majority of staff.

The Deputy, whilst supportive of the Head, had a sterner manner with the children,

> Yes, we have different, but complementary styles of dealing with the kids ... I think I tend to be the first reference point. I'm in the playground and staff room more than Jennifer can be. The dinner ladies tend to come to me, the children do too now. (white female deputy, Low Rd)

Whilst this system might appear quite pragmatic and flexible, it does nothing to challenge the traditional punitive approach to discipline that the Headteacher was trying to replace. She specifically referred to the school being 'about children now, not this patriarchal sort of system'. Yet parents, ancillary staff, children and some teachers were all familiar with this authoritarian mode of control; they constructed a hierarchy which identified the Deputy as the effective disciplinarian in the traditional male mode, and relegated Ms Court to a more marginal position. She was seen as being 'soft' and therefore less effective. This contrast undermines the Head's emphasis on understanding children's motivations, and giving them time and space to express themselves, although her rationale receives apparent support from most staff, including the Deputy. A woman teacher described Ms Court as having tried to 'change the relationships between teacher and children, being more open to individuals instead of treating everyone as a crowd'. However, this new ethos, being simply imposed, met with disruption from some children and resistance from some parents. Ms Court had responded by modifying her approach somewhat. In particular, she stressed the need for clear boundaries and structures to regulate the relationship, not just between teachers and children, but also with parents.

> After the emphasis on the children ... valuing their contributions, listening to them, there should have been a period when we clarified our learning expectations, and instead there was a short period when I felt that the children were slightly holding the reins and exploiting the openness. Then I felt we needed more differentiation. I began to be aware of things like boundaries, and a sense of belonging and appropriate activities ... I do like being called Ms Court, whereas in my last school, I was Jennifer to everyone, but it's a question of appropriateness. When I was aware that things were getting child-dictated rather than child-centred I felt we [the staff] needed to be seen by the parents as a reasonably tidy and organized group — trying to move into a more appropriate teacher mode.

Ms Court's preferred mode of discipline derives from liberal, progressive child-centred traditions, and had worked successfully in her last school which had a predominantly middle class parent body. However, it was not accepted easily by Low Rd's working class population, (Carspecken, 1990, describes a similar disjunction between parental and professional approaches to discipline). There was no dialogue or consultation with parents about discipline policies or procedures. Instead, there was a reversion to more traditional approaches which were seen as 'appropriate' for Low Rd's population.

This review of parents' experiences and perceptions of the curriculum and of discipline illustrate that both schools offer parents a nominal partnership. However, closer examination reveals that social class, occupational boundaries, and deference to historically-ascribed roles serve to keep parents in a subordinate position. Such an unequal relationship can result first, in disjunctions in parent–teacher communication (as the section on curriculum shows), and second, in the continued existence of unresolved conflicts between home and school, on issues such as discipline. In this context, a few genuinely friendly relationships between individual teachers and parents were insufficient to permanently bridge the gap caused by professional and social class differences.

Parental Roles: A Typology

This section analyzes parental interaction with the school, and seeks to identify the values and beliefs underlying different behaviours. Parents' comments on their relationship with the schools suggests that it is possible to divide them into three main groups, *supportive* parents, *detached* parents and *independent* parents. A fourth grouping, *irresponsible* parents, provides a powerful symbol, but none of the parents in this study fitted the criteria. It is worth considering these groups in more detail.

School-supportive parents appeared to accept the teachers' view of 'appropriate' parental behaviour.[3] Thus this group could be relied upon to attend school events when summoned to do so, help their children with any work that was sent home, and to take the first step in building a personal relationship with their child's teachers. However, as this chapter has illustrated, the 'good parent' ideal was one that few parents could match in actuality. Accordingly, school-supportive parents would occasionally step outside its boundaries, perhaps through too-frequent attempts (in the teacher's eyes) to monitor their child's progress, or by working with their children in a style that the classteacher disliked. However, generally, these were the parents who had the closest relationships with their child's teacher and school. Of the forty-five Hill St parents interviewed in this study, a dozen could be characterized as school supportive parents. In contrast, just four out of fifty parents at Low Rd clearly fell into this category. One obvious reason for such a divergence was the absence of any regular parent–teacher meetings or social events at Low Rd. There were consequently fewer opportunities for a clearly identifiable group of supportive parents to emerge. At both schools, this group was mostly, but not exclusively, composed of white parents.

When asked why other parents did not attend school or PA meetings, supportive parents offered two explanations. Some focussed on parental apathy, and others on the social and financial pressures in people's lives that meant sometimes 'school matters are more than they can cope with' (white mother, Hill St). Those who supported the theory of parental apathy and irresponsibility appeared to root their comments in a discourse which contrasts the 'undeserving' poor with the 'deserving', hardworking, honest poor, a division which has a long and tenacious history (Pearson, 1983; Golding and Middleton, 1982). Elements of the modern versions of the 'undeserving' poor include single mothers with often changing, often aggressive partners, and undisciplined, unruly children. Such families are portrayed as having frequent, unproductive contact with the police and social services. They do not care about the state of their home and immediate surroundings, nor about their children's education or behaviour; they do not 'hold down' steady jobs, and resist all attempts to regulate their behaviour (Murray, 1989; Golding and Middleton, 1982). This portrait receives a further brush stroke with media references to African/Caribbean families, led by single women, with disruptive children, and young black men with predilections for street crime and loud music (Thomas, 1986). Such 'folk devils' (see chapter 2 above) are portrayed as active figures, creating the circumstances in which they live. Yet certain words recurred in the descriptions given by some 'supportive parents' to describe 'irresponsible parents': 'apathetic', 'lethargic', 'not bothered', 'couldn't care less', they used the school as a 'dumping ground', and 'couldn't wait to get away'. These words suggest not the wilful rebellion of the stereotyped image, but alienated passivity (Harrison, 1983). Perhaps this is the explanation for the low parental turn-out at Hill St and Low Rd — that people had given up?

There were a few parents at both schools who felt that frequent, or even regular contact with the school was unnecessary. Nine of Low Rd's fifty parents could be classified in this way, as could eight of the forty-five Hill St parent-respondents. These *detached* parents — a group comprised of working-class adults from all ethnic groups — assumed it was the exclusive responsibility of the teacher to instill their children with 'school knowledge'. However, their limited contact with the school cannot be seen as an indicator of a lack of interest in their children's education. Certainly, they did not see themselves as educators, and the schools' somewhat weak attempts to encourage them otherwise had passed them by. They wanted their children to do well at school, but did not see any way in which they could influence their progress. However, they had not abdicated responsibility for the children's education in the broader sense, seeing their obligations as regulating the children's behaviour, introducing them to cultural and religious mores, and preparing them for the adult world.

A larger number of parents — twenty-five at Hill St and thirty-seven at Low Rd — wanted to become more closely involved with the school, but felt that various factors precluded increased contact. Therefore, although they disliked the situation, this group of *independent* parents maintained the minimum of communication with Hill St or Low Rd. As a result of not being seen at school very often, these parents were often labelled 'apathetic' by staff and other supportive parents. However, independent parents had developed to varying degrees an 'oppositional logic' (see p.5), which led them to reject the traditional roles of Parent Association member and voluntary helper (where available), doubting that such activities would make an appreciable difference to their children's education. In their relationships with teachers, parents found that they often had to take the initiative, and this independent parents were not always prepared to do. Instead, they made alternative arrangements, working with the children at home without reference to the class teacher, and/or taking them to supplementary classes.

It was also this group of parents which identified the inequality which they perceived as a defining feature of their relationships with the teaching staff. They perceived they were, in the main, excluded from any involvement in school matters. They might be called upon when a particular crisis arose, but in the normal run of events they saw no appropriate role for them to play. Some parents had internalized their exclusion to such an extent that they exhibited considerable uncertainty about approaching teachers.

> Whenever, I've gone to a teacher, she's always said how nice it was to have parents showing an interest. So perhaps some parents don't show any interest, and that's the problem. I don't know, maybe it ain't been put to them to show an interest. Alright, they really should go and fend for themselves. The children have only got one education and you have to make sure it's a good one. But maybe some people don't think of that, maybe they think well, the teacher might be busy or they might not like to go in the class and look at the work, they might feel a nuisance. (white mother, Low Rd)

Other parents were more critical, attributing their lack of influence and involvement in school to exclusive professional control.

> You have more control [at home]. You can actually choose what your child does, you can choose the books. I choose black books for my kids, but I also have lots of different books. I choose when they eat and when they don't, when they go out to play and when they don't. Here [at school] it's all been taken away from you, you don't have the right to say 'my child doesn't go to school today'. If you do, you are in trouble. (Ms Watson, African/Caribbean mother, Hill St)

Having school and home as separate spheres could result in tensions in the parent-child relationship.

> They take more notice of the teacher, and you take second place . . . you're not as important as the teacher, and they've got to do things the teachers' way. (African/Caribbean mother, Hill St)

Arguably, the exclusion these parents identify, stems not from a deliberate staff strategy, but rather from their semi-conscious agenda which gives parents a low priority. Whatever the cause, however, the result is that a significant number of independent parents feel distanced from their child's school in some way. These parents included those from all ethnic groups. Ethnic minority parents are however overrepresented in this category, reflecting the feelings of disaffection and alienation from Hill St and Low Rd that many of them described.

Collective Parental Involvement

All parent-respondents were asked their views on a parents' discussion group (see Tomlinson, 1991). Just over half responded positively, especially to the idea of discussing organizational and extra-curricular issues like playground behaviour, and uniform.[4] As noted earlier, there was more reticence where curricula issues were concerned as most parents wanted information rather than involvement in decision-making. Respondents stressed the potential of a parents' group to improve communication between parents and teacher, and to facilitate joint action, 'getting together to sort things out'.

> At the moment it's just what the school says. It [a parents' group] would give everyone a chance to have their individual say . . . No, I don't think there would necessarily be a low turn-out, parents will want to put their point-of-view to the school . . . even if the school don't take much notice, we'd have a chance to air our views. (white mother, Low Rd)

Concerns voiced by parents included the necessity of an informal, relaxed environment if people were to speak out, and the attitudes and commitment of others. 'Parents of this day and age, their attitudes aren't constructive', said one. Some, especially those who had had some involvement in Hill St's PA, doubted whether it would be possible to attract a high turn-out. Parents at Low Rd were more optimistic, perhaps because they had had fewer experiences of this sort from which to draw. Teachers also had doubts. Their view of a parents' group differed substantially from the independent, active, organization pictured by parents. Several parents suggested ways in which such a group could attain independence from staff, whereas the teachers themselves were quite openly concerned that such a group would attract the 'wrong' sort of parents, and would need someone to keep a close check on proceedings.

> I think the whole atmosphere has got to be totally different here for parents to come together as a group. If the parents wanted to do it then I think it would be better if there was a governor or a teacher as reference points within that meeting so they could address things then

and there, and the parents could get some feedback. (South Asian, female teacher, Low Rd)

I think it's important for parents to have a voice, but if something like that was set-up I feel you'd get one particular group of dominating parents that would try and take over. *A lot of the best parents are really quiet, those that take care of their children and are nice and responsible.* (white female teacher, Hill St, my emphasis)

One teacher who favoured increased parental involvement commented,

In order for the staff not to feel paranoid and attacked, I think it's important for them to start initiating things for groups of parents to join in with. To have the upper-hand I suppose. I suppose I don't want the teachers to lose control either. It's not a wonderful world, someone's got to be in control, and it's not not going to be us! If you have things going on, theatre productions and things, parents would appear. (white, male teacher, Low Rd)

A few respondents made a quite different objection, commenting on the perceived tendency of parents to concentrate on the welfare of their own child and overlook the wider interests of all children. The particularistic concerns of some parents ('If it's nothing to do with my child, I don't want to know', North African mother, Low Rd) may be explained as a rational response to the dominance of professional accountability within a producer-led education system. As discussed in chapter 2, the Conservative government's moves towards consumer accountability have also emphasized individualistic perspectives. However, the number of parents at Hill St and Low Rd who favour a parents' group suggests a willingness to adopt a broader view.

Support for the idea of parents taking a larger role in school decision-making cannot be assumed to translate unproblematically into practice. For many parents, finding time to attend meetings is a real problem. Additional commitments at school are likely to impact particularly on women (Hughes, Wikeley and Nash, 1994; David, 1993). In addition, not all teachers would react positively to such a group, especially if it threatened to affect their own actions or conditions. In order to allow a new universalistic mood to develop, it is important to promote public debate on whole school issues (Ranson and Thomas, 1989; see chapter 9). However, such a debate requires that all groups and all voices be heard and represented, whether dissenting from or supporting the status quo. This will not be achieved through the methods apparently suggested by Hill St and Low Rd's staff — the filtering of parents until only the 'good' ones remain. However, in theory at least, many parents were willing to favour involvement and participation rather than the consumer's choice — withdrawing their children from the school. In Hirschman's (1970) terms, they support 'voice' within the institution rather than 'exit' from it. One mother summed up such a choice thus:

> This is what it is — why parents are taking their kids out of school. My cousin . . . took her boy out and she's trying to get the girl out too, because all it is is, come to school, then come home, and that's it. Whereas if they [parents generally] took more interest and got more involved, to find out what the teachers get up to and how they teach, it'd be more better. (white mother, Low Rd)

Conclusion

The case studies of Hill St and Low Rd schools reveal fractured and fragmented school 'communities' (Thomas, 1986). The main division was between professional teachers and lay parents, and this was maintained by teachers' adherence to the ideal of the 'good parent' — a non-negotiated view of 'appropriate' parental behaviour imposed upon an unsuspecting parent body. However, the two main groups of parents and teachers were also further sub-divided. The majority of teacher respondents shared the same ethnicity and social class, and to a lesser extent, gender. However, teachers were also influenced by their varying pedagogical philosophies, and positions in the institutional hierarchy. Differences between them often remained submerged, subordinate to the demands of professional unity. Although most parent respondents shared the same social class and gender there was a diverse range of ethnic backgrounds, and as suggested in chapter 5, this could prevent friendships and alliances developing (see p.84 above). Parents were also divided by their different approaches to school and their role within it. Although the largest group were '*the independents*', the very nature of that grouping prevented them from coming together in order to seek common ground as parents.

Such profound fragmentation requires radical solutions. However, the participants themselves — the teachers and parents — saw the solution in reformist terms. The teachers were concerned to increase the number of overtly '*supportive*' parents. Parents' opinions were more likely to reflect their awareness of the unequal power relations between themselves and teachers. However, parents' discontent with their shared powerlessness and dependency on professionals was tempered by their perceived lack of 'school knowledge'. This acted to deter them from feeling qualified to comment on school practice, especially with regard to curricula issues. Thus, many parents also saw the solution in individualist terms, feeling that increased contact with the school would make it easier for them to state their own particular concerns, although there was some enthusiasm for the idea of collective representation, via a parents' group. However, the teachers were concerned to maintain a clear hierarchy within their relationships with parents; they cast parents as supporters and helpers, thereby encouraging individual rather than collective involvement.

Given this continued situation, some parents will become increasingly disillusioned with the rhetoric of closer contact and cooperation which does not extend beyond the role of 'supportive' parent. The next chapter focusses on an attempt to break through this impasse, through the appointment of home–school liaison officers.

Notes

1 Teachers' length of service appeared to have no effect upon their views, although it might reasonably be assumed that establishing good relationships with parents has been given a higher priority in more recent initial training. Although younger teachers were often more informal in their approach to parents, this did not mean that their relationships were substantively different to those of their more senior colleagues.

2 However, there is research evidence which suggests that many parents feel excluded by the statementing process, for example, Goacher *et al.*, 1988; Cornwell, 1987.

3 There are many similarities between 'school-supportive parents' and the ideal type, 'parents as supporter/learners', outlined in chapter three. The differences in name reflects the somewhat limited range of opportunities, available to parents at Hill St and especially Low Rd, when compared with the initiatives detailed under the supporter/learner category.

4 There was some support, especially from Bangladeshi parents at Low Rd, for separate parents' groups for particular ethnic minority groups. I have discussed this issue in more detail elsewhere (Vincent, 1995). It is worth repeating here that separate parents' groups are likely to prove highly divisive when there are few opportunities for white parents to become involved with the school (Macdonald *et al.*, 1989). An alternative strategy would be to increase the general level of parental involvement at Hill St and Low Rd, and, as part of this initiative, to make a specific appeal to minority communities (translating letters, ensuring interpreters are present, personal invitations etc).

Chapter 7

Teaching: The Low Status Profession?

Introduction

The following two chapters are concerned with change; specifically, the progress of two innovations planned by City LEA. Both aimed to intervene in home–school relations in order to increase contact and cooperation between parents and teachers. One initiative, described in this chapter, involved the appointment of three part-time workers to develop and coordinate different types of home–school liaison. The second, described in chapter 8, concerned the establishment of an advice centre for parents. The development of both projects was less straightforward than envisaged, and this account explains the conflicts and confusions that beset the process of innovation. A micropolitical perspective is advanced, as the moment of change is an especially appropriate one to explore such processes at work within an institution; it is then that 'subterranean conflicts and differences which are otherwise glossed over or obscured in the daily routines of the school,' are brought to the surface and made visible (Ball, 1987, p.28). This chapter describes the background to the project, its early progress in the three schools, and concludes by identifying some common themes.[1]

The Home–school Coordinators

The Micropolitics of Home–school Liaison

The trend towards studying educational institutions through a micropolitical perspective was developed in response to what many commentators saw as shortcomings in traditional organizational theory (Hoyle, 1986; Blase, 1991a; Ball, 1987). The latter is criticized for stressing order, consensus, a linear process of goal identification and attainment, formal sources of power, and the assumption of 'rational efficiency and effectiveness in decision-making and problem-solving', (Blase, 1991a, p.2; see also Anderson, 1991). In contrast, Ball's definition of micropolitics rests on three interrelated areas; first, the interests of participants; second, the maintenance of organizational control, and third, conflict over policy. As this chapter, and the next show, change, or its possibility, can affect all three areas. Ball (1987) comments,

I take schools . . . to be *arenas of struggle*, to be riven with actual or potential conflict between members; to be poorly-coordinated; to be ideologically diverse. (p.19, original emphasis)

It is with this description in mind that this chapter applies a micropolitical analysis to the school-based initiative described below.

City LEA's 'Home–school Partnership Project'

The home–school liaison teacher has to bargain, cajole, negotiate, trade. (CEDC, 1990, p.16)

This chapter describes the appointment and early experiences of three home–school coordinators (HSCs) in three City primary schools, St Anne's, Ladywood and Westdown. It briefly analyzes how confusion and conflict over policy, and the perception that the Project was a threat to established interests caused it to flounder in some settings. It concludes that the problems that arose stemmed from the different values and priorities held by the parties and individuals involved, a theme which recurs in chapter 8. A similar point is made by Nisbett and colleagues (1980), whose study of Scottish community education provision sought to clarify what people meant by community education. They identified common elements subscribed to by most of their respondents, but found that these were variously defined, depending on the speaker's wider value-system. This was a major feature of the early implementation of the HSC Project, as the three case studies illustrate. The broad agenda — that closer home–school relations would be valuable in supporting the children's progress — was agreed by all parties. The more detailed agenda, outlined in a project booklet pro-duced by LEA officers, had the agreement of headteachers and the coordinators. Yet the specific interpretations adopted by different individuals and groups were determined by their own professional and personal interests, and the priorities that arose from them.[2] Ball (1987) identifies three types of teachers' interests: *vested* interests, *ideological* interests and *self* interests (p.17, also Hoyle, 1986). Vested interests refer to teachers' individual and collective working conditions; ideological interests refer to the values and beliefs informing their views on the educational process; self-interest refers to teachers' self-image and self-esteem as professionals. This chapter argues that in some school set-tings, the HSC project threatened all three types of interest. Thus the likelihood of it failing to attract teachers' support was high, and it was, in one case, rejected totally.

The History of HSC Posts

The idea of appointing, to a school-based post, a person with responsibility for developing closer home–school relationships is one that has been taken up around the country. Schemes vary in their emphasis and organization but they also share considerable similarities, derived from a common origin. As earlier chapters show, the issue of parent–teacher relationships, and their correspond-ing effects upon the experience of school students, came to prominence during the 1960s' compensatory programmes (CEDC, 1990; Powell, 1995). The LEAs that still have, or have had HSCs posts recently, serve mainly inner city areas (Bastiani and Bailey, 1992; Bastiani, 1993). Some local authorities in areas with a mixed social class population direct HSCs at those schools with predominantly poor working class and/or ethnic minority populations. Middle class parents, by contrast, are not thought to be in particular need of either lessons in childcare, nor anyone to 'interpret' the education system. However, sustained criticism (for example, Tizard *et al.*, 1981; ACER, 1986; David, 1993) of the compensat-ory approach has led to a corresponding shift in the language of policy goals and aims for HSCs. While a focus on the family and child remains important in most projects, some HSCs also work with teachers to alter their practice and attitudes (CEDC, 1990).

City's project was first mooted by a local headteacher, David Sandford, who had been impressed by a visit to a recently-appointed parent coordinator at a nearby secondary school. The coordinator's role was primarily to organize other parents to help in the school, either in the classroom or with various non-teaching tasks (for more details, see Mayall, 1990). Mr Sandford saw the potential for developing such a post. He commented, 'this particular secondary school was saying [to parents] "This is what we want provided", and I felt that was important. But the other part was to say, "Well, what do you want from us?"'. Eventually, after negotiations with the LEA and several charitable trusts, funding was made available for three part-time coordinators over a period of two years. City LEA's initial proposal to the funders appeared to disassociate itself from the traditional compensatory role for HSCs by stressing that the Project sought to include all parents.

> The central aim . . . is to explore ways in which parents from all racial, cultural and social backgrounds can be encouraged to play a greater role in their child's early learning and educational achievement. To do this, it is proposed to establish parent coordinators in three primary schools, each with a different intake in racial, cultural and social terms.

However, a more detailed statement of intent reveals a lack of clarity concern-ing the Project's aims. The proposal to the trusts attempted to quote the LEA's Education Development Plan, where it notes the importance of finding ways in which the contribution of 'parents, schools and pupils in the education process might be more clearly defined so that shared objectives can be pur-sued in a spirit of partnership and understanding'. However in the proposal to the trusts, *shared* [objectives] has become *school*, which considerably alters the tone of the paragraph.

Senior officers involved with the Project felt its main priority was to encourage increased parental involvement in their individual child's learning and thereby raise standards. They did not reject the possibility that this might lead to discussion or even modification of school policies and practices, although this was not emphasized. Thus the scheme fits the *supporter/learner* category identified in chapter 3, although it was not conceived as being wholly teacher-directed — a point not appreciated by some of the teachers involved. However, the Director of Education had a slightly different interpretation from senior officers. While they emphasized that the main focus for the HSCs would be school-based developments, the Director saw the HSCs also 'working very closely with community groups in generating a greater degree of interest and involvement on the part of the wider community in issues of schooling in the locality'. During the Project, it became clear that similar differences in interpretation existed amongst teachers and the HSCs. They were often subtle and rarely made explicit, but nevertheless had crucial implications for the Project's future.

Officers felt that it was important schools should nominate themselves if they wished to have a coordinator based at their school. Such self-selection was seen as indicative of positive staff attitudes, even if the institution could not demonstrate any particular progress in developing parental involvement to date. However, these events occurred in the first year after the abolition of the ILEA, timing which no doubt contributed to the low school response rate, and the subsequent administrative delays. Thus the coordinators were not appointed until June 1991, which meant that there was a gap of over a year between the school's initial expression of interest, and the arrival of a coordinator. The three schools chosen had populations which represented a rough spread of the social class and ethnic groups present in the borough — a deliberate decision on the part of officers. All three headteachers were involved in the interview process. The coordinator's precise activities were purposively left vague as they were seen to be dependent on the existing situation in the school and the wishes of teachers and parents. The three successful candidates were white women in their thirties who all had a background in community or voluntary work, and had children. In keeping with officers' views about the specific nature of the job, and, much to the disapproval of the local NUT, none of them were teachers.

Events, Reactions and Interpretations

St Anne's CE School

St Anne's was a small, popular school situated near a busy and somewhat shabby shopping area. Statistical data from 1990/91 reveal that the largest ethnic group was children from African/Caribbean families who accounted for just over half the population. The families were more equally distributed between socioeconomic groups than the population of the other two schools, and St Anne's recorded figures for free school meal eligibility (43 per cent) and English as a second language (14 per cent) were below the borough averages of 50 per cent and 24 per cent respectively. The teaching staff were predominantly white, well-established at the school, and turnover was low. The school's Headteacher, a white man, David Sandford, had been at the school for eleven years, five of those as Head. The school also had a Parents' Association which organized several well-attended social and fundraising events.

St Anne's HSC, Lydia, differed from the other coordinators in one important respect. She had been involved in a voluntary capacity at the school for some eleven years, helping in the classrooms, as a PA Committee member and lately as a parent governor, assuming, in the latter role, considerable responsibility for admissions. This last served to give her more status than experience as an ancillary helper alone would have done. Lydia saw herself as part of the school — although not part of the teaching staff, a point I'll return to — and was the only coordinator who referred to staff as 'we' rather than 'they'. She was similarly accepted by staff and many parents, having as one officer remarked 'credibility [with the teachers] before she moved a muscle'. Lydia also had a very positive relationship with David Sandford. He had clear goals for the development of parental involvement at St Anne's and saw Lydia's post as crucial to their realization. However, in contrast to the other two Project schools, Lydia's role was not perceived as a threat by the St Anne's teachers. David Sandford advocated 'leading by example', so that Lydia worked only with teachers already enthusiastic about increased parental involvement. These teachers also had considerable freedom to expand that parental involvement as and when they chose. Lydia herself felt that teachers were within their rights to do this. Consequently, she presented no direct or immediate threat to their sense of autonomy within their own classrooms.

Both the teachers and Lydia herself perceived her main link as being with the school, not City's Education Offices. She preferred to concentrate on practical, school-based developments and her easy incorporation into the school establishment meant that she had less involvement with the LEA than the other two HSCs who turned to officers for support.

In her first few months, Lydia worked on several new initiatives encouraging parents to come into school either as helpers or to meet with the teachers and governors. A 'drop-in' room was established, the written format for home–school communication was revised, and a survey conducted to discover parents' concerns regarding the school. This last was a preliminary step to planning a home–school contract, an issue David Sandford was particularly interested in, and which he saw as a mechanism for developing a parental role beyond an exclusive school-supportive orientation. He was aware that contracts have attracted criticism for presenting as a partnership what is really a school-dominated model of parental involvement (see chapter 3), and therefore emphasized that a contract should be formed through extensive consultation. He hoped to use it to involve parents in the school's governance, and thereby widen the number of roles on offer to them, to include a status analogous to that of participant.

> Instead of saying [to parents], 'What do you want from the school?' and leaving it vague, [we'll] give [them] a list from which they can prioritize some areas and we can look at them in depth, so we've already got a mandate from parents about what we should be doing ... Lydia has now got ... parents ... to come in and [help]. I think that's brilliant. But that's only one side of it. I want to know what parents expect from St Anne's School — you can't have a one-way partnership. What I hope we'll have eventually is an agreement between teachers, parents and children as to what we're about. This will then be presented as a discussion document for anyone who comes to school, but instead of something presented by one person it will be agreed ... This is an equally important function of [the co-ordinator], it's great to have people come in and do things, but this is their school, [parents] have got to have a clear voice in it. (David Sandford)

However, developments were at an early stage at St Anne's. Many potential problems had not yet arisen. The notion of consultation itself is problematic (see chapters 1, 8 and 9), and the task of ensuring that a representative body of parents was involved in formulating a home–school contract would be a difficult one. There was also, as the Headteacher was aware, the possibility of negative and hostile teacher reaction in the face of parental criticisms or even questioning. However, the Project's initial progress at St Anne's was smooth. The agenda was written by the Headteacher, and implemented by the coordinator, with enthusiastic support from some teachers, and relatively passive acceptance from others. Parental involvement at St Anne's was in a transitional phase. Some aspects — parents as helpers and parents as active fund-raisers — consigned parents to the more traditional reaches of the *supporter/learner* category. However, there were signs that the headteacher wished to develop more opportunities for parents to act as participants. His moves in this direction contained the potential for altering considerably teacher-parent relationships, but they were also vulnerable to the pitfalls described above. However, the Project at St Anne's was specifically defined, and within those boundaries, and from its progress in its first six months, participants judged it successful.

Ladywood School

Ladywood was a large school situated in a residential part of the borough. Statistical data suggested a growing polarization in the school population between parents with professional jobs (40 per cent) and those without a job at all (34 per cent). The number of children eligible for free school meals was slightly above the borough average of 50 per cent. The school's population was ethnically diverse, and included a small, but significant, number of Turkish-speaking children, most of whom were recent arrivals in England. The number of children with English as a second language was 25 per cent, a figure in line with the borough average. The teaching staff were predominantly white, and included new and established staff. The Headteacher, a white woman, Eleanor Keatley, had been in post for two years.

The existing school ethos emphasized traditional, teacher-directed forms of parental involvement (including socials and parent helpers). This is illustrated by the Head's response to a question about home–school policies.

> Oh, we have got one [a policy], but I don't quite see . . . [pause] . . . It's just the usual thing of why we want parental involvement, and that we try and encourage it. Parental involvement in the classroom and on outings, special occasions, and to a lesser extent, discipline. (Eleanor Keatley)

The headteacher's perception was that the HSC's job was to help staff with initiatives *they* had planned by relieving them of much of the 'leg-work'.

> Given that we've made these tentative steps [in parental involvement], and it has to be said that all these things have involved masses of teacher time. The booklet, the socials, the newsletter, all that type of thing the teachers could initiate, but there's an awful lot of leg-work the coordinator could do . . . [I want her to encourage parental involvement] in the curriculum really. We were thinking of PACT and Maths PACT, that takes an awful lot of time to get together — the parents could help make the games [used in maths PACT]. They're much more likely to play them at home if they had a hand in making them. So although the co-ordinator's role might appear a bit . . . [pause] servant-ish, it wouldn't be at all really. It's just doing things we don't have time to do. (Ms Keatley)

However, Ladywood's coordinator, Claire, had a broader view of her role, believing that teacher attitudes towards parents needed to change. She felt that Ladywood teachers had little interest in communicating with parents beyond a few narrow areas where teachers wanted information or compliance, and that the staff would feel their autonomy threatened by further parental incursions. The importance of Claire's non-teaching background cannot be underestimated. She sympathized readily with parents who felt bemused or excluded by the school; indeed, this was often her experience. Therefore, she was more parent-centred in her approach than were the staff. She suggested that a new computer club should be open to all parents, so that some could learn alongside their children. However, the teacher involved wanted to recruit solely those parents who already had computer skills and could share them with the children (see p.94) for other examples of parents as experts). Claire's plans for making contact with parents by visiting them in their homes received a lukewarm reception from the Headteacher; home-visits were seen as appropriate only if the HSC was visiting children identified by staff as giving cause for concern.

Thus Claire's early initiatives — trying to build up links with the children in the reception class and their parents, starting a Parents' Group for parents of children with statements of special educational need, and developing contacts with members of the Turkish-speaking communities — displayed some progress, but were hampered by the rapid cooling of relationships between herself and Eleanor Keatley. She felt increasingly marginalized, having little contact with the Headteacher and not being involved in the planning of a school social event. Her position was symbolized by her lack of space within the school. The Head originally insisted that there was nowhere available for Claire to use as a base and as a meeting place for parents. LEA officers eventually intervened to ensure she was given a room.

Another source of contention was Claire's initial approach to her new role. Officers had suggested that HSCs conduct interviews with teachers and parents to establish perceptions about existing relationships in the school, and to use this as a baseline from which to work. The Head considered this research of little importance compared with the 'real' work going on in the school, and she felt disenchanted by Claire's 'failure' to be socialized into professional norms of behaviour (see also Epstein, 1993).

> There was quite a lot of talking in the staffroom on the day she was here . . . If you want to get into a school, you have to work with the kids, there's no way round that . . . I thought I was very specific about what we wanted [from the Project], it was the way it was going to be accomplished that I didn't insist on enough probably . . . It had to be in the classroom with the kids, and then moving out from there, and that if there were talks and meetings and so on, it had to be out of class hours. (Ms Keatley)

The Head is describing a key feature of the canon of accepted professional values; that what is important in school is teacher-child interaction. Obviously this is a central concern of any educational institution. Claire, however, was not a teacher, and she was concerned with a set of relationships other than those between student and teacher. The HSC's role was premised on the assumption that the quality of the home–school relationship affects teacher and student interaction. By privileging the latter, the Headteacher was denying the potential of the former, and, consequently, denying the rationale for the HSC posts. In this way, the position of the teacher as trained professional was judged preeminent. Claire's first public role in the school was to have been that of ancillary helper, rather than as a worker concerned with broader educational issues than those contained within the immediate classroom environment. The Headteacher's perception that the HSC was insufficiently open to professional norms was further aggravated by her belief that Claire was in school for very little time, and spent too long at the Education Offices, involved in the production of policy documents that were themselves abstracted from developments at the 'chalk-face'.

Ms Keatley's general point is corroborated by research literature which identifies the gap between policy and practice as a major reason for the failure of innovations, particularly those imposed from outside the school (Fullan, 1992; Troyna and Williams 1986). Her attitude also contained hints of a traditional teacher-administrator hostility (Tyler, 1986; Blase, 1991c). Since administrators are not in the position where they are judged by their ability to work with children, but can exert some influence over teachers' working conditions, they are often regarded with suspicion by school staff. To the Headteacher, the HSC appeared to identify with administrators rather than teachers. On arriving at Ladywood, Claire was faced by what one officer described as a 'sink-or-swim' attitude. While the staff awaited action, Claire felt unable to plan any developments before she was familiar with the school's ethos and culture. She became marginalized as teachers perceived 'nothing' was happening. As the Project did not develop as she wished, Ms Keatley apparently lost interest, commenting that it was 'not at the top of my mind'. Finding the situation increasingly hard to manage, the HSC turned to LEA officers for advice and support. Unfortunately, this served to confirm the Head's impression that this was not the active, school-based project she wanted, and the spiral of disenchantment grew. Ironically it was the apparently unwelcome reception that Claire received from school staff that made her more critical of teachers' attitudes towards parental involvement. In the Project's early stages, she would have agreed to any positive suggestions for initiatives from the teachers, even those informed by strong self-interest. However, her feeling that she lacked interest, support and structure at Ladywood, undoubtedly contributed to the development of her parent-centred approach at an early stage. At one point, this resulted in her working exclusively with parents, setting up meetings unconnected with the school. As she explained, 'I'm trying the other tack now [working with parents rather than teachers]. Bringing parents into [the Parents' Room] . . . I just carry on on my own' (HSC).

In summary, a clash of perspectives between the Headteacher and the HSC over the purposes of the Project impeded its development at Ladywood. An officer suggested that the staff's professional status led them to devalue alternative definitions of parental involvement.

> That school does have parents involved, not necessarily how we'd like, but . . . Claire comes in and they have to show her what the maths scheme is, so she can show it to parents, what the language curriculum is, anything really . . . [Teachers think] 'What's the point of us showing [the HSCs] what to do? If they were teachers they would already know what we want done.' . . . [The Ladywood teachers] do get parents who are experts in certain areas to do things, they do

fundraise, they do have socials, but they don't want to start anything too drastic . . . it's the general thing — 'we want parents involved but how we want them involved, and if you want it different, we're not going to jump up and help you'. (officer)

This fundamental disjunction caused a split to open up between staff and the HSC. Although this was sometimes bridged (for instance the HSC collaborated with teachers on a booklet for parents about reading), joint activity was uncommon. The situation is analogous to the separation of the 'community' and the 'school' sides of a community school, causing both to operate independently (see p.18 above). The HSC and the teachers both interact with parents, but in different ways, and with different purposes. Thus, in its first six months at Ladywood, the Project was unable to encourage whole-school development in this area.

Westdown School

Westdown was situated in a residential street close to a busy market. Fifty per cent of the school's pupils were eligible for free school meals, an average figure for City. Fifty-three per cent of children had English as a second language, which was double the borough average. The school's population was ethnically diverse, and over 80 per cent of families either had no wage earner at home or were classified as engaged in semi/unskilled manual work. There was, however, a small minority of parents (nearly 12 per cent) who held non-manual jobs. This social polarization affected staff views of home–school relations, with some staff perceiving some of the middle class parents as 'interfering', a point to which I will return. The staff were predominantly white and mostly well-established at the school. The Headteacher, a white woman, Lorna Blake, had been Deputy before becoming Head two years previously. All the teachers (including the Head) were NUT members, a factor which developed considerable symbolic importance during events at Westdown.

Prior to the HSC's appointment there had been a few initiatives in improving home–school relations, including the publication of a book written by parents and children. However these projects had not formed a coherent programme. Like Ladywood's Headteacher, Lorna Blake viewed the project as support for activities already going on in school. The staff were initially very enthusiastic, although their interest rapidly diminished when a Westdown parent who had applied for the post was unsuccessful.

The successful candidate, Jenny, found that, with the exception of one or two teachers, staff seemed largely uninterested in her role. Right from the start, therefore, she worked separately from the teachers, consulting with parents on the establishment of a parents' group. Friction with the teachers first arose over her plans for 'drop-in' sessions in the newly-designated Parents' Room. The staff disliked the idea of parents having unimpeded access to the room; first, because the children themselves used the room occasionally, and second, because of the perceived likelihood of theft. Space is again employed to denote status; the marginal position of both parents and the HSC herself is reinforced by the school's insistence on the absolute control of its territory (this contrasts with St Anne's where, despite the smallness of the premises, the HSC had an office).

Several senior teachers continued to be hostile towards Jenny and the Project, and their position within the school appeared to be such that no-one openly opposed their views, although Ms Blake remained personally positive and supportive towards the HSC. The degree of teacher suspicion was encapsulated in an incident when teachers, acting without consulting or informing Jenny, drew up guidelines designed to regulate parental involvement in the classroom, and distributed copies to the HSC and LEA officers.

By Christmas 1991, the Project had withdrawn from Westdown. The immediate cause was a discussion between the headteachers, officers and the HSCs which proposed that the reception children at all three schools should be assessed at the beginning and end of the year, 'with the contribution of home–school cooperation estimated — if only subjectively by teacher and parent', (minutes, 27 September 1991). The Westdown teachers interpreted the minutes as proposing formal, external testing of reception children, a prospect they found disturbing. A senior teacher commented,

> I think people — it wasn't that they were specifically mistrustful of the Project, but . . . aren't very trusting of the educational climate . . . It might start out as a fairly innocent thing, but can soon turn into a more formal test, as we saw a year ago with the SATs [Standard Assessment Tasks].

However, Jenny maintained that the teachers' real concern was a more fundamental doubt about the Project itself. She attended a final staff meeting,

> I made it clear to the staff what it [the assessment] was all about . . . asking parents' opinions about how they felt their child was doing, asking teachers' opinions . . . I said it was no-way imposed . . . No-one said they didn't agree with that. They didn't have a reason, it was just an excuse.

Consequently, when the HSC forced the issue with the teachers, they refused to give the Project their clear support, and instead requested a meeting with officers. This did not occur as Jenny felt her position to be untenable. After consultation with Lorna Blake, senior officers withdrew the Project. A flurry of meetings with governors and parents followed as both the LEA and the staff offered their explanations of events. The governors finally supported the teachers. A meeting with parents put the teachers' case: that they had understood that the HSC's post was to have concentrated on 'practical initiatives', rather than 'research', and that their concerns had not been recognized by the LEA who had withdrawn the Project 'without consultation with the staff' (Head-teacher's statement, December 1991). A few parents criticized the staff's actions, but most, unaware of the complicated background to the withdrawal, remained silent. The meeting also discussed the continuation of plans for a parents' group and a system of class representatives, initiatives which the teachers proposed to implement themselves, although with few results.

Both teachers and LEA officers (including Jenny, the HSC) identified sim-ilar factors which explained the Project's downfall. Unsurprisingly, however, their interpretations differed.

The first issue was one of power relations. LEA officers felt that Lorna Blake had been outmanoeuvred by a group of powerful teachers on her staff. They argued that she had continued to be supportive of the Project, but had avoided open discussion with those staff who opposed it, thus allowing tensions to escalate beyond her control. However, when discussing the events with me, Lorna Blake presented a united front with her staff, arguing that the Project's emphasis had changed from a 'practical' one, with the HSC contributing to developments initiated by the staff, to a research and assessment programme.

Although officers arranged a preliminary meeting with staff to discuss the siting of an HSC in their school, they assumed the schools operated on a traditional, hierarchical model, and therefore officers communicated regularly only with the headteachers, giving them the freedom to decide what issues they should discuss with their staff. However, Westdown did not operate on this model; what the LEA saw as a weak Headteacher and a strong staff group was presented by senior teachers as a democratic, collegiate relationship.

Furthermore, as at Ladywood, the HSC post was not seen as a high status one, but rather as 'chatting to parents' which was not a 'real' job like teaching. 'The underlying current,' suggested Jenny, 'was that it was a cushy job' (see also Tomlinson, 1984, for similar views of HSC posts).

The other area where the balance of power in the school was important was teacher relationships with parents. The influence of the shared profes-sional ethos that brought the teachers together to form a defined 'interest set' (Hoyle, 1986), superseded any shared perceptions that might have arisen between teachers and Westdown's group of professional parents. On the contrary, for some of the (largely white, middle class) staff, the involvement of these parents was seen as a sign that the HSC was seeking to involve the 'wrong' parents.

> The irony was that the few, very few, handful, of parents she [the HSC] did seem to contact . . . were somewhat dissenting about the school; white, middle class parents who maybe feel they don't have enough control here . . . It's not all the white, middle class parents, there are some lovely ones who are very involved, very supportive, not hostile to the teaching staff, [but] that group of dissenting parents, are used to power and control in their jobs and their situations, and,

> consciously or unconsciously, feel they should be [used to it] here too . . . It was an unhappy alliance. (senior teacher)

The second issue which teachers and officers identified as bringing about the Project's downfall was the differing definitions of parental involvement held by the different parties. The coordinator and the officers felt that staff were willing to allow parental involvement only on their own terms. However, Jenny, like Claire at Ladywood, saw parental involvement as wider than having parents help in class, hence her interest in developing a parent's group. In contrast, the teachers had expected the Project to increase the number of parents coming into school to work under their direction. Accordingly, there was the same emphasis, as at Ladywood, on 'doing something'. As the senior teacher explained,

> This is the kind of place you have to roll your sleeves up, people don't like you to sit and take notes first, they like you to do something. I think there was always a feeling that if a parent from the school had got the job, they could have got started straight away on something practical, because they would have already known parents who could have helped.

However, what this teacher does not acknowledge was that a 'school-supportive' parent would be more likely to become coopted into the school's ethos, and therefore find it harder to develop a critical view of the institution, or to challenge the staff. Jenny commented,

> [The staff] thought, 'we'll get our candidate in and carry on what we are doing now.' . . . [A teacher] said in a meeting . . . 'we already have parents working with us. They work with us in the way we want them to work with us.'

A third issue was the existing tension in the relationship between the LEA and the local NUT branch. Officers, already scathing of the union's values and perceived intransigence, simply transferred this distrust to the Westdown teachers, although not all staff were active union members. The suspicion was fully reciprocated by the teachers, who complained of the LEA's hidden motives and top-down style of implementation which, several felt, were encapsulated by the HSC Project. The teachers' 'interest set' was undoubtedly solidified by their shared union membership (Hoyle, 1986). This coalition may have contributed to their readiness to confront the LEA over the HSC's role, rather than simply 'overlook' her, the alternative tactic employed by Ladywood teachers.

In short, a key explanation for the events at Westdown School was that the teachers were defending their autonomy and independence from what they perceived as actual or potential incursions by parents and the LEA. The presence of the home–school coordinator seemed likely to induce such developments, so the teachers denied her an effective role, and when she persisted, they succeeded in having the position removed altogether.

Issues Arising

This section highlights several general themes arising from the preceding discussion. The primary issue is the problematic nature of implementing change. From this, three subsidiary issues specific to this case study are explored: first, the critical role of the headteachers; second, the LEA's part in organizing the Project; third, the teachers' reactions. The Project as a whole is seen as an instance of a flawed understanding of the process of implementing change (Fullan, 1992). As suggested earlier, conventional administrative theory views change as a linear process working towards clearly defined goals, susceptible to 'rational' planning. Alternative modes of analysis, emphasizing micropolitical theory, suggest that this is an oversimplification, overlooking the interests of participants in manipulating developments to secure their own positions (Ball, 1987). In this particular case, the administrators were unaware of the teachers' embattled perception of their status, and were therefore unable to respond effectively when this issue obstructed the Project's planned development.

Innovation — The Spread of 'Good Practice'?

Curricula development in schools commonly proceeds by establishing and publicizing a series of activities and attitudes which taken together are labelled 'good practice' (Brown, 1992). Often initiators are 'elevated practitioners' (Partington and Wragg 1989), such as advisers, or lecturers in higher education. Those learning about and implementing 'good practice' are classroom teachers or students. This immediately points to an imbalance in power between those who innovate and those who initiate, and between theory and practice. The 'ordinary' teacher, though, has one particular source of power, rooted in her autonomy within the classroom, which allows her to resist, reject or re-interpret locally imposed strategies and approaches, (Corbett, 1991; Bowe, Ball and Gold, 1992). Brown (1992), writing about influences and approaches to primary maths, identifies another reason why particular approaches do not automatically flourish when transposed from one school to another — the fundamental flaw in the concept of spreading 'good practice'.

> a high degree of control of the circumstances in which teachers work is presumed . . . Such a view . . . is untenable, as there are contingencies that . . . make the circumstances in one school or classroom, possibly very different from another within the same administrative, policy and resourcing framework. (p.46)

The City Home–School Partnership Project comprised an innovation developed by those external to the school (LEA officers) who believed that increased contact and communication with parents was 'good practice'. The HSC's role was to develop ways in which this increase could take place, thereby necessarily altering teachers' present practice, and then to publicize successes to other schools. As this chapter has illustrated, the teachers at Ladywood and Westdown resisted, successfully blocking major changes to working conditions, and preserving their classroom autonomy. Events at the two schools illustrate the key role of teacher consent in implementation. Corbett (1991) also argues that 'failure to account for such powers has rendered predominant models of school change ineffective for affecting practice' (p.76). Thus, individual school cultures can negate a successful innovation 'borrowed' from another school setting (Ball and Bowe, 1991; Blase, 1991c; Fullan, 1992). If, as suggested above, one teacher can successfully resist the initiative, group resistance can be even more effective.

Headteacher style

The headteacher is a key figure in the process of innovation in a school, and usually has a position as a 'critical reality definer' (Riseborough, 1981), although particular constraints are provided by individual school settings (Ball, 1987; Pollard, 1987; Burgess, 1983). This section again draws on the models of headship presented by Ball (1987), but its focus is different, concentrating specifically on the Headteacher's attitude towards the Project and the HSC appointed to the school, and not, as in chapter 4, the Head's relationship with the staff group.

The Head of St Anne's, David Sandford, had an *interpersonal* approach to the HSC and to the Project. He was informal in his manner, relying on constant face-to-face communication in his dealings with Lydia, the HSC. Indeed, this was his preferred style with all members of the school population. He laid considerable emphasis on the need to build up personal relationships with parents, and was at the school gate every day, talking to the adults who came to deliver their children. This also gave him an opportunity to persuade or cajole as necessary. Interpersonal heads operate by building up a sense of loyalty and obligation amongst individual members of the school community thus avoiding outright confrontation (Ball, 1987).

> Lead by example, that's the only way, but not spending hours trying to convert someone. You have to select carefully who's going to work with the co-ordinator . . . It's clear in my mind where we're going, but not in everyone else's. I have to do some work on that. (Mr Sandford)

Personal contact, persuasion, few direct challenges to an individual's autonomy, but retaining executive decision-making powers — these are the hallmarks of an interpersonal style. There was no doubt that, at St Anne's, it was Mr Sandford who targeted home–school relations as an area for development, and identified possible strategies. The home–school contract took shape under his direction, and although he consulted with the HSC frequently, he was very much the initiator.

Lorna Blake, Westdown's Headteacher was in a much less secure position. Throughout the HSC's time at the school, she maintained a low profile. Some of her difficulties stemmed from the specifics of her position, as she had only been appointed to permanent headship during 1991, after a period as Acting Head. Her previous position as Deputy meant that she had existing relationships and allegiances with the staff. This, combined with their shared membership of the same union, may also have contributed to her reluctance to challenge some of the assertive members of her staff. It appears, from the (limited) evidence of the Project, that she was unable to attain a position as 'critical reality definer' within the school. There are indications that the Project became contentious at a speed and to a degree that took her unawares, and left her with little room to manoeuvre. However, publicly, Lorna Blake appeared willing to be identified with her staff's position, and let the Project fail, (despite the risk to her own reputation and that of the school), rather than tackle the dominance of some teachers.

In her response to the Project, Ladywood's Headteacher, Eleanor Keatley was *authoritarian* in manner. Ball (1987) comments that this type of head reacts negatively to opposition, and that it is 'avoided, disabled or simply ignored' (p.109). This describes Eleanor Keatley's approach on several occasions. When the HSC acted in a way the Head considered unsuitable, she stated her objections firmly, apparently unwilling to accept alternative viewpoints. When contacted by an LEA officer wishing to arrange a meeting to discuss the obvious difficulties besetting the Project, she delayed the date, and appeared unwilling to spare the time. It seems likely that the staff group were influenced to some extent by their Headteacher's attitude and took their cue from her. This study does not cover Eleanor Keatley's relationships with her staff, and it cannot be assumed that these were necessarily authoritarian. Having decided that the Project would not be as beneficial as she originally supposed, she may have been trying to minimize the staff's workload by encouraging them to concentrate on their classroom responsibilities, rather than dissipating their energy on the Project.

The role of the LEA

The Project's implementation was affected by the officers' working conditions. The dominance of 'crisis management' and staff cut-backs meant that the HSC project did not receive undivided officer attention. Thus a clearly defined view of the type of parental involvement the Project was seeking to encourage was not forthcoming from the authority. Leaving individual schools to define the Project's exact aims backfired on the officers to some extent, as it relied on the headteachers, and preferably the staff, being enthusiastic enough to do so.

This happened only at St Anne's. Although officers ensured that schools nominated themselves for the Project, they over-estimated the amount of commitment this implied, whereas a consideration of the schools' current practices may have given them more accurate information. The Project's general goals and their manner of attainment were (deliberately) presented in vague terms in order to encourage consensus, and more detailed guidance was not produced (Troyna and Williams, 1986). However this allowed staff to make their own assumptions about the HSC's role. At all three schools the Project's practical side was valued above the research aspects by teachers, hence the emphasis on 'doing something'. There were few signs of teachers feeling 'ownership' of the Project; it was seen as an LEA initiative, and, at Westdown especially, a threatening imposition from above.

Teachers' reactions

Some of the teachers' concerns regarding the Project were illustrated by the views of a group at Greensea School. The school had been an original contender for the Project, but withdrew before the appointment of the HSCs. Some of reasons behind their disenchantment are due to the school's specific circumstances, but the staff cited other more general reasons which are outlined here. First, the Project itself, and to some extent parental involvement in general, was seen as being an extra pressure upon teachers trying to implement the National Curriculum. Second, and more fundamental was the question of teacher autonomy. The staff felt their professional credibility under attack from all levels — the government, the media, and now parents. Closer involvement of 'unqualified' people in the education process, through parental choice of school and the new responsibilities of parent governors was seen as a 'dangerous encroachment upon teacher autonomy' (Greensea teacher).

> What qualifications do these people have? What are their credentials?
>
> What happens if parents are at odds with teachers over educational methods? Who has the final say?
>
> If parental involvement is so important for achievement, where does that leave the teacher? (Greensea staff)

The preferred form of parental involvement for the Greensea teachers, echoing those at Ladywood and Westdown, was to initiate parents into the school's own practices and values. This way, as one said, they could retain their own status as professionals and boost parents' self-worth and confidence: 'Parents are welcome' — within limits. However, this should not be taken to imply that the teachers were unthinkingly reactionary. An alternative explanation is that their behaviour is a logical response to the weakness of their structural position (Ozga and Lawn, 1981). Although the Greensea teachers focus their criticism on recent changes in education, Blase (1991c) comments that the position of an 'ordinary' teacher has always been subject to insecurity.

> Teachers are extremely vulnerable to school administrators, students, parents and others. As a result, their political behaviour tends to be reactive, protectionist and covert. (p.247)

This describes the situation at Ladywood, where 'apathy or lack of interest were very effective delaying tactics, and as a result discussions would get nowhere, action would not be taken,' (Ball, 1987, p.51). At Westdown, the teachers' actions were more proactive than reactive, and more overt than covert. However, their aim matched that of their Ladywood counterparts — the protection of their interests. At St Anne's, the innovation was carefully directed and controlled by the Headteacher, and implemented by a known person, maintaining a 'responsive' role towards staff (Mayall, 1990, pp.60–1). Thus the Project was not perceived as an external imposition, nor did it appear to threaten the teachers' independence.

Conclusion

This chapter has described and analyzed developments in the three schools throughout the early stages of the HSC Project. It concludes that the process of encouraging increased parental involvement through siting an HSC in a school emerges as a far more complex process than was expected. After the Project's first few months, the LEA officers acknowledged this, although they identified teacher intransigence as the main problem.

> We went into the Project looking at how to involve different social and ethnic groups of parents, but we've found ourselves looking at the problems of involving schools and teachers. (officer)

It seems that such schemes are more likely to progress smoothly if kept within certain boundaries (see also examples in Jowett *et al.*, 1991). As professionals have a vested interest in retaining their position as the dominant 'partner' in the parent–teacher relationship, their view of an HSC's role is likely to be a conservative one. Experiences at St Anne's suggest that if HSCs are placed in a school where they are supported by the powerful actors in that particular institution, and if the change-agent proceeds cautiously, planning events which do not diverge too much from the teacher's own view of parental involvement, then developments are possible (also Mayall, 1990). More radical change would attack the heart of teachers' claims to professional status, by extending influence to lay people, and is a strategy that could not be attempted without much debate and discussion. Certainly, the task placed too high a demand upon three individuals in three different schools in one local authority. The next chapter looks at an additional and concurrent attempt by the LEA to improve parent–teacher relationships, this time by siting the mediator *outside* any one school.

Postscript

Although this chapter describes only the first six months of the HSC Project, the pattern for developments in St Anne's and Ladywood was established for the remainder of the Project; Lydia continued to work at St Anne's largely without reference to the LEA, although a serious illness on the part of the Headteacher affected the pace of change. Claire also stayed at Ladywood, although the situation remained difficult. Towards the end of the Project, the school claimed the Parents' Room for the children's use, and Claire, feeling this was the last straw, resigned.

Notes

1 This chapter and the next focus mainly on the views of LEA officers and other professionals rather than parents. My original research plan was to study the development of the coordinator scheme over a prolonged period of time, and to collect parental views as part of this. However, there was a delay of well over a year in appointing the coordinators, which meant that I could only study the first six months of the scheme, concentrating mostly on the coordinators' first term at school. By the end of this period, at least two of the coordinators had had little opportunity to develop links with parents, and therefore, few would have gained an impression of the project. While the coordinator scheme was delayed, the Parents' Centre was being established. However, similar time constraints meant that, unfortunately, I also had little contact with parents who visited the Centre.

2 Earlier chapters have argued that home–school relations, like community education, is particularly vulnerable to this phenomenon because of the high level of generality and incidence of condensation symbols present in discussions of the issues (see chapter 5).

Chapter 8

The Local Approach

Introduction

In this chapter I will consider the potential roles for an LEA in extending opportunities for parental participation within its own boundaries. The particular focus of the chapter is on the establishment of City Parents' Centre — a local authority initiative designed to encourage parental participation in the local education system, primarily by providing help and support for parents in their dealings with schools or the LEA. This is presented as an example of the 'enabling authority' approach, a local state project informed by a social democratic model of participation, which aims to facilitate citizen access to, and involvement in, state institutions.

First, this chapter reviews some relevant aspects of participation theory. Second, it critically considers the model of an 'enabling authority' that has been adopted by many LEAs in an apparent attempt to make themselves more accessible to school and lay influence. Third, it describes the establishment of the Centre, identifying its four main goals, and the differing definitions and priorities ascribed to those aims by the actors involved. The chapter concludes that, despite shortcomings in local authority approaches to increasing lay participation, the local state potentially has a key role to play in facilitating such initiatives. However, this role cannot be fully realized under the current restraints imposed by central government.

A Note on Lay Participation

In chapter 1 reference was made to Pennock's four reasons for introducing participatory democracy: namely, to make the organization concerned seem *responsive* to its clients or electorate; to *legitimize* its actions; to *aid the personal development* of individuals 'reached' by the new participatory ethos; or to *overcome the alienation* of those groups supposedly served by the organization (Pennock, 1979). The first two reasons are conservative in character, as their prime aim is to ensure the smooth-running of the institution. The third and fourth aims are capable of a more radical interpretation, as they are concerned with minimizing the powerlessness felt by those formerly excluded from the system (Beattie, 1985).

The critique of social democratic initiatives in participation offered in chapter 1 suggests that apparent attempts to increase participation often prove illusory in substance. Furthermore, moves to introduce participatory processes are often motivated by a wish to legitimate the general profile of the institution concerned. In drawing attention to such phenomena, Lukes (1974) highlights what he calls the 'sheer weight of institutions' (p.38) which serves to limit decision-making to a particular group of professionals. The process of exercising power includes 'individual and intentional' acts (*ibid.*, p.39), but also transcends them; indeed, Lukes stresses the effectiveness of institutional inactivity and structures which work against efforts to devolve power beyond the institutional elite. His focus on institutions as well as individual actions serves to emphasize two points. First, that 'the collective consequences of following [institutional] rules . . . and the norms, habits, symbols and . . . assumptions [which] underlie them' (Young, 1990, p.41) can have unplanned, but oppressive, consequences for client groups outside the institution. Second, the actions of individuals employed within the institution, even those in seemingly powerful positions, are subject to constraints caused by entrenched procedures and attitudes (Young makes a similar point, see pp.5–6 above). Therefore, fundamental change is necessary if the traditional patterns of domination and exclusivity are to be altered (Clune, 1990). Such developments are rare, but not impossible. Stephen Ball's depiction of schools as 'arenas of struggle' (p.115 above) can be applied to other organizations, including, in this case, local education authorities (Troyna and Williams 1986). This is supported by Ball's comment that there is, seemingly, 'space' to be exploited in most organizations.

> Clearly, micropolitical processes in the organization operate to maintain the status quo. Yet attention to micropolitical processes also highlights the degree of 'tenuousness, dysfunction, interruption and possibility' (Whitty, 1985, p.45) that is inherent in the educational context. (Ball, 1987, p.279)

However, the influence of New Right ideologies on this 'degree of . . . interruption and possibility' cannot be forgotten. As chapter 1 argued, predominant New Right approaches shun the social democratic rhetoric of collective citizen participation, which underpins participatory initiatives, preferring instead an emphasis upon the role of the individual consumer. As this emphasis pervades *central* government, this chapter turns next to a consideration of current approaches to participation at the level of the *local* state.

The 'Enabling' LEA

As chapter 2 noted, the 1986 (no.2) and the 1988 Education Acts ensured that the financial and managerial responsibilities connected to the operation of a school were devolved from the local education authority to individual schools. In addition, the establishment of schools with grant maintained status created a new tier of institutions independent from their erstwhile employers. Such developments, set in the context of the Conservative governments' long-standing antipathy towards the local state reinforced the perception of those who worked in local government, and particularly in LEAs, that their position was a precarious one. Thus during the late 1980s and early 1990s many LEAs sought to develop a new role for themselves. This was one which stressed consultation and participation, rather than didactic approaches, and one which sought to disrupt the process of 'mainstreaming' (as described on p.33 above). These developments can be considered under the general heading of the '*enabling authority*' (Clarke and Stewart, 1991; Ranson, 1992; Raab, 1993).[1] A useful summary of this model is provided by Kathryn Riley (1992), although she uses an alternative title of the 'interactive LEA'.

> The interactive LEA is pro-active, seeking to find a new and creative role for itself, rather than being buffeted about on a sea of legislative changes. This new role locates the LEA centrally in the local education arena, but also recognises the centrality of other key movers . . . The interactive LEA actively encourages participation . . . and [is] account-able for the quality of the educational experience offered locally. It is the strategic planner for services and the linchpin between the centre and the locality. (p.21)

However, the emphasis on increased participation requires careful examination. Whilst LEA rhetoric includes references to greater public participation (see Ranson, 1992, for examples), it is arguable that the bulk of initiatives and strategies, if directed towards parents at all, seems to concentrate on the provision of information. Meanwhile, the main recipient of opportunities for consultation are *schools*. Indeed some LEA officers openly identify the rationale behind their new found emphasis upon 'partnership' as being its effect as a deterrent to dissuade schools from opting-out. As one officer from an LEA in the North of England commented:

> [The LEA has tried to] draw schools into a debate, in a kind of part-nership, a better understanding of how the department ran so that they felt some ownership of some of the funding decisions that were being made . . . [Heads and governors] have come up with some of the same conclusions and decisions that we've come up with, but they've come up with them with a better understanding, rather than [the outcomes] being imposed on them. (officer, 'Metropolitan' LEA)[2]

However, efforts at widening the consultative base have not been entirely confined to other educational professionals. In recent years local authorities have sought to minimize any association that their electorate might make between themselves and remote bureaucracy (Hampton, 1991). Thus 'one-stop shops' have been established, and a plethora of charters and associated information has poured from town and county halls (Taylor, 1992). However, there are several possible rationale for such initiatives. As Pennock suggested, apparent attempts to increase public involvement may be primarily concerned with the legitimation of the institution's existing ways of working, and decisions that have already been taken. As the earlier quotation from the officer in 'Metropolitan' LEA implies, such an emphasis gains in importance in a climate of financial stringency, when unpopular decisions are being made. Parents may therefore find that they are better informed to enter into local educational debates, but they cannot assume that their views will be heeded by decision-makers. Colin Ward (1976) made a similar criticism of exercises justified as encouraging public participation in planning, claiming that they were designed to achieve little more than the dissemination of information; 'a propagandist exercise to fob off opposition to decisions which have already been made elsewhere,' (p.124; see also p.24).

However, there are also examples of LEAs attempting to go beyond the simple measure of increasing their publicity and information, and making more wide-ranging attempts to enhance opportunities for community participation (Ranson, 1992 and 1993). The ways in which an LEA tries to achieve this are dependent upon an authority's past and present political and administrative cultures. In the case of an authority like City, its political antecedents are as a 'radical' left-wing borough seeking to make the council more accountable to its electorate (for comments on the partial realisation of this aim by the Labour left councils see Lansley *et al.*, 1989). Most traces of this incarnation have now vanished, although a residual emphasis on involving local people still survives to influence its particular interpretation of an 'enabling authority'. This pre-exisiting emphasis on public participation — even if it existed largely at the level of rhetoric — goes some way to explain the genesis of two projects, undertaken by the LEA. Both were apparently designed to provide parents with information and advice regarding the local education service, and also to allow parental and other 'community' voices access into the formal decision-making process. One innovation, the Parents' Centre, I will consider in some depth later in this chapter. The second initiative was a forum, instigated by the Chair of the Education Committee, in which local educational issues could be debated by representatives from different groups. Ranson (1992) has suggested that such locally-based groups could,

> enfranchise citizens within the community to influence and take re-sponsibility for their own learning environment. They can negotiate with the providers to use educational resources so as to meet the learning needs of the community as a whole. (pp.184–5)

However, the process of convening this group (known as City Education Forum, CEF) was slow and uncertain, and its exact role was obscure. It was proposed that the agenda for CEF meetings would not to be fixed by the LEA, but remain open to ensure its members were free to discuss any issues of concern to them. However, in practice, officers suggested that the representatives would be confined to an advisory role.[3]

Even if one allows that forums such as CEF do have the potential to increase the available channels for consultation and communication between local government departments and the electorate, another caveat remains. These procedures tend to most fully accessible to, and most often employed by, middle class individuals and groups who are familiar with the formal and often bureaucratic consultative mechanisms (Hampton, 1991; Thomas, 1986). Therefore, the second project, the City Parents' Centre, was viewed by the LEA as an attempt to ensure advice, support and opportunities for contact with the LEA, were available to *all* parents within the borough. The process of establishing the Centre provides the focus for the next section.

The Establishment of The City Parents' Centre

Beginnings

The data on which this chapter is based traces the development of the Centre from the first proposals for its establishment through its first year of life. At this time, it was located in temporary premises in a ground floor room of a secondary school. It was staffed by three female workers, all from different ethnic backgrounds, who shared the two full-time posts. Although it took the Centre several months to establish itself, after this initial period the workers spent a large proportion of their time dealing with parental enquiries. The most common problems concerned special educational needs assessment and provision, admissions and appeals, and disputes with schools concerning a child's progress or behaviour.

The impetus for the Parents' Centre came from a small group of parent governors during an LEA consultation exercise. Their original ideas suggest an alternative conception of the Centre's premises to the 'office-like' surroundings that evolved.

> We made it quite clear that what we were looking for was a shop-front, somewhere we could sell educational materials and have parents drop-in, like a sort of Early Learning Centre, a community centre . . . but that would have cost too much money, so when we were offered the room in the school . . . the project came off the ground. (parent governor)

LEA officers greeted the proposal with enthusiasm, and there appeared to be an immediate consensus over the Centre's suggested aims and functions. The Centre's publicity employed the language of participation and partnership. It described itself as 'something more than a centre for advice', which would 'make a reality of the concept of a partnership between the education service and parents'. The Director of Education commented that it was 'not just somewhere parents can go for advice and information (but a place that encouraged the adoption of) a proactive role in home–school partnership'. However, such vague descriptions serve only to offer symbolic reassurance, a gloss of community participation. The generalities of the rhetoric attracted an apparent consensus from the different groups and individuals concerned with the Centre's establishment, whilst at the same time acting to conceal considerable differences over priorities and interpretations.

Four groups played a key role in the Centre's formation: officers from the LEA; the Director of Education, who was not involved with day-to-day developments but kept quite closely in touch with the Centre's progress; the Centre's workers; and the group of parent governors from whom the idea originated (referred to here as parent volunteers). From interviews with these four groups and examination of the Centre's literature, it is possible to outline four aims for the Centre that all were superficially agreed upon. They were:

- to provide information;
- to provide a channel of communication between the LEA and parents;
- to provide advice and support to parents on an individual basis;
- to help schools and parents develop closer relationships.

This chapter continues by outlining the positions taken by the various groups on these four aims, in order to clarify and illustrate the nature of the diversity of views.

Interpretations

The *Director of Education* saw the Centre as an example of the LEA's willingness to encourage closer parental involvement in City's education service, and as offering opportunities for parental participation at a higher level than had hitherto been possible. He commented:

> The local authority has a responsibility to empower parents by providing them with information that gives them power or access to power, and to create an environment whereby *groups* of parents have opportunities to begin to detect that there is space in the system for them to play a role. (my emphasis)

While the Director acknowledged that work with schools and individual parents was important, he saw the key to the change and improvement of the state education system as lying in another direction — the establishment of independent parents' and students' groups. He felt that organization within the local community was of particular importance in encouraging excluded groups of parents — black parents or white working class parents — to find an effective voice with which to influence the education system.

> It's always been my intention that the Parents' Centre should be a catalyst for the development of [parent] groups, so that parents themselves are having discussions about their experiences, [and] articulating their needs and demands . . . The first strategy, I think, is ensuring that those [community] groups who are already organized have the capacity to work in partnership with and influence service delivery in education.

The Director saw the Parents' Centre as a bridge between schools, the LEA and local communities. By contrast, *senior policy officers* stressed the function of the Centre as a channel for communication, allowing the LEA to keep an 'ear to the ground', and enabling it to respond with advice and information to any issues causing particular concern. However, the authority appeared to wish to limit closer citizen participation to issues which it saw as relatively non-contentious, and accordingly, restricted the available agenda (Lukes, 1974). Thus different issues received different treatment. The Centre organized a workshop for parents on secondary transfer, for example, whilst the introduction of national testing for 7-year-olds was ignored, despite the existence of a local parent-led campaign to withdraw children from the tests. The Centre workers had planned to hold a parents' meeting on the issue, but were advised against this by other officers, who warned that such meetings might be 'hijacked' by the local branch of the NUT who also supported a boycott.

Senior officers were keen for Parents' Centre workers to work in schools. They took the view that to get 'locked into' case-work and advocacy with individual parents would prove too time-consuming for the workers, and would not be cost-effective. Instead the workers should act as 'arrows' to other departments within the LEA, and deal with most queries by simply referring them to other parts of the organization. In schools it was felt that the Centre workers could act as an extra resource for hard-pressed teachers who wanted to extend their relationships with parents but did not have the time. In this model the workers' role is as an aid to the school, encouraging parents to be more closely involved on the school's terms.

Whilst the Director and his senior officers subscribed to all four of the aims outlined earlier, there is a discernible contrast in their priorities. The Director stressed the importance of parents having an influence in the local education system apart from, and quite separate to, their relationship with their child's teachers. This would require some degree of power shifting from the authority and schools to parents, both individually and as a group. Officers preferred a model in which the authority was more *accessible* to parents, but not necessarily more *susceptible*. Thus they stressed the improvement of individual relationships between teachers and parents, rather than parental independence and solidarity.

The attitudes of the *Parents' Centre workers* themselves contained elements of both these philosophies. They felt that the Parents' Centre could and should function as a channel of communication between parents and the LEA, but that effective structures did not exist to relay around the authority the information and issues they reported. Furthermore, the workers felt that the LEA was reluctant to share any of the information it held with parents.

> I still feel that the [authority] like any body that has power, wants to keep information away from parents. The least they can give parents the better. If we have a parent who wants to see the figures for exclusions . . . management are like [gives a shocked gasp], 'What do they want that for? How can we put them off?' There's not enough sympathy or understanding of the rights of parents. (Parents' Centre worker)

With regard to the third function — that of giving advice and support to individual parents — the workers felt case-work was extremely important but time-consuming. As the project was new, they felt under a certain amount of pressure to show results. Advocacy often involved long, complicated cases to which there was no simple solution, and which were, they perceived, harder to justify in terms of the administrative norms of the LEA environment.

> It's the whole values thing really. At [section] meetings . . . everyone says what reports they've written, what meetings they've been to, and when it gets to me, I've done case-work. It looks as if I've done nothing — talked to parents . . . It's like it's not real work. (Centre worker)

They felt that outreach work to schools was important if teachers were not to view them solely as 'trouble-shooters', or even worse as trouble-makers. They were aware that although their interaction with particular schools had gone well, teachers were generally suspicious of them, at least initially. The workers felt they had to justify their role to staff, as they had no established professional standing, unlike say, educational psychologists or welfare officers (see also Tomlinson, 1984).[4] Although the workers were critical of what they saw as teachers' often deficit attitudes towards parents, particularly working class parents, they themselves displayed a tendency to view their 'cases' as individual families with particular problems, often at home, which spilled over to affect the children's school life. Thus, in theory, the workers acknowledged that working class parents were in a structurally powerless position when facing the school. Yet in practice, their answer was pragmatic and reformist as they concentrated on trying to resolve individual concerns. In essence, they were engaged in 'teaching' parents how to 'fit in' to the state system and operate it to gain what they wanted with the minimum disturbance.

> We're always saying, 'How can you get the best out of it, bearing in mind that the school has all the power? At the end of the day, you've got to work in a certain way to benefit your child and yourself'. It does seem unfair, you can sympathize with them [parents] when they think it's unfair. It's explaining the system. (Centre worker)

In their casework the workers were reactive, responding to situations which were brought to them. In their proposed work with schools, they were more proactive, for instance, setting up parents' groups within special schools, but in common with senior officers, they saw their role as working closely with teachers, and within any already-existing structures.

The *parent volunteers*, as the only group who were not employed by City LEA, wanted the Centre to have much more independence, and disliked what they saw as LEA dominance. One example they identified was that the LEA wanted to have little contact with the parent and teacher pressure group, CENS (City's Education Needs Support), and did not wish the Parents' Centre to maintain any links either. Thus CENS was not allowed to use the Parents' Centre resources, although they were theoretically available for parents' groups. The LEA's attitude stemmed from their tense relationship with the local NUT, and CENS's close links with the trade union branch. However, the parent volunteers felt that the Centre should work with any group of parents who were concerned about education locally, and that taking up issues such as Key Stage 1 testing of 7-year-olds, where there were already signs of parental interest and concern, was vital if links with parents were to spread. They were less concerned about outreach to schools, preferring instead that the Centre should establish itself as a community-based organization, offering parents a range of educational and non-educational activities and services. They were also of the opinion that case-work was integral to the Centre's existence, and very much wanted to be part of that. However, this was an area from which they were largely excluded, due to the officers' belief that it was not a suitable task for non-professionals to perform. This attitude was resented by the parent volunteers, a point to which I shall return later.

Thus the confusion concerning the Centre revolved around three key issues: the status of the workers; who was in control; and the exact function of the Centre. First, the status of the workers: were they community outreach workers, or officers liaising between one level of the local state (the education offices) and another (the schools)? Second, the control of the Centre: was it an 'outpost of the LEA' as described by a senior officer, or in the process of evolving into an independent centre? Third, the exact function of the Centre: was it to direct its energies into harmonising relationships between parents, the local authority and schools, or encouraging parents to organize independently?

This lack of a clearly articulated conception of the role and status of the Centre and its workers was one of the biggest obstacles to its successful establishment. With many potential areas for action, workers and volunteers frequently expressed feelings of confusion and a lack of support in defining their roles. This was heightened by erratic staffing at the Centre due to the personal circumstances of the workers, and by the situation within the LEA itself. As chapter 4 noted, City was subject to a number of severe organizational and financial problems, which had greatly increased the workload of senior officers. As the Parents' Centre had not itself presented such problems, it had, to some extent been left to develop at its own (slow) pace by managers.

Parental Participation in the Parents' Centre

The next few pages explores the devolution of power to parents, both with regard to the daily running of the Centre, and through the Centre, the local education service generally. The Director saw City's Centre as a pilot project, and the ideal as a series of local centres helping to promote an approach to education that emphasized community involvement.

> It is a matter of having one of these things [a Parents' Centre] operating cheek by jowl with every school just about. In other words, there is a centre for education in this locality, it's called a school . . . where you do not have the concept of an expert, but ordinary people sharing skills, experiences and frustrations and finding ways of negotiating through all that a particular perspective on education, belief in themselves, belief in their capacity to influence things. (Director)

The parent volunteers had envisaged an independent community centre run by paid workers and parents for parents. Their Centre would also have had links with, offer support to, and provide resources for a number of other community education groups, or school-based parents' associations. Thus, it would provide opportunities for parents to participate at a number of levels in the delivery of City's education service.

Given that at least two groups involved with the Centre saw this as important, why did City's Parents' Centre become an organization under close council control rather than developing into a community-based organization funded by the LEA? Several explanations can be identified: the status of the parent volunteers; the management structure of the Centre and the resulting constraints laid upon the workers actions; the LEA's perception of 'activist' parents, and the pressurized environment in which the LEA operated. These issues will be considered in turn.

The parent volunteers were a small group of working and middle class women who were closely involved in the early stages of establishing the

Centre. Their continued contribution might have given it a distinctive ethos, distinguishing it from a wholly Council-run project. However, they soon became disillusioned. Having originally expected to have to battle hard to get the Council to fund their nascent Centre, they had been surprised by the LEA's enthusiasm, and then started to feel coopted and absorbed by the authority. Worse still, they believed that council control and bureaucracy was responsible for the inertia that periodically affected the Centre. The women wanted to carry out case work and be involved in the management of the Centre. Paradoxically, in seeming to welcome and acquiesce to their ideas, the LEA's involvement had effectively marginalised them.

Majority opinion amongst the Centre workers was that routine jobs (for example, filing and mailing) were the most appropriate for parent volunteers, unless parents had specialist skills like word-processing or translating. There is an obvious parallel here with many teachers' views on the role of parents within a school (see pp.93–4 above; also Mayall, 1990). Both groups are concerned that close parental involvement might encroach upon their professional expertise. It has already been mentioned that the workers felt it was important for them to establish their jobs as high-status ones. In doing so, they were responding to what they perceived as the demands of teachers and administrators to fit into two structured and relatively hierarchical environments. This placed constraints upon them, causing them to view all parents who visited the Centre, including the parent volunteers, as clients rather than participants. Sharing their workload with the parent volunteers would have meant risking an interpretation of their work as something needing no particular expertise, and thereby putting their own positions in jeopardy. A junior officer remarked on this phenomenon.

> I've been there [Parents' Centre] when it's 'Oh, we don't want them [parents] to see that!' There are jokes now, 'Oh God, a parent!' The sort of things you get teachers saying! When you hear jokes, people take them for fun, but there's a hidden element of truth in them often. They [Parents' Centre workers] need parents obviously, but in the same way schools need parents to want to send their kids there. Once it becomes an institution, it's like you [as an outsider] can come so far and you can know so much, then that's it.

This resulted in the parent-volunteers being expected to play a role rather akin to that of *supporter/learner* (see chapter 3), which for the most part, they were unwilling to do.

Thus the workers concern with professionalism was one factor which stopped the Centre devolving management power to parent-volunteers. Professionalism also helps to explain why the Centre workers concentrated on case work dealing with individual problems. The workers were using their expertise to ease 'problem' families smoothly back into their existing school situations. Again, this strategy was imposed on them, to a certain extent, by the constraints under which they worked. During their case-work they were often in the difficult position of being LEA employees, supporting parents in their grievances against other LEA employees. In addition, there was little two or three workers could do to alter any negative teacher attitudes towards parents. In the same way their proposed outreach to schools was likely to consist in a large part of supporting schools in planning initiatives that were already part of the institution's repertoire such as curriculum evenings. The workers were sometimes able to influence the way in which these were planned, so that the events more closely matched up with parents' interests and concerns, but their role remained reformist. The workers were aware of these limitations, commenting that parental participation was not seen as integral to the operation either of schools or the education offices, but rather as something separate, an experiment, and an extra. One of the workers drew a parallel with the introduction of equal opportunities initiatives.

> A lot of people saw the race relations' unit and the women's unit as the people who 'did' equal opps, when it should be everybody. Now it's better, it's not perfect, but it's more of a norm. That's how parental involvement should be.

Therefore, encouraging parents from particular schools to organize themselves into groups in order to negotiate with their schools was not a tactic the Centre workers could easily adopt, despite the Director's apparent support for such a move. It would put them into conflict with the very groups of professionals at the LEA and in schools with whom they were trying to establish themselves.

Another pertinent factor restraining the development of a community-managed and run Centre was the LEA's suspicion of 'activist' parents. This was defined by the workers as follows,

> *Worker 1*: I think definitely with our line management there is a phobia about anyone who ever says anything negative about the Council. It's never true!

> *Worker 2*: There's this thing about who's a 'genuine' parent. If a parent becomes politicized enough or angry enough to campaign, like stand outside the Town Hall . . . they're no longer a 'genuine' parent . . . or again there is this fear that they have been dominated or taken over by the [teachers' union] or CENS.

> *Worker 1*: It's very patronising. [It's as if] parents don't have enough brain to get that far on their own!

The LEA's attitude is doubtless influenced by officer and member awareness that any attempts at increasing participatory decision-making would be experimental, and therefore of high risk to the LEA. As a small Labour authority providing services for an area of social and economic deprivation, the LEA's priority was to establish itself as the provider of an efficient and effective service. Therefore it was disinclined to listen to any parties which might make demands that would hinder progress towards this goal. By keeping the Centre in particular, and the decision-making process in general, under its own control, the LEA could minimize this possibility.

The Parents' Centre: Summary

This account has demonstrated that the rhetoric of City Parents' Centre does encapsulate Pennock's (1979) two more radical aims for citizen participation, namely, aiding the personal development of individuals and overcoming group alienation. However, various constraints minimized the visibility of these objectives whilst highlighting Pennock's first two motivations — legitimizing the LEA's work and making it more responsive to its clients. The changes required to fulfil these two aims can be more easily incorporated into the LEA's current structure as they demand little power-sharing with lay actors. The constraints that rendered the more radical aims peripheral operate at a variety of levels, both general and more specific to this case. Lukes (1974) was cited earlier, referring to the immutability of institutional structures, which works against devolving decision-making power beyond the institutional elite. As an example of this, I have identified the ideology of professionalism, or what Iris Young (1990) calls 'the ideology of expertism' (p.80), as one way in which City Education Authority retained sole exercise of power. Professionalism ensured that decision-making powers were restricted to a small group of people who justified their position with reference to their knowledge and experience, and who also had a vested interest in ensuring that this situation remained constant (Ball, 1987). Thus, for example, even if CEF meetings had continued (see Postscript, p.147), the body was unlikely to have advanced beyond a repository for information and occasional consultation. Furthermore, existing hierarchies and systems were so entrenched that the Centre workers would have encountered great difficulty in opposing or radically departing from, accepted ways of working in schools and the LEA offices.

Various contextual factors also made the possibility of radical innovation less likely. Throughout the previous decade, central government had cultivated an ideological climate which emphasized the individual's role as a consumer; an emphasis which is antithetical to the aims of collective citizen participation. This created a situation in which City LEA, part of a weakened local state, attempted to implement initiatives encouraging collective citizen participation, which ran counter to the values espoused by central government. The Parents' Centre was not immune from the pervasive image of parent-as-consumer. Thus it concentrated on helping individual families fit in to the existing school system, and take up their 'rightful' responsibilities with regard to the education of their own children. The power-relations between the authority and parents remain unchanged. Nor are parents encouraged to join together in defence of their shared interests as parents. One officer suggested that the Centre may evolve to become a 'complaints point' — a wholly different conception to one which emphasizes the Centre as a focus for collective parental participation. Furthermore, central government's ideological dislike of the local state, especially when manifested in financial constraints, creates the highly pressurized environment in which the LEA operates. This increases the likelihood of a hesitant approach to innovation, especially that informed by an 'oppositional' logic. Therefore, although this attempt at citizen participation appears to date to be little more than symbolic reassurance, it is perhaps unfair to castigate the authority for not encouraging a model of government that has not yet been fully attempted by other areas of the central or local state (Harlow and Rawlings, 1984).

Conclusion

Local education authorities have been boxed into a corner by the education policies of central government. This has resulted in a situation in which the opportunities for LEAs to develop and innovate have been severely constrained by the provisions of the 1988 Education Reform Act.

As chapter 2 noted, the 1993 Education Act places further obstacles in the paths of local authorities. However, this does not mean that there is no scope for local authority development. There are signs that some LEAs are attempting to provide educational leadership in their localities, through, for example, supporting and monitoring school practice and provision. Indeed Ball, Bowe and Gold (1992) point to signs suggesting that in some instances, schools and LEAs are involved in reinterpreting central government policy. However, the potential of such strategies within a strongly centrally-controlled system is necessarily limited (Hatcher and Troyna, 1994). Experiments with radical potential, such as those outlined in this chapter are even more susceptible to making erratic progress and, like the Parents' Centre and CEF, prove short-lived, thereby illustrating the difficulties of extending lay participation within the political, financial, and/or cultural restrictions of the local state environment (Ranson, 1993). It is the existence of these restrictions, emanating from both inside and outside an LEA, that are highlighted by those critics who doubt the potential of the 'enabling' model. As Charles Raab (1993) comments,

> It is open to question how far local authorities have the scope to act in this way, or in the more wide-ranging and creative modes that are suggested by the eloquent evangelists of the 'enabling' approach . . .
> Even if [LEAs] are able to re-insert themselves into a position of influence locally, it is unlikely that they will be able to remedy the

reproduction of inequalities that opting-out and market choice rein-
force. (pp.162 and 159)

Postscript

In 1992 open elections were held to elect parent representatives for CEF.
Nominally, any parent in the borough could stand as a candidate. In actuality,
most (but not all) of those parents who did stand had some previous involvement with local education groups or was a governor. The parent representatives met once with the Director of Education and the Chair of the Education
Committee. However, LEA officers felt that the CEF parent representatives all
had their own particular agendas, and that this made them a difficult group to
consult with. No more meetings were planned. The LEA then sought alternative consultation procedures. In 1995, the City Education Conference was held
to discuss a range of educational issues. It was envisaged that such a conference
could become an annual event. However, it is interesting to note that the
conference was organized through the schools and each institution invited to
send their Headteacher, a governor and one other representative. It is difficult
to see how such arrangements would allow parents an independent voice
within the local education system.

The Parent's Centre had been affected by unstable staffing since its establishment, and by 1993 the workers had all left and the Centre was closed,
while its position was reviewed. It will not reopen in that form again, but City
LEA have plans to develop another advice and information service for parents
which would focus on increasing parental involvement in their children's learning, combined with some element of parent education.

Notes

1 Cochrane (1993) makes the point that the notion of the 'enabling authority' was
  initially used to describe market-based approaches to the delivery of services, whereby
  authorities issued contracts to other agencies, thereby 'enabling' them to deliver
  services. However, the concept was developed by local government professionals
  and academics to include notions of greater openness, participation and public
  accountability.
2 *Source*: an ESRC-funded project (R000233586), *The Effect of Local Management of
  Schools on Special Educational Needs Provision.*
3 One officer when asked whether CEF would have a decision-making role replied
  succinctly, 'God, no!'
4 This process of integration with school staff was also important in case the Parents'
  Centre was delegated under local management, leaving schools with the choice of
  buying into the service.

Chapter 9

Conclusion

Introduction

This concluding chapter provides a summary of the preceding analysis, and considers future developments in home–school relations. It provides a brief critique of the directions taken, and solutions provided, by communitarian authors who argue for a regeneration of 'community' with the school taking a leading role in such a process. School-based developments in the area of home–school relationships are considered next, but while such strategies form an important part of the picture, a broader perspective is needed, one which locates the school within a social and political context. As communitarian-ism is found to be too one-dimensional in its approach, an alternative way of viewing community and citizenship is suggested. These definitions emphasize heterogeneity and diversity, and are seen to provide a framework in which relationships between teachers and pupils can be reconsidered, and ultimately redefined towards greater parental participation.

Throughout this book I have argued that teachers are able to maintain a position as dominant 'partners' in their relationships with parents, especially working class parents. This contributes to a situation in which parental 'par-ticipation' is largely limited to the involvement of individual parents. Earlier chapters suggest that previous social democratic initiatives (such as the statist reform model of community education) which aimed to increase lay parti-cipation in state institutions were informed by the discourse of 'benevolent paternalism' (CCCS, 1981). Therefore, they proved to pay little more than lip service to their stated goals, and failed to create the necessary climate for change (see chapter 1). Thus the New Right's rhetoric of individual self-determination and consumer power struck a chord among many groups within the electorate (see chapter 2). However, the Conservative Party has emphasized parents' roles as individual consumers. As a result, some parents are able to exercise a greater degree of control over which school their children attend. Yet, once a school is found, involvement for the majority of parents revolves around a *supporter/learner* model, carrying out specific curricular or extra-curricular tasks under the guidance of a teacher (see chapter 3). A minority of parents become involved in the management of the school through the gov-erning body. However, although elected by other parents, parent governors are not encouraged to see themselves as parent representatives, but rather to consider their individual duty to the governing body as a whole. Whilst some parents are more able than others to adopt and exploit a consumer-oriented role, those groups, whose beliefs and practices differ from the prevailing values structuring school norms, can find themselves at a disadvantage. They are also the most vulnerable to attempts by education professionals to change parenting, and particularly 'mothering' practices, to make them fit accepted norms (see chapters 3 and 5). This is illustrated by the case studies of Hill St and Low Rd schools which highlight the established professional ideal of a 'good parent' (see chapter 6). These two case studies also analyze the school 'communities' to show that they consist of diverse interest groups, fragmented by differences, which include social class, ethnicity, professional status and philosophy. However, the primary division is between professionals and lay parents. Pedagogical differences between teachers are submerged in favour of professional unity, resulting in teacher discourse that attempts to place parents (of whatever background) in a subordinate position in relation to the professionals. In a context in which the 'norm' for parental involvement is for parents to act individually as *supporter/learners*, it is far more likely that parents who reject this role will take up another individualist stance, that of an *independent* parent, rather than seek to form collectives, although there was support amongst Hill St and Low Rd parents for the principle of parents' groups.

Chapter 7 reinforces the argument that the ethos of the teaching profession is strong enough to defeat any joint interests that may arise from parent and teacher sharing gender and/or social class positions. This tendency towards professional defensiveness and insularity is seen as a result of the positional insecurity of the teaching profession, unsure of its exact status or the extent of its responsibilities.

Having examined parent–teacher relationships within schools, and concluded that even with a mediator (the Home–School Coordinators featured in chapter 7) the professionals remain largely in control of the parent–teacher relationship, chapter 8 looks at City's Parents' Centre. It examines the potential of such an organization, devoted to supporting parents and independent of any one particular school. However, the Parents' Centre is seen as an example of both the limitations of social democratic approaches to citizen participation and the continuing influence of professionalism in incorporating people into existing ways of working. Chapter 8 also highlights the current financial and political constraints operating upon LEAs, which significantly limit and constrain the range of initiatives likely to emanate from the local state. With this situation in mind, this concluding chapter continues by examining several proposals for future developments in relationships between citizens and state institutions.

New Directions?

Communitarianism

The 1990s have witnessed an upsurge in interest in 'community', both in the UK and the USA. Communitarianism focuses on the development of strong, interactive communities possessed of a moral voice. As John Gray argues, this literature has grown out of an acceptance of market individualism and therefore has a very different theoretical basis to the social democratic strategies of the 1970s.

> There is little in the communitarian literature that focuses on the economic sources of decay of communities — that addresses the reality of endemic job insecurity or the poverty that now afflicts even many of those in work. Instead much communitarian discourse in Britain echoes American anxieties about family breakdown and . . . develops a fundamentalist restoration of the 'traditional' family. (Gray, 1995)

As Gray notes, much of this literature is American, and one of the key figures is Amitai Etzioni (see for example Etzioni, 1993 and 1994). Etzioni asserts that the solution to the social breakdown which he perceives, is to promote 'the numerous values we share as a community . . . such as the inappropriateness of racial and gender discrimination, the rejection of violence, and the desirability of treating others with love, respect and dignity' (1993, p.97, cited in Kahne, 1995, p.2). However, as Joseph Kahne points out, even if we agree that these are all shared values, no consensus exists regarding how these commitments should be translated into policy. Etzioni's assumption of consensus ignores the way in which policy 'solutions' are articulated primarily by members of particular social groups (i.e. middle-aged, middle-class, white, professionals), whilst other perspectives are overlooked.

One writer who applies communitarian arguments to Britain is Dick Atkinson (1994a and 1994b) who attempts to define a new interpretation of the term 'community' and the school's place within it. He argues that 'self-governing' (ie grant maintained schools) are more innovative institutions and more accountable to 'the community' than schools controlled by the LEA. His argument bears some resemblance to that of Chubb and Moe (1990) in that all three commentators portray direct democratic control as being responsible for rampant bureaucracy, the stifling of innovation, and the fostering of a 'dependency culture'. However Atkinson's solutions are couched in more moderate terms than those deployed by Chubb and Moe. He envisages the retention of a 'slim and visionary Town Hall' (1994b, p.48), one that would not interfere with the increasing 'self-reliance' of schools and their surrounding 'urban villages' (*ibid.*, p.42).

> In place of the old model of a local authority as a monopolist of power, we can build networks and clusters of institutions — collaborating groups of self-governing institutions — that can help communities cohere, and give them fresh purpose and pride. (*ibid.*, p.2)

Leaving aside for the moment the question of the extent to which schools operating within a competitive, quasi-market framework where they are necessarily engaged in a struggle to retain their market share (Ball, 1994a), can be expected to maintain voluntary, cooperative groups on any large scale,[1] I want to focus on Atkinson's view of the school operating within 'the community'. He appears to be influenced by managerial theories imported from private sector businesses, and refers to the 'simple commonsense theory' of British industrialist John Harvey-Jones (1994a, p.44). He talks of organizations developing from being shaped like a pyramid (ie controlled from above) to a 'maypole' with its component parts becoming autonomous units.[2] Atkinson feels this would be an appropriate model for schools. A cluster of schools could come together to form each maypole, every individual institution being one ribbon. Maypoles should share a common set of values with which to hold their diverse parts together. These should then be transmitted to parents.

> The kind of school advocated here necessarily sharpens and clarifies the 'informal' messages it gives to children and adults. It shows them that their worlds of family and school complement and reinforce each other. (1994b, p.27)

What is missing from Atkinson's liberal analysis is a recognition of inequalities of power. He employs a model of social justice, which is concerned with improving individual access to resources, rather than focusing on patterns of structural discrimination (Troyna and Vincent, 1995).[3] Through this perspective, he acknowledges (yet does not root his analysis in) social deprivation and the pressures arising from poverty, and also the inequalities of power that arise between large institutions (such as the town hall) and the individual. However, he seems to be suggesting that these inequalities would somehow be avoided on a smaller scale, in the relationships between teachers and parents for instance or between what he refers to as 'social entrepreneurs' (community leaders) and other individuals and groups. Yet he foresees these powerful actors attempting to disseminate particular conservative values, such as a traditional family structure (1994b, pp.15–18). For instance,

> fast food and a fast lifestyle may have their attractions, but the family gathered around the meal table should be advocated. (*ibid.*, p.17)

Not only does Atkinson fail to recognize the difficulty of generating pluralist procedures under such circumstances, he also ignores the likelihood of diverse voices within his apparently homogeneous 'community'. He talks of '*the* unwritten agenda of the wider community' which is apparently not being met by the present system of party political representation in local government (*ibid.*, p.42), and later, he speaks of 'the will of the community' (*ibid.*, p.49). Etzioni (1993) assumes similar homogeneity of values and priorities, placing the school unproblematically in the position of moral arbiter,

> If the moral infrastructure of our communities is to be restored, schools will have to step in where the family, neighbourhoods and religious institutions have been failing. (p.89)

As Iris Marion Young (1990) notes, this position contains a strong logic towards exclusion of those who do not share the values and beliefs propagated by powerful actors within 'the community'.

> Proponents of community . . . deny difference by positing fusion rather than separation as the social ideal . . . In many towns, suburbs and neighbourhoods people do have an image of their locale as one in which people will all know one another, have the same values and life style and relate with feelings of mutuality and love. In modern American society such an image is almost always false; while there may be a dominant group with a distinct set of values and life style, within any one locale one can usually find deviant individuals and groups. Yet the myth of community operates strongly to produce defensive exclusionary pressures. (pp.228 and 235)

Accordingly, I suggest that an alternative model to communitarianism would share its focus on grass-roots developments, but would emphasize people defining for themselves what interests and concerns they share with others about their local surroundings including educational provision. Such an exercise of 'voice', or to be more accurate, voices, would involve considerable changes at the level of the individual school, and this chapter turns next to this issue.

Democratic Schools?

Advocating increased powers for such a heterogeneous group as parents raises a classic liberal dilemma, namely, if groups of parents employ their greater say in school affairs to achieve reactionary and discriminatory goals, what response should be made? Some of the most bitter, recent cases of parents fighting for their rights to determine their children's education have concerned those individuals who wish their children to have a 'traditional', monocultural education. For example, parents at Dewsbury and Cleveland insisted that their children should not attend multiracial schools, and eventually received the backing of the courts for their stance (Naylor, 1989; Vincent, 1992). It was argued earlier that exclusion from sites of decision-making was a contributory factor to such reactions (see p.99 above; also Formisano, 1991). Awareness of the rationale supporting progressive teaching methods, including multicultural and anti-racist approaches has been largely confined to the teaching profession. Yet such approaches are a favourite demon of the tabloid press. Given the extreme levels of non-communication, revealed by earlier chapters, between some homes and schools, the media may be an important source of information on teaching methods and curriculum content for a parent. Therefore, it is unsurprising that the adoption of progressive methods may result in confused, dissatisfied parents and occasionally vocal media opposition.[4]

However, this is not a complete explanation for all such examples. The Dewsbury and Cleveland cases were also informed by deeply embedded, powerful racist discourses and beliefs (see Vincent, 1992). So parental exclusions by schools is not, of course, a sufficient explanation for all instances of reactionary parental opinion. Despite this, attempting to remedy the imbalance of power between home and school may be the best available option for those seeking to defend progressive initiatives. Thus, there is a need for those teachers to make good the deficiencies in communication with non-professionals. This requires them to leave the confines of their professional groups and enter the public arena, prepared to be proactive in the explanation and defence of their policies and practices.

Amy Gutmann (1987) argues that decision-making in the education system needs to find an alternative to both the 'family state' where all decisions are taken by the state, and the 'state of families' where education is exclusively in the hands of parents. Gutmann asserts that neither party has the right to exclusive authority over children's education. Parents have rights to educate their children to become members of their family and immediate community, but the state has a responsibility to all children to educate them for life in the world outside the family, and to make them aware of ways of living different from their own (Jonathan, 1989). This approach aims to disentangle a child's rights from parents' wishes to impose their own cultural values. Gutmann therefore suggests a broadly-based decision-making procedure. All parties, parents and teachers and the state, would have an input, and discussion and debate would be crucial in determining some type of consensus. However certain qualities for example, mutual respect, non-repression and non-discrimination (for example, ensuring open access to educational provision and a full curriculum) are, she argues, essential to a democratic state. Therefore the achievement of these, admittedly rather general, principles allows the state to encroach upon parents' absolute freedom in respect of their children's education (Gutmann, 1987). The MacDonald Report, commenting on the wishes of some parents for monocultural education, reaches similar conclusions. It defends children's rights not to have a 'nostalgically remembered version' of their parents' education imposed on them. Schools should not simply 'bend to parents' prejudices,' (MacDonald *et al.*, 1989, p.337).

However, if the position of education as a social and public rather than a private good means that parents' rights to determine their child's education must be amenable to qualification by the state, then it is also arguable that it would be neither desirable nor feasible to return to the days of exclusive control of the education system by state employees. Therefore, developments in home–school relations should aim, not to convert *independent* and *detached* parents so that they adopt a *school supportive* stance, (see chapters 3 and 6) but rather to concentrate on procedures to strengthen parental participation within the school (Vincent, 1992). This would require a range of strategies, in an attempt to establish opportunities for parental participation at different levels.

The case studies of Hill St and Low Rd show that the existing, albeit infrequent, interaction between home and school tends to operate at the level of individual parents and teachers. Indeed, this relationship is a key one. This could be supported by the school introducing relatively straightforward measures, particularly concentrating on improving parent–teacher communication. Regular, private, parent–teacher consultations are important here, and Macbeth (1995) also suggests 'phone-in' surgeries when staff are available at advertised times. Other initiatives include the provision of clear accessible information on school organization, whole school policies, and teaching methods; curriculum workshops, home reading and maths schemes; opportunities for parents to visit and take part in classroom activities, and so on. These are all ways in which an individual parent can learn more about the way in which the school functions, and can, through parent–teacher consultations, voice her own opinions about her child's needs, interests and progress. It is on this level that many schools concentrate when seeking to develop their home–school relations.

However a participatory role for parents requires a broader focus than the individual child. It is at this stage — the inclusion of parents into whole school and local educational issues — that many initiatives fail, a point illustrated by the account of City's HSC scheme in chapter 7. Various strategies have been suggested by commentators. Hughes, Wikeley and Nash (1994) argue that schools should undertake consultation exercises with parents, *providing* that teachers are willing to act on the subsequent information. Macbeth (1995) recommends the creation of 'mini-PTAs' [Parent–Teacher Associations] at class or year group level. This would involve inviting parents to school to talk about the organization of that year, meet each other, and perhaps adopt a system of class representatives whereby one parent, known to all can act as a link between the teacher and other parents.

Sally Tomlinson (1991) argues that legislation is necessary to combat the inertia that dominates schools' approaches to home–school relations (see also Sallis, 1987). She suggests statutory Home–School Associations (HSAs) in each school (see chapter 3 above). They would be open to all parents, teachers, older pupils and governors. Their function would extend beyond the extra-curricular concerns of most parent–teacher groups to,

> discuss matters relating to children's learning, progress and development . . . HSAs would be statutorily consulted at local level . . . when important decisions are being made on education and their representatives would be consulted at national levels. (Tomlinson, 1991, p.16)

Thus parents would have the opportunity to participate at each level — the individual child, the class, the whole school, and perhaps beyond, in the locality. However, even legislating to compel schools to establish HSAs would be unlikely to propel parents unproblematically into a role as participants. Such changes would require profound alterations in current relationships between teachers and parents. As chapter 2 noted, the Taylor Report assumed in the late 1970s, that giving parents a place on the governing body would result in an immediate increase in their influence. Yet many parent governors, particularly women, still operate as peripheral members of their governing body (Golby *et al.*, 1990; Deem, Brehony and Heath, 1995). Similarly, previous experiments with parent advisory bodies in the USA concluded that their advice and opinions were often ignored, and that their work was confined to consideration of the more mundane matters involved in school governance (Malen, Ogawa and Kranz, 1990; Hess, 1991). However, despite these caveats, statutorily-based HSAs could have some effect in disrupting the existing notions of 'appropriate' parental roles which serve to confine parents within a supporter/learner role.

Despite the difficulties faced by the City Parents' Centre, similar organizations could be valuable for their ability to offer support to parents from a source independent of any one school. A network of such centres could offer parents advice and information, develop links between schools and locally-based groups, and provide facilities and resources for parents' groups attached to individual schools. In order to avoid some of the pitfalls identified in chapter 8, the planning and operation of parents' centres would need to involve members of local communities at all stages, thereby requiring the LEA to avoid or relinquish a tight hold upon the process.[5] Such centres could have a useful, reciprocal relationship with the dwindling band of community workers which some schools still manage to employ. Astin (1986) suggests broadening the role of these workers to extend beyond their traditional goal of helping individuals to access the education system, to encompass support for collective action (*ibid*, p.15). This would involve community workers trying to make links between different groups in a locality, and ascertaining what their needs and interests were with regard to the school. A community worker could provide parents with the encouragement and space to organize independently of educational professionals.

Such strategies can only offer partial solutions. Each on their own is limited, hence the importance of opportunities for parents to participate in that work at a variety of different levels, and in different settings. However government educational policy encourages parents to exercise their influence as consumers. A focus on community action and school-based change would redefine and redirect that principle of consumer sovereignty away from a consumer model towards a model of democratic participation (Locke, 1974; Ranson, 1986). However, an approach that is wider than school-based change alone is necessary. The strength of communitarianism, and perhaps a contributory factor to its popularity, is the scope of its 'vision'. The next section takes similar themes to those identified by the communitarian movement, but begins to articulate an alternative model stressing diversity.

Developing Citizenship

The developments already suggested oppose the policy priorities of recent Conservative governments, which suggest a particular definition of the role of 'the parent', and by extension, 'the citizen'. As detailed in chapters 1, 2 and 3, the 'responsible' parent of Conservative legislation is concerned with making choices which benefit his or her own circumstances. Likewise New Right approaches to citizenship promote 'the active consumer, customer or client' (Oliver, 1991b, p.35) whilst depoliticizing and discouraging grassroots, political activity.

Chapter 2 argues that the Parents' Charter encourages parents, once they have chosen a school, to be supportive of the professionals. If they have great cause for dissatisfaction, parents can 'exit', but opportunities for exercising 'voice' remain dependent on individual circumstances. Statutory bodies or forums in which all parents have a right to voice their opinion have not received central government backing. Thus Carr (1991) comments that the 'market' model of democracy encourages an 'individualistic society' and a 'politically passive citizenry' (p.379). The market model of social welfare contains a notion of 'rights that extends only as far as consumer rights, and is thus incomplete. It does not address structural inequalities that limit the ability of a citizen, perhaps in her role as parent, to compete in the market place (see chapter 2). If a broader definition of rights is adopted, the Conservative Party's model is exposed as limited to responsibilities rather than entitlement (Marshall, 1950). Citizenship then becomes 'a burden, a set of obligations which a citizen owes,' (Oliver, 1991a, p.164). This is illustrated by the emphasis on parental obligations in both the *supporter/learner* and the *consumer* model; such a focus overlooks the possibility of a broader, more participative role for parents.

The development of such a role requires an acknowledgement that 'education is a public good as well as a private benefit' (Ranson, 1992, p.183), demanding collective as well as individual involvement. It is through participation in public dialogues that citizens can recognize areas of commonality in their concerns, and thus build a grass roots movement to support and improve state education (Troyna and Carrington, 1990). As Ranson and Thomas (1989) comment,

> It requires the opportunity for citizens to express their view, for their voice to be heard, so that the inescapably diverse constituencies of education are enabled to present, discuss and negotiate their account. (p.74)

As suggested earlier, this mention of diversity is crucial. Similarly, Oliver's writing refers to 'multiple citizenship' (1991a, p.162). This is defined as a sense of belonging to more than one community. It can be understood as acknowledging that every individual has links with several social communities; links which primarily result from the interaction of class, ethnicity and gender variables. This appreciation may go some way towards overriding expectations of easy consensus, based on simplistic notions of the uniformity of geographical communities (see chapter 1 above).

Iris Marion Young develops the point by referring to the need for a heterogeneous public sphere which encourages self-organization of groups and group representation in decision-making. In proposals which run directly counter to Dick Atkinson's calls for decentralization, Young argues for regional government which could protect minority interests which she argues are at risk under plans for decentralisation and local autonomy. Decentralization in itself does little to challenge, and indeed may contribute to, a homogeneous view of 'the community' which is likely to result in the exclusion of some voices and some perspectives. As Young (1990) says, 'the problems of atomism are the same whether the atoms are individuals, households or cities' (p.250). She continues by stressing that local participation is vital, but within a context that guarantees minority rights. Therefore she suggests a system of neighbourhood assemblies, including workplace and school councils. Representatives of these forums would constitute a regional government which guaranteed the representation of minority groups. Young's writing reveals her determination, not merely to acknowledge, but to *centre* her analysis around 'issues of social and cultural diversity, the need to protect the voices of society's marginal thinkers, and the importance of reflective and critical dialogue,' (Kahne, 1995, p.1). Such a focus has implications for the way in which we think about relationships between schools and parents, and accordingly, the potential to affect changes to what many parents experience as schools' alienating and exclusionary practices.

Conclusion

This book has argued that parent–teacher relationships are shaped by the unequal power relations between the two groups. I have outlined various attempts at reconstitution, including national developments such as community education (chapter 1) and parental involvement in the curriculum (chapter 3), as well as local initiatives, such as the HSC scheme (chapter 7) and the Parents' Centre (chapter 8). These accounts suggest that such innovations have a marked tendency to be reformist, not in their rhetoric perhaps, but in their aims and outcomes. At each site, whether at school or LEA level, policies are likely to be the focus for conflict and competition. This may mean that 'oppositional' policies calling for change to the current balance of power have a relatively small chance of finding their way onto the political agenda. This is especially so at national level, where successive Conservative governments have strengthened central government powers and reconstructed the political agenda to focus on individual rather than collective strategies. However, it is not my purpose to suggest that change is impossible within the current structures. The erosion of autonomy for education professionals remains incomplete, and teachers and local administrators still have opportunities to address the issues of home–school relationships. It is also possible that some parents may be able to extend their consumer 'powers' of school choice to participate in the life of the school (Vincent, 1992).

Therefore, although progress in increasing opportunities for parental participation is likely to be fragmented and erratic, I suggest that future developments should endeavour to increase democratic control of the school, rather than promote stewardship by the market. It is the former which has the potential to affect relationships, not just between individual teachers and parents, but also between citizens and agencies of the state. For as Stewart Ranson comments, 'participation in education can . . . help foster not only effective schooling, but also the conditions for a more vital accountability for citizenship' (1986, p.96).

Notes

1 Lunt *et al.*, (1994) detail some of the difficulties facing schools trying to share resources and provision and develop joint approaches to, in this case, just one area — special education.
2 Indeed, the necessity for LEAs to delegate the majority of their budgets under LMS, combined with the influence of managerial ideologies, are leading many LEAs to develop in this direction. For a critique of managerialism, see Pollitt (1990).
3 The same criticism can be levelled at Philip Woods' notion of a consumer-citizen, an interesting, but in my view, ultimately flawed attempt to develop a concept inclusive enough to encompass the complexities of changing relationships between citizens and public services (Woods, 1993). Whilst Woods acknowledges briefly that individual consumer resources are variable, he does not appear to concede that the inequalities inherent in peoples' access to these resources — he identifies money, information, legal rights and 'cultural capital' — are such that they constitute a profound challenge to the concept of consumer-citizen. He downplays the ways in which inequalities are structurally produced and sustained, suggesting instead that 'cultural capital' can be equalized by providing everyone with equal information, and providing advice and support for disadvantaged groups (Woods, 1994b). However, as inequalities based on class, gender and ethnicity are not so easily affected by reformist attempts to increase the influence of individual service-users, new opportunities are likely to be taken up by those middle class groups already in possession of considerable social and economic resources.
4 An example is provided by the experience of Culloden Primary School in East London which in 1991 became the target for a virulent media campaign directed at its progressive teaching methods.
5 During 1994/95, a project along these lines was being developed by parents' groups in several locations with the support of the Advisory Centre for Education.

Appendix — Interview Details

In terms of ethnicity and gender, the breakdown is as follows:

	African/ Caribbean	ESWI*	South Asian	Other groups	Total
Women	28	67	18	7	120
Men	4	21	10	3	38
					Grand Total
Total	32	88	28	10	158

*ESWI = English, Scots, Welsh and Irish

In order to preserve the anonymity of individual respondents, a further breakdown is given only for the first two case study schools, Hill St and Low Rd. Both governing body Chairs were white and male. At Hill St I interviewed forty-five parents in total, and all the full-time teachers (sixteen including the Head). At Low Rd I interviewed fifty parents, and fifteen of the twenty full-time teachers (including the Head). This breaks down as follows:

Hill St parents:
10 African/Caribbean women
8 South Asian parents (3 men, 5 women)
3 Cypriot women (2 Greek Cypriot, 1 Turkish)
5 Turkish Kurdish parents (2 men, 3 women)
19 ESWI (5 men, 14 women)

Hill St teachers:
1 South Asian woman
3 African/Caribbean teachers (2 women, 1 man)
11 ESWI (7 women, 4 men)
1 other European

Low Rd parents:
12 African/Caribbean parents (1 man, 11 women)
15 Bangladeshi parents (7 men, 8 women)
23 ESWI (2 men, 21 women)

Low Rd teachers:
2 South Asian women
3 African/Caribbean teachers (2 women, 1 man)
9 ESWI (7 women, 2 men)
1 other European

Bibliography

ACER (1986) *Parents' Voices in Early Childhood Education*, London, ACER.

ADLER, M. (1993) *An Alternative Approach to Parental Choice*, London, National Commission on Education, Briefing Paper no.13, London, NCE.

ADLER, M., PETCH, A. and TWEEDIE, J. (1989) *Parental Choice and Education Policy*, Edinburgh, Edinburgh University Press.

ALEXANDER, R. (1992) *Policy and Practice in Primary Education*, London, Routledge.

ALLEN, G., BASTIANI, J., MARTIN, I. and RICHARDS, K. (Eds) (1987) *Community Education: An Agenda for Reform*, Milton Keynes, Open University Press.

ALLEN, G. and MARTIN, I. (Eds) (1992) *Education and Community: The Politics of Practice*, London, Cassell.

ALLEN, J. (1990) 'Does feminism need a theory of "the state"?', in WATSON, S. (Ed) *Playing the State*, Sydney, Allen & Unwin.

ANDERSON, G. (1991) 'Cognitive politics of principals and teachers: Ideological control in an elementary school', in BLASE, J. (Ed) *The Politics of Life in Schools*, London, Sage.

APPLE, M. (1986) *Teachers and Texts*, London, Routledge and Kegan Paul.

APPLE, M. (1993) *Official Knowledge: Democratic Education in a Conservative Age*, London, Routledge.

ARNOWITZ S. and GIROUX H. (1993) *Education Still Under Siege*, Westport, CT, Bergin and Garvey.

ARNSTEIN, S. (1969) 'A ladder of citizen participation', *American Institute of Planners' Journal*, **35**, 4, pp.216–24.

ASSOCIATION OF LONDON AUTHORITIES (1991) *London's Charter for Education*, London, ALA.

ASTIN, B. (1986) 'Community work: Education for action', *Journal of Community Education*, **5**, 2, pp.12–15.

ATKIN, J., BASTIANI, J. and GOODE, J. (1988) *Listening to Parents*, London, Croom Helm.

ATKINSON, D. (1994a) *Radical Urban Solutions*, London, Cassell.

ATKINSON, D. (1994b) *The Common Sense of Community*, London, Demos.

BACHRACH, P. and BARATZ, M. (1970) *Power & Poverty — Theory & Practice*, New York, Oxford University Press.

BALL, S. (1987) *The Micro-Politics of School*, London, Methuen.

BALL, S. (1990) *Politics and Policymaking in Education*, London, Routledge.

Bibliography

BALL, S. (1994a) *Education Reform: A Critical and Post-structural Approach*, Buckingham, Open University Press.

BALL, S. (1994b) 'Some reflections on policy theory: A brief response to Hatcher and Troyna', *Journal of Education Policy*, **9**, 2, pp.171–82.

BALL, S. and BOWE, R. (1991) 'The micropolitics of radical change: Budgets, management, and control in British schools', in BLASE, J. (Ed) *The Politics of Life in Schools*, London, Sage.

BALL, S., BOWE, R. and GEWIRTZ, S. (1994) 'Choice, class and complexity', a project paper, Centre for Educational Studies, King's College, London.

BALL, W. (1992) 'Critical social research, adult education and anti-racist, feminist praxis', *Studies in the Education of Adults*, **24**, 1, pp.1–23.

BALLARD, P. (1937) *Things I Cannot Forget*, London, University of London Press.

BARON, S. (1988) 'Community and the limits of social democracy', in GREEN, A. and BALL, S. (Eds) *Progress and Inequality in Comprehensive Education*, London, Routledge.

BARON, S. (1989) 'Community education: From the Cam to the Rea', in BARTON, L. and WALKER, S. (Eds) *The Politics and Processes of Schooling*, Milton Keynes, Open University Press.

BASH, L. and COULBY, D. (1989) *The Education Reform Act: Competition and Control*, London, Cassell.

BASH, L., COULBY, D. and JONES, C. (1985) *Urban Schooling*, London, Holt, Rinehart & Winston.

BASTIANI, J. (Ed) (1987a) *Parents and Teachers 1*, Windsor, NFER-Nelson.

BASTIANI, J. (1987b) 'From compensation . . . to participation? A brief analysis of changing attitudes in the study and practice of home–school relations', in BASTIANI, J. (Ed) *Parents and Teachers 1*, Windsor, NFER-Nelson.

Bastiani, J. (1987c) 'Professional ideology versus lay experience', in ALLEN, G., BASTIANI, J., MARTIN, I. and RICHARDS, K. (Eds) *Community Education: An Agenda for Reform*, Milton Keynes, Open University Press.

BASTIANI, J. (Ed) (1988a) *Parents and Teachers 2*, Windsor, NFER-Nelson.

BASTIANI, J. (1988b) 'Staffroom mythology and teacher ignorance', in BASTIANI, J. (Ed) *Parents and Teachers 2*, Windsor, NFER-Nelson.

BASTIANI, J. (1989) *Working with Parents: A Whole School Approach*, Windsor, NFER-Nelson.

BASTIANI, J. (1993) *UK Directory of Home–School Initiatives*, London, Royal Society of Arts.

BASTIANI, J. (1994) 'The accreditation of parental learning', *Parents in a Learning Society, Royal Society of Arts News*, **3**, pp.1–2.

BASTIANI, J. and BAILEY, G. (1992) *Directory of Home–School Initiatives in the UK*, London, Royal Society of Arts.

BATTERN, J., RALPH, S. and SEARS, M. (1993) 'Communities in crisis: An example of community-based adult education', *Adults Learning*, **4**, 6, pp.169–72.

BEATTIE, N. (1985) *Professional Parents: Parent Participation in Four Western European Countries*, London, Falmer Press.

BEN-TOVIM, G., GABRIEL, J., LAW, I. and STREDDER, K. (1986) *The Local Politics of Race*, London, Macmillan.

BENNETT, N. (1976) *Teaching Styles and Pupil Progress*, London, Open Books.

BENNINGTON, J. (1977) 'The flaw in the pluralist heaven', in RAYNOR, J. and HARRIS, E. (Eds) *The City Experience*, London, Ward Lock.

BERNSTEIN, B. (1975) *Class, Codes and Control: Vol.1*, London, Routledge and Kegan Paul.

BLASE, J. (Ed) (1991a) *The Politics of Life in Schools*, London, Sage.

BLASE, J. (1991b) 'Introduction', in BLASE, J. (Ed) *The Politics of Life in Schools*, London, Sage.

BLASE, J. (1991c) 'Analysis and discussion: Some concluding remarks', in BLASE, J. (Ed) *The Politics of Life in Schools*, London, Sage.

BOLAND, N. and SIMMONS, K. (1987) 'Attitudes to reading: A parental involvement project', *Education 3–13*, **15**, 2, pp.28–32.

BOSTON, J., MARTIN, J., PALLOT, J. and WALSH, P. (1991) *Reshaping the State*, Oxford, Oxford University Press.

BOURNE, J. (1980), 'Cheerleaders and ombudsmen: The sociology of race relations in Britain,' *Race and Class*, **20**, 4, pp.331–52.

BOWE, R., BALL, S. with GOLD, A. (1992) *Reforming Education and Changing Schools: Case Studies in Policy Sociology*, London, Routledge.

BOWE, R., GEWIRTZ, S. and BALL, S. (1994) 'Captured by the discourse? Issues and concerns in researching "parental choice"', *British Journal of Sociology of Education*, **15**, 1, pp.63–78.

BOWLES, S. and GINTIS, H. (1976) *Schooling In Capitalist America*, London, Routledge and Kegan Paul.

BRIDGES, D. (1987) 'The "problem" of the non-attending parent', in BASTIANI, J. (Ed) *Parents and Teachers 1*, Windsor, NFER-Nelson.

BRITO, S. and WALLER, H. (1993) 'Partnership — at what price?', in MERTTENS, R., MAYERS, D., BROWN, A. and VASS, J. (Eds) *Ruling the Margins: Problematising Parental Involvement*, London, University of North London Press.

BROWN, A. (1992) 'Mathematics: Rhetoric and practice in primary teaching', in RILEY, J. (Ed) *The National Curriculum and the Primary School: Springboard or Straitjacket?*, London, Kogan Page.

BROWN, A. (1993) 'Participation, dialogue and the reproduction of social inequalities', in MERTTENS, R. and VASS, J. (Eds) *Partnership in Maths*, London, Falmer Press.

BROWN, P. (1990) 'The "Third Wave": Education and the ideology of parentocracy', *British Journal of Sociology of Education*, **11**, 1, pp.65–85.

BUCI-GLUCKSMANN, C. (1980) *Gramsci & the State*, London, Lawrence & Wishart.

BURGESS, R. (1983) *Experiencing Comprehensive Education: A Study of Bishop McGregor School*, London, Methuen.

BURGESS, R. (Ed) (1985) *Strategies of Educational Research: Qualitative Methods*, London, Falmer Press.

BURGESS, R. (Ed) (1989) *The Ethics of Educational Research*, London, Falmer Press.

BURGESS, R., HUGHES, C. and MOXON, S. (1991) 'Parents are welcome: Head-teachers' and matrons' perspectives on parental participation in the early years', *Qualitative Studies in Education*, **4**, 2, pp.95–107.

BUTCHER, H., LAW, I., LEACH, R. and MULLARD, M. (1990) *Local Government and Thatcherism*, London, Routledge.

CACE (CENTRAL ADVISORY COUNCIL FOR EDUCATION) (1967) *Children and their Primary Schools* (The Plowden Report), London, HMSO.

CARR, W. (1991) 'Education for citizenship', *British Journal of Educational Studies*, **39**, 9, pp.375–85.

CARSPECKEN, P. (1990) *Community Schooling and the Nature of Power: The Battle for Croxteth Comprehensive*, London, Routledge.

CATTERALL, B. (Ed) (1990) *London 2000: Education Strategies for the Whole Community (conference report)*, London, London Research Centre.

CCCS (CENTRE FOR CONTEMPORARY CULTURAL STUDIES) (1981) *Unpopular Education*, London, Hutchinson.

CCCS (1982) *The Empire Strikes Back*, London, Hutchinson.

CCCS (1991) *Education Limited*, London, Unwin Hyman.

CEDC (COMMUNITY EDUCATION DEVELOPMENT CENTRE) (1990) *Home–School Liaison Teachers*, Coventry, CEDC.

CHITTY, C. (1989) *Towards A New Education System: The Victory Of The New Right*, London, Falmer Press.

CHUBB, J. and MOE, T. (1990) *Politics, Markets and America's Schools*, Washington, DC, The Brookings Institution.

CLARKE, M. and STEWART, J. (1991) *Choices for Local Government for the 1990s and Beyond*, London, Longman.

CLUNE, W. (1990) 'Introduction', in CLUNE, W. and WITTE, J. (Eds) *Choice and Control in American Education: Volume 2*, London, Falmer Press.

CLUNE, W. and WITTE, J. (Eds) (1990) *Choice and Control in American Education: Volume 2*, London, Falmer Press.

COARD, B. (1971) *How a West Indian Child is Made ESN*, London, New Beacon.

COCHRANE, A. (1993) *Whatever Happened to Local Government?*, Buckingham, Open University Press.

COHEN, S. (1980) *Folk Devils and Moral Panics*, New York, St Martin's Press.

COLE, I. and FURBEY, R. (1994) *The Eclipse of Council Housing*, London, Routledge.

CONSULTATIVE COMMITTEE (1931) *Report on Infant and Nursery Schools* (The Hadow Report), London, HMSO.

CORBETT, H. (1991) 'Community influence and school micro-politics: A case study', in BLASE J. (Ed) *The Politics of Life in Schools*, London, Sage.

CORNWELL, N. (1987) *Statementing and the 1981 Education Act*, Bedford, Cranfield Press.

COWBURN, W. (1986) *Class, Ideology and Community Education*, London, Croom Helm.

COWIE, C. and LEES, S. (1981) 'Slags or drags?', *Feminist Review*, **9**, pp.11–13.

CROFT, S. and BERESFORD, P. (1992) 'The politics of participation', *Critical Social Policy*, **35**, pp.20–44.

CROFT, S. and BERESFORD, P. (1993) *Citizen Involvement*, London, Macmillan.

CULLINGFORD, C. (Ed) (1985) *Parents, Teachers and Schools*, London, Robert Royce.

DAHL, R. (1961) *Who Governs? Democracy and Power in an American City*, New Haven, CT, Yale University Press.

DALE, R. (1989) *The State & Education Policy*, Milton Keynes, Open University Press.

DALE, R. (1994) 'National reform, economic crisis, and "New Right" theory', *Discourse*, **14**, 2, pp.17–29.

DAVID, M. (1978) 'Parents and education politics', in BROWN, M. and BALDWIN, S. (Eds) *The Year Book of Social Policy in Britain 1977*, London, Routledge and Kegan Paul, pp.87–107.

DAVID, M. (1993) *Parents, Gender and Education Reform*, London, Polity Press.

DAVID, T. (1990) *Under Five — Under-educated?*, Milton Keynes, Open University Press.

DEEM, R. (1989) 'The new school governing bodies — are gender and race on the agenda?', *Gender and Education*, **1**, 3, pp.247–60.

DEEM, R., BREHONY, K. and HEATH, S. (1995) *Active Citizenship and the Governing of Schools*, Buckingham, Open University Press.

DEHLI, K. and JANUARIO, I. (1994) *Parent Activism and School Reform in Toronto*, Toronto, Ontario Institute for Studies in Education.

DES (DEPARTMENT OF EDUCATION AND SCIENCE) (1975) *Language for Life* (The Bullock Report), London, HMSO.

DES (1988) *School Governors: A New Role*, London, HMSO.

DES (1991) *The Parents' Charter*, London, HMSO.

DFE (Department for Education) (1992) *The White Paper*, London, HMSO.

DFE (1994) *Our Children's Education: The Updated Parents' Charter*, London, HMSO.

DHASMANA, L. (1994) 'Asian parents' perceptions and experiences about innercity schools — a local perspective', *Multicultural Teaching*, **12**, 2, pp.24–8.

DUNLEAVY, P. (1991) *Democracy, Bureaucracy and Public Choice*, London, Harvester Wheatsheaf.

DUXBURY, S. (1987) 'Childcare ideologies and resistance: The manipulative strategies of pre-school children', in POLLARD, A. (Ed) *Children and Their Primary Schools*, London, Falmer Press.

DYE, J. (1989) 'Parental involvement in curriculum matters: Parents, teachers and children working together', *Educational Research*, **31**, 1, pp.20–33.

EADE, J. (1989) *The Politics of Community*, Aldershot, Avebury.

EDELMAN, M. (1964) *The Symbolic Uses of Politics*, Chicago, IL, University of Illinois Press.

EDWARDS, V. and REDFERN, A. (1988) *At Home In School*, London, Routledge.

ELLIS, T. *ET AL.* (1976) *William Tyndale: The Teachers' Story*, London, Writers and Readers Publishing Company.

EPSTEIN, D. (1993) *Changing Classroom Cultures*, Stoke, Trentham.

EPSTEIN, J. (1994) 'Family math that's above average: Take home activities for kids and their parents', *Instructor*, **103**, 8, pp.17–18.

EPSTEIN, J. and HERRICK, S. (1991) *Implementation and Effects of Summer Home Learning Packets in the Middle Grades*, Baltimore, MD, Centre for Research on Effective Schooling for Disadvantaged Students.

ETZIONI, A. (1993) *The Spirit of Community*, New York, Touchstone.

ETZIONI, A. (1994) *The Parenting Deficit*, London, Demos.

FINCH, J. (1984a) 'It's great to have someone to talk to: The ethics and politics of interviewing women' in BELL, C. and ROBERTS, H. (Eds) *Social Researching: Politics, Problems, Practice*, London, Routledge and Kegan Paul.

FINCH, J. (1984b) 'A first class environment? Working class playgroups as preschool experience', *British Educational Research Journal*, **10**, 1, pp.3–17.

FITZ, J., HALPIN, D. and POWER, S. (1993) *Grant-Maintained Schools: Education in the Market Place*, London, Kogan Page.

FLEW, A. (1987) *Power To The Parents*, London, Sherwood Press.

FORMISANO, R. (1991) *Boston Against Busing*, Chapel Hill, NC, University of North Carolina Press.

FOSTER, P. (1990) *Policy and Practice in Multicultural and Anti-Racist Education*, London, Routledge.

FOUCAULT, M. (1977) *Discipline and Punish*, New York, PANTHEON Books.

FOUCAULT, M. (1980) 'Truth and power', in GORDON, C. (Ed) *Power/Knowledge Selected Interviews and Other Writings, 1972–1977*, New York, Pantheon Books.

FRIERE, P. (1972) *Pedagogy of the Oppressed*, London, Sheed & Ward.

FREIRE, P. (1985) *The Politics of Education*, London, Macmillan.

FULLAN, M. (1992) *School Improvement: The Implementation Perspective and Beyond*, Milton Keynes, Open University Press.

GANS, H. (1977) 'Urbanism and suburbanism as a way of life', in RAYNOR, J. and HARRIS, E. (Eds) *The City Experience*, London, Ward Lock.

GASKELL, J. and McLAREN, A. (Eds) (1987) *Women and Education: A Canadian Perspective*, Alberta, Detselig Enterprises.

GAUTREY, T. (1937) *Lux Mihi Laus: School Board Memories*, London, Lint House.

GEE, J. (1989) 'The narratization of experience in the oral style', *Journal of Education*, **171**, 1, pp.75–96.

GEORGE, V. and WILDING, P. (1976) *Ideology and Social Welfare*, London, Routledge and Kegan Paul.

GEWIRTZ, S., BALL, S. and BOWE, R. (1995) *Markets, Choice and Equity in Education*, Buckingham, Open University Press.

GIBSON, D. (1987) 'Hearing and listening: A case study of the "consultation" process undertaken by a local education department and black groups', in TROYNA, B. (Ed) *Racial Inequality in Education*, London, Tavistock Press.

GILBERT, R. (1992) 'Citizenship, education and postmodernity', *British Journal of Sociology of Education*, **13**, 1, pp.51–68.

GILLBORN, D. (1990) *'Race', Ethnicity & Education*, London, Unwin Hyman.

GILLBORN, D. (1993) 'Racial violence and harassment', in TATTUM, D. (Ed) *Understanding and Managing Bullying*, London, Heinemann Books.

GILLBORN, D. (1995) *Racism and Antiracism in Real Schools*, Buckingham, Open University Press.

GIROUX H. (1983) 'Theories of reproduction and resistance in the new sociology of education: A critical analysis', *Harvard Education Review*, **53**, 3, pp.257–95.

GIROUX, H. (1994) *Disturbing Pleasures*, London, Routledge.

GITLIN, A., SIEGEL, M. and BORU, K. (1989) 'The politics of method: From leftist ethnography to educative research', *Qualitative Studies in Education*, **2**, 3, pp.237–53.

GLATTER, R. (Ed) (1989) *Educational Institutions and their Environments: Managing the Boundaries*, Milton Keynes, Open University Press.

GOACHER, B., EVANS, J., WELTON, J. and WEDELL, K. (1988) *Policy and Provision for Special Educational Needs*, London, Cassell.

GOLBY, M. and BRIGLEY, S. (1988) 'Where are the parents coming from?', *Forum*, **30**, 3, pp.90–2.

GOLBY M. with BRIGLEY, S., LANE, B., TAYLOR, W. and VIANT, R. (1990) *The New Governors Speak*, Tiverton, Fair Way Publications.

GOLDING, P. and MIDDLETON, S. (1982) *Images of Welfare & Poverty*, Oxford, Martin Robinson.

GORE, J. (1990) 'What can we do for you: What *can* "we" do for "you"?' *Educational Foundation*, **4**, 3, pp.5–26.

GORE, J. (1993) *The Struggle for Pedagogies*, London, Routledge.

GRACE, G. (1978) *Teachers, Ideology and Control*, London, RKP.

GRAMSCI, A. (1971) *Selections from the Prison Notebooks*, (ed and tr. by HOARE, Q. and NOWELL SMITH, G.), New York, International Publishers.

GRAY, J. (1995) 'Hollowing out the core', *The Guardian*, 8 March.

GREEN, A. (1990) *Education & State Formation: The Rise of Education Systems in England, France & the USA*, London, Macmillan.

GRETTON, J. and JACKSON, M. (1976) *Collapse of a School — or a System?*, London, Allen & Unwin.

GRIFFITH, A. and SMITH, D. (1987) 'Constructing cultural knowledge: Mothering as a discourse', in GASKELL, J. and McLAREN, A. (Eds) *Women and Education: A Canadian Perspective*, Alberta, Detselig Enterprises.

GUTMANN, A. (1987) *Democratic Education*, Princeton, NJ, Princeton University Press.

GUTTING G. (1989) *Michel Foucault's Archaeology of Scientific Reason*, Cambridge, CUP.

GYFORD, J., LEACH, S. and GAME, C. (1989) *The Changing Politics of Local Government*, London, Unwin Hyman.

HALL, S. (1983) 'The great moving rights show', in HALL, S. and JACQUES, M. (Eds) *The Politics of Thatcherism*, London, Lawrence & Wishart.

HALL, S. (1989) *The Hard Road to Renewal*, London, Verso.

HALL, S. and JACQUES, M. (Eds) (1983) *The Politics of Thatcherism*, London, Lawrence & Wishart.

HALPIN, D. and TROYNA, B. (Eds) (1994) *Researching Education Policy*, London, Falmer Press.

HALSEY, A., HEATH, A. and RIDGE, J. (1980) *Origins and Destinations*, Oxford, Oxford University Press.

HAMPTON, W. (1991) *Local Government and Urban Politics*, London, Longman.

HANCOCK, R. (1993) 'Professional language, literature and parents', *Language Matters*, **3**, pp.16–19.

HANNON, P. (1987) 'A study of the effects of parental involvement in the teaching of reading on children's reading test performance', *British Journal of Educational Psychology*, **57**, pp.56–72.

HANNON, P. (1989) 'How should parental involvement in the teaching of reading be evaluated?', *British Educational Research Journal*, **15**, 1, pp.33–40.

HANNON, P. and JACKSON, A. (1987) 'Educational home-visiting and the teaching of reading', in BASTIANI, J. (Ed) *Parents and Teachers 1*, Windsor, NFER-Nelson.

HARLAND, J. (1988) 'Running up the down escalator — crisis management as curriculum management', in LAWTON, D. and CHITTY, C. (Eds) *The National Curriculum*, London, Institute of Education, Bedford Way Papers no.33.

HARLOW, C. and RAWLINGS, R. (1984) *Law and Administration*, London, Weidenfield & Nicholson.

HARRISON, P. (1983) *Inside the Inner City*, Harmondsworth, Penguin Books.

HATCHER, R. and TROYNA, B. (1994) 'The "policy cycle": A Ball by Ball account', *Journal of Education Policy*, **9**, 2, pp.155–70.

HATCHER, R, TROYNA, B. and GEWIRTZ, D. (1993) *Local Management of Schools and Racial Equality*, Final report to the Commission of Racial Equality.

HAVILAND, J. (1988) *Take Care, Mr. Baker*, London, Fourth Estate.

HAYEK, F. (1944) *The Road to Serfdom*, London, Routledge and Kegan Paul.

HESS, G. (1991) *School Restructuring, Chicago Style*, California, Corwin Press.

HEWISON, J. (1985) 'The evidence of case studies of parents' involvement in schools', in CULLINGFORD, C. (Ed) *Parents, Teachers and Schools*, London, Robert Royce.

HEWISON, J. and TIZARD, J. (1980) 'Parental involvement and reading attainment,' *British Journal of Educational Psychology*, **50**, pp.209–15.

HEWITT, N. (1992) 'Compounding differences', *Feminist Studies*, **18**, 2, pp.313–26.

HILLCOLE GROUP (1993) *Falling Apart: The Coming Crisis of Conservative Education*, London, Tufnell Press.

HIRSCH, D. (1995) 'School choice and the search for an education market', *International Review of Education*.

HIRSCHMAN, A. (1970) *Exit, Voice & Loyalty*, Cambridge, MA, Harvard University Press.

HOLUB, R. (1992) *Antonio Gramsci: Beyond Marxism and Postmodernism*, London, Routledge.

HOOD, C. (1990) 'De-Sir Humphreying the Westminster model of bureaucracy: A new style of governance?', *Governance*, **3**, 2, pp.205–14.

HOWARD S. and HOLLINGSWORTH A. (1985) 'Linking home and school in theory and practice', *Journal of Community Education*, **4**, 3, pp.12–18.

HOYLE, E. (1986) 'Micropolitics of educational organisations', in WESTOBY, A. (Ed) *Culture and Power in Educational Organisations*, Milton Keynes, Open University Press.

HUGHES, M., WIKELEY, F. and NASH, T. (1994) *Parents' and Their Children's Schools*, Oxford, Basil Blackwell.

ILEA (INNER LONDON EDUCATION AUTHORITY) (1985) *Parents and Primary Schools*, London, ILEA.

ILEA (1989) *The Primary Language Record: Handbook for Teachers*, London, ILEA.

ISAAC, J. (1990) 'The New Right and the moral society', *Parliamentary Affairs*, **43**, 2, pp.209–26.

JEFFS, T. (1992) 'The state, ideology and the community school movement', in ALLEN, G. and MARTIN, I. (Eds) *Education and Community: The Politics of Practice*, London, Cassell.

JENKINS, J. (1987) 'The green sheep in Colonel Gaddaffi Drive', *New Statesman*, 9 January.

JOHN, G. (1990) 'Launch speech for London 2000', in CATTERALL, B. (Ed) *London 2000: Education Strategies for the Whole Community* (conference report), London, London Research Centre.

JOHN, G. (1992) unpublished paper on the supplementary school movement.

JOHNSON, R. (1991) 'A new road to serfdom? A critical history of the 1988 Act', in CCCS *Education Limited*, London, Unwin Hyman.

JONATHAN, R. (1989) 'Choice and control in education: Parents' rights, individual liberties and social justice', *British Journal of Educational Studies*, **37**, 4, pp.321–38.

JONATHAN, R. (1990) 'State education service or prisoner's dilemma: The "hidden hand" as source of education policy', *British Journal of Educational Studies*, **38**, 2, pp.116–32.

JONATHAN, R. (1993) 'Parental rights in schooling', in MUNN, P. (Ed) *Parents and Schools: Customers, Managers or Partners*, London, Routledge.

JONES, G., BASTIANI, J., BELL, G. and CHAPMAN, C. (1992) *A Willing Partnership*, London, Royal Society of Arts.

JONES, K. (1989) *Right Turn*, London, Hutchinson.

JONES, M. and ROWLEY, G. (1990) 'What does research say about parental participation in children's reading development?', *Evaluation and Research in Education*, **4**, 1, pp.21–36.

JONES, V. (1986) *We Are Our Own Educators*, London, Karia Press.

JOWETT, S., BAGINSKY, M. and MACDONALD MACNEIL, M. (1991) *Building Bridges: Parental Involvement in School*, Windsor, NFER-Nelson.

KAHNE, J. (1995) 'Lacking democracy: Etzioni's "Spirit of Community"', Paper presented at the annual meeting of the American Educational Research Association, San Francisco, April.

KNOX, P. (1982) *Urban Social Geography: An Introduction*, London, Longman.

LABOUR PARTY (1989) *Parents in Partnership*, London, The Labour Party.

LABOUR PARTY (1991) *Labour's Charter for Parents*, London, The Labour Party.

LANSLEY, S., GOSS, S. and WOLMAR, C. (1989) *Councils In Conflict*, London, Macmillan.

LAREAU, A. (1989) *Home Advantage: Social Class & Parental Intervention in Elementary Education*, London, Falmer Press.

LAWRENCE, E. (1982) 'In the abundance of water, the fool is thirsty: Sociology and black "pathology"', in CCCS *The Empire Strikes Back*, London Hutchinson.

LAWTON, D. (1994) *The Tory Mind on Education 1979–1994*, London, Falmer Press.

LE GRAND, J. (1991) 'Quasi markets in social policy', *Economic Journal*, **101**, pp.1256–67.

LOCKE, M. (1974) *Power and Politics in the School System*, London, RKP.

LONDON EDINBURGH WEEKEND RETURN GROUP (1980) *In and Against the State*, London, Pluto Press.

LOUGHREY, D. (1991) 'Time for me . . . involving parents in their children's education', *Primary Teaching Studies*, **6**, 1, pp.114–23.

LOVELAND, I. (1991) 'Legal rights and political realities: Governmental responses to homelessness in Britain', *Law and Social Inquiry*, **16**, 2, pp.249–319.

LOVELAND, I. (1996) *Constitutional Law*, London, Butterworths.

LOVETT, T. (1982) *Adult Education, Community Development and the Working Class*, Nottingham, University of Nottingham.

LOVETT, T., CLARKE, C. and KILMURRAY, A. (1983) *Adult Education and Community Action*, London, Croom Helm.

LUKES, S. (1974) *Power*, London, Macmillan.

LUNT, I., EVANS, J. NORWICH, B. and WEDELL, K. (1994) *Working Together: Inter-school Collaboration for Special Needs*, London, David Fulton.

LYSAGHT, Z. (1993) 'Partnership with parents in primary education', *Irish Educational Studies*, **12**, pp.196–205.

MAC AN GHAILL, M. (1988) *Young, Gifted and Black*, Milton Keynes, Open University Press.

MACBETH, A. (1984) *The Child Between: A Report on School-Family Relationships in the Countries of the EC*, Education series 13, Brussels, Commission of the European Communities.

MACBETH, A. (1989) *Involving Parents*, Oxford, Heinemann.

MACBETH, A. (1995) 'Partnership between parents and teachers in education' in MACBETH, A., McCREATH, D. and AICHISON, J. (Eds) *Collaborate or Compete? Educational Partnerships in a Market Economy*, London, Falmer Press.

MACDONALD, I., BHAVNANI, R., KAHN, L. and JOHN, G. (1989) *Murder In The Playground* (The Macdonald Report), London, Longsight Press.

MACINTYRE S. (1985) 'Gynaecologist-woman interaction', in UNGERSON, C. (Ed) *Women and Social Policy*, London, Macmillan.

MACLEOD, F. (1985) *Parents In Partnership: Involving Muslim Parents In Their Children's Education*, Coventry, Community Education Development Centre.

MACLURE, S. (1990) *A History of Education in London 1870–1990*, London, Penguin.

MALEN, B., OGAWA, R. and KRNZA, J. (1990) 'What do we know about school-based management? A review of the literature — a call for research', in CLUNE, W. and WITTE J. (Eds) *Choice and Control in American Education Volume 2*, London, Falmer Press.

MARSHALL, T. (1950) *Citizenship and Social Class*, Cambridge, Cambridge University Press.

MARTIN, I. (1987) 'Community education: Towards a theoretical analysis', in ALLEN G., BASTIANI, J., MARTIN, I. and RICHARDS, K. (Eds) *Community Education: An Agenda for Reform*, Milton Keynes, Open University Press.

MARTIN, I. (1992) 'Community education: LEAs and the dilemmas of possessive individualism', in ALLEN, G. and MARTIN, I. (Eds) *Education and Community: The Politics of Practice*, London, Cassell.

MARTIN, J., RANSON, S. and RUTHERFORD, D. (1995) 'The annual parents' meeting: Potential for partnership', *Research Papers in Education*, **10**, 1, pp.19–49.

MAYALL, B. (1990) *Parents in Secondary Education*, London, Calouste Gulbenkian Foundation.

MCAUSLAN, P. (1980) *The Ideologies of Planning Law*, Oxford, Pergammon Press.

MCCARTHY, C. (1990) *Race and Curriculum*, London, Falmer Press.

MEASOR, L. (1985) 'Interviewing: A strategy in qualitative research', in BURGESS, R. (Ed) *Strategies of Educational Research: Qualitative Methods*, London, Falmer Press.

MEIGHAN, R. (1986) *A Sociology of Education*, London, Cassell.

MERTTENS, R., MAYERS, D., BROWN, A. and VASS, J. (Eds) (1993) *Ruling the Margins: Problematising Parental Involvement*, London, University of North London Press.

MERTTENS, R. and VASS, J. (1987) 'Parents in schools: Raising money or raising standards?', *Education 3–13*, **15**, 2, pp.23–7.

MERTTENS, R. and VASS, J. (1993) *Partnerships in Maths*, London, Falmer Press.

MIDWINTER, E. (1972) *Priority Education*, London, Longman.

MILES, M. and GOLD, B. (1981) *Whose School Is It Anyway?*, New York, Praegar Publishing.

MILIBAND, R. (1984) *Capitalist Democracy in Britain*, Oxford, Oxford University Press.

MINISTRY OF HOUSING (MoH) (1969) *People and Planning* (The Skeffington Report), London, HMSO.

MIRZA, H. (1992) *Young, Female and Black*, London, Routledge.

MOORE, D. (1990) 'Voice and choice in Chicago', in CLUNE, W. and WITTE, J. (Eds) *Choice and Control in American Education: Volume 2*, London, Falmer Press.

MUNN, P. (1993) (Ed) *Parents and Schools: Customers, Managers or Partners?*, London, Routledge.

MURRAY, C. (1989) 'Underclass', *Sunday Times*, 26 November.

MUSGRAVE, P. (1979) *The Sociology of Education*, London, Methuen.

MYERS, K. (1990) 'Review of "equal opportunities in the new ERA"', *Education*, 5 October, p.295.

NAYLOR, F. (1989) *Dewsbury: The School Above the Pub*, London, Claridge Press.

NEAL, S. (1995) 'Researching powerful people from a feminist and anti-racist perspective: A note on gender, collusion and marginality', *British Educational Research Journal*, **21**, 4, pp.517–31.

NEWHAM, M. (1983) 'Community', in TIGHT, M. (Ed) *Education for Adults — Vol.1 Adult Learning and Education*, London, Open University/Croom Helm.

NEWTON, K. (1976) *Second City Politics*, Oxford; Clarendon Press.

NISBETT, J., HENRY, L., STEWART, C. and WATT, J. (1980) *Towards Community Education*, Aberdeen, Aberdeen University Press.

OAKLEY, A. (1981) 'Interviewing women: A contradiction in terms', in ROBERTS, H. (Ed) *Doing Feminist Research*, London, Routledge and Kegan Paul.

O'CONNOR, M. (1994) *Giving Parents A Voice*, London, Research and Information on State Education Trust (RISE).

O'HAGAN, B. (1987) 'Community education in Britain: Some myths and their consequences', in ALLEN, G., BASTIANI, J., MARTIN, I. and RICHARDS, K. (Eds) *Community Education: An Agenda for Reform*, Milton Keynes, Open University Press.

O'HAGAN, B. (Ed) (1991a) *The Charnwood Papers: Fallacies in Community Education*, Ticknall, Education Now Books.

O'HAGAN, B. (1991b) 'Empowerment fallacy: Knowledge is power', in O'HAGAN, B. (Ed) *The Charnwood Papers: Fallacies in Community Education*, Ticknall, Education Now Books.

OLIVER, D. (1991a) 'Active citizenship in the 1990s', *Parliamentary Affairs*, **140**, pp.157–71.

OLIVER, D. (1991b) *Government in the United Kingdom*, Milton Keynes, Open University Press.

OZGA, J. and GEWIRTZ, S. (1990) 'Partnership, pluralism and education policy: A reassessment', *Journal of Education Policy*, **5**, 1, pp.37–48.

OZGA, J. and LAWN, M. (1981) *Teachers, Professionalism and Class*, London, Falmer Press.

PARENTS TALKING ABOUT EDUCATION STEERING GROUP (1994) *National Conference 1993: A Report on the Conference and Developments*, One Year On, London, Parents Talking About Education.

PARTINGTON, J. and WRAGG, E. (1989) *Schools and Parents*, London, Cassell.

PASCAL, C. (1988) 'Democratised primary school government: Policy in practice', *British Educational Research Journal*, **14**, 1, pp.17–29.

PASCAL, C. (1989) 'Democratised primary school government: Conflicts and dichotomies', in GLATTER, R. (Ed) *Educational Institutions and Their Environments: Managing the Boundaries*, Milton Keynes, Open University Press.

PATEMAN, C. (1970) *Participation and Democratic Theory*, Cambridge, Cambridge University Press.

PEARSON, G. (1983) *Hooligan: A History of Respectable Fears*, London, Macmillan.

PENNOCK, J. (1979) *Democratic Political Theory*, Princeton, NJ, Princeton University Press.

PETERS, M. (1994) 'Individualism and community: Education and the politics of difference', *Discourse*, **14**, 2, pp.65–78.

POLLARD, A. (1987) *The Social World of the Primary School*, London, Holt, Rinehart & Winston.

POLLITT, C. (1990) *Managerialism and the Public Services*, Oxford, Basil Blackwell.

POSTER, C. and KRUGER, A. (Eds) (1990) *Community Education in the Western World*, London, Routledge.

POWELL, J. (1995) 'The work of a home–school liaison teacher', in MILLS, J. and MILLS, R. (Eds) *Primary School People: Getting to Know Your Colleagues*, London, Routledge.

PUGH, G. and DE'ATH, E. (1989) *Working Towards Partnership in the Early Years*, London, National Children's Bureau.

PUNCH, M. (1986) *The Politics and Ethics of Fieldwork*, Beverley Hills, CA, Sage.

RAAB, C. (1993) 'Parents and schools: What role for education authorities?', in MUNN, P. (Ed) *Parents and Schools: Customers, Managers or Partners?*, London, Routledge.

RANSON, S. (1986) 'Towards a political theory of public accountability in education', *Local Government Studies*, **12**, 4, pp.77–98.

RANSON, S. (1988) 'From 1944 to 1988: Education, citizenship and democracy', *Local Government Studies*, **14**, 1, pp.1–19.

RANSON, S. (1990) 'Towards education for citizenship', *Educational Review*, **42**, pp.151–66.

RANSON, S. (1992) *The Role of Local Government in Education: Assuring Quality and Accountability*, London, Longman.

RANSON, S. (1993) 'Markets or democracy for education', *British Journal of Educational Studies*, **41**, 4, pp.333–52.

RANSON, S. and THOMAS, H. (1989) 'Education reform: Consumer democracy or social democracy?', in STEWART, J. and STOKER, G. (Eds) *The Future of Local Government*, Basingstoke, Macmillan.

RAWLING, J. (1988) 'School and community: The case of the urban primary school', in WATSON, L. (Ed) *Primary School, Home and Community: Headteachers' Perspectives on Purpose, Organisation and Management*, Sheffield, Sheffield City Polytechnic, Papers in Education Management no.66.

RENNIE, J. (1985) *British Community Primary Schools*, London, Falmer Press.

RICHARDSON, A. (1983) *Participation*, London, Routledge and Kegan Paul.

RILEY, K. (1992) 'The changing framework and purposes of education', *Research Papers in Education*, **7**, 1, pp.3–25.

RISEBOROUGH, G. (1981) 'Teachers' careers and comprehensive schooling: An empirical study', *Sociology*, **15**, 3, pp.352–81.

RIZVI, F. (1993) 'Williams on democracy and the governance of education', in DWORKIN, D. and ROMAN, L. (Eds) *Views Beyond the Border Country: Raymond Williams and Cultural Politics*, London, Routledge.

SALLIS, J. (1987) 'Parents and the 1986 Education Act', *Journal of Education Policy*, **2**, 4, pp.347–51.

SALLIS, J. (1991) 'Home/school contracts: A personal view', *Parents in a Learning Society, Royal Society of Arts News*, **4**, p.7.

SCHATTSCHNEIDER, E. (1960) *The Semi-Sovereign People*, New York, Holt, Rinehart & Winston.

SEDDON, T., ANGUS, L. and POOLE, M. (1990) 'Pressures on the move to school-based decision-making management', in Chapman, J. (Ed) *School-Based Decision-Making and Management*, London, Falmer Press.

SHARP, R. and GREEN, A. (1975) *Education and Social Control*, London, Routledge and Kegan Paul.

SHOWSTACK-SASSON, A. (1983) 'Dear Parent . . .' in WOLPE, A.-M. and DONALD, J. (Eds) *Is There Anyone Here From Education?*, London, Pluto Press.

SIDERS, M. and SLEDJESKI, S. (1978) *How to Grow a Happy Reader: Report on a Study of Parental Involvement*, Research monograph no.27, Gainsville, FL, University of Florida.

SILVER, H. (1990) *Educational Change and the Policy Process*, London, Falmer Press.

SIMON, R. (1977) 'Gramsci's concept of hegemony', *Marxism Today*, March.

SIMON, R. (1993) *Gramsci's Political Thought*, London, Lawrence & Wishart.

SMITH, T. (1988) 'Parents and pre-school', in BASTIANI J. (Ed) *Parents and Teachers 2*, Windsor, NFER-Nelson.

SONYEL, S. (1987) 'The silent minority: Turkish children in British schools', *Multicultural Teaching*, **5**, 3, pp.15–19.

STACEY, M. (1991) *Parents and Teachers Together*, Milton Keynes, Open University Press.

STANLEY, L. and WISE, S. (1983) *Breaking Out: Feminist Consciousness and Feminist Research*, London, Routledge and Kegan Paul.

STANWORTH, M. (1981) *Gender and Schooling*, London, Women's Research and Resources Centre Publications.

STEEDMAN, C. (1985) 'Listen how the caged bird sings: Amarjit's song', in STEEDMAN, C., URWIN, C. and WALKERDINE, V. (Eds) *Language, Gender & Childhood*, London, Routledge and Kegan Paul.

STEEDMAN, C., URWIN, C. and WALKERDINE, V. (Eds) (1985) *Language, Gender & Childhood*, London, Routledge and Kegan Paul.

TAYLOR, D. (1992) 'A big idea for the nineties? The rise of the citizen's charters', *Critical Social Policy*, **33**, pp.87–94.

TAYLOR-GOOBY, P. (1985) *Public Opinion, Ideology, and State Welfare*, London, Routledge and Kegan Paul.

THOMAS, D. (1986) *White Bolts, Black Locks*, London, Allen & Unwin.

TIZARD, B., BLATCHFORD, P., BURKE, J., FARQUHAR, C. and PLEWIS, I. (1988) *Young Children at School in the Inner City*, London, Lawrence Erlbaum Press.

TIZARD, B. and HUGHES, M. (1984) *Young Children Learning*, London, Fontana.

TIZARD, B., MORTIMORE, J. and BURCHELL, B. (1981) *Involving Parents in Nursery And Infant Schools*, Oxford, Grant McIntyre.

TIZARD, B., MORTIMORE, J. and BURCHELL, B. (1988) 'Involving parents from minority groups', in BASTIANI, J. (Ed) *Parents and Teachers 2*, Windsor, NFER-Nelson.

TIZARD, J., SCHOFIELD, W. and HEWISON, J. (1982) 'Collaboration between teachers and parents in assisting children's reading', *British Journal of Educational Psychology*, **52**, pp.1–15.

TOMLINSON, S. (1984) *Home and School in Multicultural Britain*, London, Batsford.

TOMLINSON, S. (1991) 'Home–school partnerships', in TOMLINSON, S. and ROSS, A. (Eds) *Teachers and Parents*, London, Institute of Public Policy Research.

TOMLINSON, S. (1992) 'Disadvantaging the disadvantaged: Bangladeshis and education in Tower Hamlets', *British Journal of Sociology of Education*, **13**, 4, pp.437–46.

TOMLINSON, S. and HUTCHISON, S. (1991) *Bangladeshi Parents and Education in Tower Hamlets*, London, Advisory Centre for Education (ACE).

TONNIES, F. (1955) *Community & Association*, London, Routledge and Kegan Paul.

TOOLEY, J. (1992) 'The "pink-tank" on the Education Reform Act', *British Journal of Educational Studies*, **40**, 4, pp.335–49.

TORKINGTON K., (1986) 'Involving parents in the primary curriculum', in Hughes, M. (Ed) *Involving Parents in the Primary Curriculum, Perspectives 24*, Exeter, University of Exeter, School of Education.

TOWNSEND, H. and BRITTAN, E. (1972) *Organisation in Multiracial Schools*, London, NFER.

TROYNA, B. (1993) *Racism and Education*, Buckingham, Open University Press.

TROYNA, B. (1994) 'Blind faith? Empowerment and educational research', *International Studies in Sociology of Education*, **4**, 1, pp.3–24.

TROYNA, B. and CARRINGTON, B. (1989) 'Whose side are we on? Ethical dilemmas in research on "race" and education' in BURGESS, R. (Ed) *The Ethics of Educational Research*, London, Falmer Press.

TROYNA, B. and CARRINGTON, B. (1990) *Education, Racism and Reform*, London, Routledge.

TROYNA, B. and HATCHER, R. (1992) *Racism in Children's Lives: A Study of Mainly-White Primary Schools*, London, Routledge.

TROYNA, B. and VINCENT, C. (1995) 'The discourses of social justice', *Discourse*, **16**, 2, pp.149–66.

TROYNA, B. and WILLIAMS, J. (1986) *Racism, Education and the State*, Beckenham, Croom Helm.

TYLER, W. (1986) 'The organisational structure of the school', in WESTOBY, A. (Ed) *Culture and Power in Educational Organisations*, Milton Keynes, Open University Press.

UPTON, S. (1987) *The Withering of the State*, Wellington, Allen & Unwin.

URWIN, C. (1985) 'Constructing motherhood: The persuasion of normal development', in STEEDMAN, C., URWIN, C. and WALKERDINE, V. (Eds) *Language, Gender & Childhood*, London, Routledge and Kegan Paul.

VINCENT, C. (1992) 'Tolerating intolerance? Parental choice and race relations — the Cleveland case', *Journal of Education Policy*, **7**, 5, pp.429–43.

VINCENT, C. (1995) 'School, community and ethnic minority parents', in TOMLINSON, S. and CRAFT, M. (Eds) *Ethnic Relations and Schooling*, London, Athlone Press.

VINCENT, C., EVANS, J., LUNT, I. and YOUNG, P. (1995) 'Policy and practice: The changing nature of special educational provision in schools', *British Journal of Special Education*, **22**, 1, pp.4–11.

WALFORD, G. (1991) *Doing Educational Research*, London, Routledge.

WALFORD, G. (1992) *Selection for Secondary School*, National Commission on Education, Briefing Paper no.7. London, NCE.

WALKER, J. and CRUMP, S. (1995) 'Educational options: Democracy, diversity and equity', Paper presented at the annual meeting of the American Educational Research Association conference, San Francisco, April.

WALKERDINE, V. (1985) 'On the regulation of speaking and silence: Subjectivity, class and gender in contemporary schooling', in STEEDMAN, C., URWIN, C. and WALKERDINE, V. (Eds) *Language, Gender & Childhood*, London, Routledge and Kegan Paul.

WALKERDINE, V. and LUCEY, H. (1989) *Democracy In The Kitchen*, London, Virago.

WALLER, W. (1932) *The Sociology of Teaching*, New York, Wiley Press.

WARD, C. (1976) *Housing — An Anarchist Approach*, London, Freedom Press.

WATSON, S. (Ed) (1990a) *Playing the State*, Sydney, Allen & Unwin.

WATSON, S. (1990b) 'The state of play: an introduction', in WATSON, S. (Ed) *Playing the State*, Sydney, Allen & Unwin.

WATSON, S. (1990c) 'Conclusion', in WATSON, S. (Ed) *Playing the State*, Sydney, Allen & Unwin.

WATTS, J. (1990) 'Community education and parental involvement', in Macleod, F. (Ed) *Parents and Schools: The Contemporary Challenge*, London, Falmer Press.

WESTOBY, A. (1989) 'Parental choice and voice under the 1988 ERA', in Glatter

R. (Ed) *Educational Institutions and their Environments: Managing the Boundaries*, Milton Keynes, Open University Press.

WESTWOOD, S. (1992) 'When class became community: Radicalism in adult education', in RATTANSI, A. and REEDER, D. (Eds) *Rethinking Radical Education: Essays in Honour of Brian Simon*, London, Lawrence & Wishart.

WHITE, L. and SMITH, D. (1993) 'The partnership between parent, teacher and pupil', *Headteacher Review*, Spring, pp.16–18.

WHITEHEAD, J. and AGGLETON, P. (1986) 'Participation and popular control on school governing bodies: The case of the Taylor Report and its aftermath', *British Journal of Sociology of Education*, **7**, 4, pp.433–49.

WHITTY, G. (1985) *Sociology and School Knowledge*, London, Methuen.

WHITTY, G. and EDWARDS, T. (1993) 'Deregulation in education' Paper presented at a conference on 'Liberalisierung im Bildungswesen', Basel, Switzerland, October.

WHITTY, G., EDWARDS, T. and GEWIRTZ, S. (1993) *Specialisation and Choice in Urban Education: The City Technology College Experiment*, London, Routledge.

WHITTY, G. and MENTER, I. (1989) 'Lessons of Thatcherism: Education policy in England & Wales 1979–1988', *Journal of Law & Society*, **16**, 1, pp.46–64.

WILDING, P. (1982) *Professional Power and Social Welfare*, London, Routledge and Kegan Paul.

WIRTH L. (1964) 'Urbanism as a way of life', in REISS, A. (Ed) *Louis Wirth on Cities and Social Life*, London, University of Chicago.

WITTE, J. (1993) 'The Milwaukee parental choice program: The first thirty months', paper presented at the annual meeting of the American Educational Research Association conference, Atlanta, April.

WOLFENDALE, S. (1992) *Empowering Parents and Teachers: Working for Children*, London, Cassell.

WOLFENDALE, S. (1994) 'Parents views of home–school links', Parents in a Learning Society', *Royal Society of Arts News*, **4**, p.5.

WOODS, P. (1988) 'A strategic view of parent participation', *Journal of Education Policy*, **3**, 4, pp.323–34.

WOODS, P. (1993) 'Parents as consumer-citizens', in MERTTENS, R., MAYERS, D., BROWN, A. and VASS, J. (Eds) *Ruling the Margins: Problematising Parental Involvement*, London, University of North London Press.

WOODS, P. (1994a) 'Parents and choice in local competitive arenas', paper presented at the annual meeting of the American Educational Research Association conference, New Orleans, April.

WOODS, P. (1994b) 'Giving parents real influence: Empowerment and responsiveness as neglected themes in partnership', paper presented at the 42nd Annual Canadian Education Association conference, Banff, May.

WRAGG, T. and PARTINGTON, J. (1989) *Schools And Parents*, London, Cassell.

WRIGHT, C. (1987) 'Black students, white teachers', in Troyna, B. (Ed) *Racial Inequality In Education*, London, Tavistock.

Bibliography

WRIGHT, C. (1992) *Race Relations Within the Primary School*, London, David Fulton.

YEATMAN, A. (1990) *Bureaucrats, Technocrats, Femocrats*, Sydney, Allen & Unwin.

YOUNG, I. (1990) *Justice and the Politics of Difference*, Princeton, NJ, Princeton University Press.

YOUNG, M. and WILMOTT, P. (1957) *Families and Kinship in East London*, London, Routledge and Kegan Paul.

Index